MY
ORPHANS OF THE WILD
RESCUE AND HOME CARE OF NATIVE WILDLIFE

MY ORPHANS OF THE WILD

RESCUE AND HOME CARE OF NATIVE WILDLIFE

ROSEMARY K. COLLETT
WITH CHARLIE BRIGGS

*Best Wishes —
Rosemary Collett*

**J. B. LIPPINCOTT COMPANY
PHILADELPHIA AND NEW YORK**

Figures 1 through 4 in "Cages and Housing" were drawn by
Clark H. Briggs.

Grateful acknowledgment is made to George D. Suddaby, D.V.M.,
who reviewed the text and acted as professional consultant on veterinary information included here.

U.S. Library of Congress Cataloging in Publication Data

Collett, Rosemary K   birth date
My orphans of the wild: rescue and home care of
native wildlife.

Bibliography: p.
1. Wildlife rescue.   2. Naturalists—Correspondence,
reminiscences, etc.   I. Briggs, Charlie, birth date
joint author.   II. Title.
QL83.2.C64   639'.9   74–1111
ISBN–0–397–01021–4

Foreword

Wild animals along a part of the west coast of Florida have much to be thankful for in the person of Rosemary Collett. She and her husband, George, are the founders of a unique facility known as Felicidades Wildlife Foundation, Inc., located in Venice, in their own home and on the grounds surrounding it. Here she has nursed hundreds of sick and injured wild birds and mammals back to health and then released them. For those that were unfortunate enough not to be able to return to the wild, she has provided shelter and food so that they may live out their lives in security and safety.

Rosemary Collett is not the type of person who just talks about wildlife problems; she gets things done. On any given day she may swim out in the Gulf of Mexico to bring a seabird with a broken wing back to shore. Or she may risk being snagged by a panic-stricken pelican bristling with rusty fishhooks when she attempts to rescue it. She exposes herself constantly to the very real possibility of serious injury from the beaks, talons, and teeth of the creatures she is trying to help.

The real measure of her devotion, however, is shown by the tremendous amount of time she freely gives in the care, feeding, and nursing of her wild friends. Many hours are spent each day in the preparation and feeding of different diets to the various birds and mammals at the home. Cages must be cleaned and sick birds medicated, which consumes many more hours. Calls may come at any time requesting assistance in rescuing a sick or injured creature. Add to this her frequent appearances before schoolchildren and many other groups, and you should be getting the idea by now that she is a rather special individual. Few people have such dedication to a cause.

Her many years of caring for wild animals and the invaluable personal observations she has been able to make on her patients' behavior in captivity make her very well qualified to write a book such as this. It will be a useful reference for anyone involved in the care and treatment of many different birds and mammals. There is a wealth of information on feeding and caring for the young of numerous species that are frequently found as orphans. She suggests a number of diets that are easily prepared and readily obtainable by anyone.

Rosemary goes into detail on the housing and cages that she utilizes for the young and adult of many species. The very important fact that all young animals need a warm place to stay is brought out, along with the methods that work for her in providing warmth.

Those who may desire to do some of the same type of work that she is doing will benefit from the precautions that she includes in her book. There is a good deal of useful information, much of it painfully acquired, I am sure, on handling wild mammals and birds. The need for due care in preventing the handler from contracting a contagious disease from the sick animal is also emphasized.

There are chapters on first aid for birds and mammals as well as a list of medications that have worked well for her in caring for her patients. Suggestions for vaccinating certain species against some of the contagious diseases are also given in the book. Certainly her methods of caring for oil-damaged seabirds will be of interest to many persons who become involved in rescue efforts when massive accidental releases of oil occur along our shores and bays. And her experiences in releasing healthy mammals and birds to return to the wild have produced some uniquely informative and delightful portions of the book.

Although her primary purpose here is to inform, Rosemary's light touch and sense of humor have produced plenty of entertaining anecdotes, as have her perceptive insights into the personalities of her patients.

GEORGE D. SUDDABY, D.V.M.

Contents

Introduction

It all started when we took in a pregnant guinea pig. At least, I think that's how it started. As I write these words, looking out my window at eight sea gulls limping around my patio, nine pelicans bathing in the wading pool, and a tall storky wood ibis serenely sunning itself while awaiting its fish dinner, I wonder.

How *did* it all begin? Eight years after that guinea pig, our six-room house, set on an acre of flat sandy land three blocks from the Gulf of Mexico in Venice, Florida, has become Casa de Felicidades, home of Felicidades Wildlife Foundation. (Nonprofit? An understatement—the scramble for money to feed and care for the animals never ends.) We now treat and release dozens of wild animals monthly, and we have over a hundred animal patients at our home. We have a newsletter mailing list of close to a thousand animal lovers. My dining room table is always covered with cages full of baby birds. My house is devoted more to wildlife than to me, my husband, George, and my daughter, Janice, and there is always a pelican in the bathtub.

Somehow, after taking in that guinea pig, and after George brought home a flying squirrel with the plaintive explanation, "I've always wanted a flying squirrel," we began to get really

11

interested in animals. At first, we thought we were just interested in collecting a few. We began to haunt the pet shops and animal dealers, and we acquired a colorful toucan and a pair of white-tailed antelope squirrels. ("They never breed in captivity," the dealer gravely assured us. Although the toucan has long since died, the antelope squirrels multiplied to several dozen and now occupy four large cages in the family room.)

Then the word got around that the Colletts liked animals and had a way with them. People began to appear at our door with a bird with a broken wing or a pair of baby raccoons turned up by a bulldozer or a pelican hurt by a fisherman's hook.

Our phone began to ring constantly. It might be the local police department saying a mute swan had flown into a power line and would we take it and care for it? Or a lady saying, "You don't know me, but there's a strange bird on our beach and I think it's hurt—can you come and get it?"

I found myself experimenting with pet formulas and pet nursing bottles, buying more and more fish and seed and dry dog food, and looking for information on how to feed, treat, and care for sick, injured, and orphaned wild creatures. There are no complete reference books on this subject, and in eight years of experimenting and learning, in thousands of hours of caring for wild creatures, I finally became my own authority. With the invaluable help and advice of Dr. Suddaby, our veterinarian, who is always willing at any hour to try to help a suffering animal, we have achieved a very high rate of cured and released patients.

Since our involvement with wildlife, we have given up gardening, flower beds, and other niceties we once enjoyed as home owners. We don't mow the lawn often—it disturbs the pelicans. We let drooping branches droop—the ducks nest in them. We have let our trees—bamboo, Surinam, palm, and other tropical foliage—grow tall and lush to provide privacy for our patients. A six-foot cypress fence completely encloses our acre now, for more wildlife privacy and to keep out marauding animals. Our backyard, our family room, and our screened porch are lined with cages for patients. We use our entire home—three bedrooms, two baths, kitchen-dining area, living room, family room, and porch—for our work. Our bookshelves are jammed with wildlife reference works. Our carport is used for storage.

I constantly juggle patients indoors and out. Some of our wonderful junior high school Ecology Club students are building new cages for us. We have drawn plans for an aviary and hope someday to have sufficient funds for enough land and buildings so the animals can live in their own environment and we can live in ours. In the meantime, it means scrupulous daily cleaning of the house, grounds, cages, and backyard wading pools, most of which I do myself.

After our work grew so large and our personal funds ran out, we organized the Felicidades Wildlife Foundation, which is actually on and in our home and grounds. We share it with the wildlife patients who need our help; our welcome sign, "Casa de Felicidades," is posted in our front yard, along with our proudly flown green and white ecology flag. Tax-deductible donations to the foundation have made it possible for us to put up that cypress fence, build some new cages, buy food and supplies for the animals and birds, and keep the program going. As part of the foundation's work, we travel to Florida west coast schools, giving slide lectures and taking some of our patients for the children to see.

In this book, I will try to pass on what we have learned, so that when you find an injured bird or orphaned mammal, you will know what to do to help it and how to care for it. In return, I ask only that you always return your patient to the wild when it has recovered, giving back to nature as freely as she has given to you. In this way we can all make sure that the earth's creatures will be replenished and that an endangered species may always be found in nature, not just in a zoo.

I would hate to think that the day might come when the only place you could see a brown pelican was in our backyard.

ROSEMARY K. COLLETT
Venice, Florida
September 1973

1
THE MASKED BANDIT
Raccoons

I have raised and released over thirty raccoons, twenty-five of them from infancy on the bottle. Just as no two humans are precisely identical, the raccoons I've known were distinct individuals, varying in both physical appearance and personality. We had one, Mischief (named for a characteristic that all of them seem to share), who regularly sucked her "fingers." None of the others did this. Mischief was one of the sweetest we ever raised, and we had her longer than any of the others. Most of our raccoons have been ready to leave at about eight months of age, but Mischief was fifteen months old before I decided it was time to release her. Or rather, she decided it was time. I was putting her back in her cage one day, and she didn't want to go into it. She bit me. She'd never done that before. When it happened again a week later, despite her loving and trusting nature, it was clear that she was growing up, probably going into her first mating season.

Although raccoons do not mature until they are about two years old, they can mate and bear young at an earlier age. Experts say that in the far South, as in Florida, raccoons mate in December (in the North, we are told, they mate in February). This was April. Apparently there is no such set rule, for we have had tiny orphans brought to us in May, August, November, December, and January.

*Mischief, the "finger"-sucking raccoon I raised from infancy.
She later returned to the wild via the Coonrad Hilton.*

The gestation period for raccoons is nine weeks, and the mother usually has from three to six babies, born with soft fuzzy coats, black masks, and faint tail rings. Raccoons can den in many places, but they are especially fond of hollow trees. The babies are blind at birth, and their eyes open at about three weeks. They are generally weaned at three months, but they begin making foraging trips with their mothers at about eight weeks old.

As they mature, the physical characteristics that so easily identify them develop and sharpen—the stocky bushy-haired body, the clear black mask, the pronounced black rings on the tail. Their hair can vary in color from brownish to grayish, often with black guard hairs. Some raccoons are quite red; some are albinos. Their feet are long-toed, with sharp claws, and their black front paws, so much like hands, are sensitive and as soft as kid. Raccoons average 36 inches long, with their weight ranging from 10 to 25 pounds, though some grow larger, up to 40 pounds. The Florida raccoon is smaller and has longer legs than its cousins elsewhere in the United States. Some theorists believe the Florida type may have developed longer legs to adapt to life in swampy regions.

The raccoon is often hunted with dogs especially trained for this purpose. With its shuffling, loping gait, it cannot make a fast getaway, but it is very clever. The raccoon is a great climber, often going up trees to avoid its enemies. It will break the trail in a stream, and if a dog follows it into the water, it may drown its tormentor simply by holding the dog's head under water.

Classified as omnivorous, raccoons will eat just about anything, though they seem to consume more vegetable than animal food. Their natural food is varied, depending on the habitat. They eat crayfish, snails, frogs, fish, and insects and grubs of all sorts. They love turtle eggs, and they raid sea-turtle nests on our Florida beaches. They catch mice. They like corn and other grain, wild berries and grapes of many kinds, and they love persimmons. They like nuts, such as pecans. And, as we have discovered in working with infant and adult raccoons, they also like many varieties of food from our own table, as well as canned or dried cat and dog foods.

Infant Diet and Care

The first requirement of an orphaned baby raccoon is warmth. The best way I've found to provide this is to put a heating pad, set at low heat, under a box which is lined with clean soft towels. I fill a water bottle with hot water, wrap it in a towel so the baby will not be burned, and put it in the box. The warm soft bottle is a good mother substitute and gives the small one something to snuggle against.

Sometimes I use a ten-gallon aquarium tank to house my babies, again with the heating pad underneath. The solid sides give protection against drafts, and the glass lets me watch their antics without disturbing them. Mischief, whom we fetched from Sarasota twenty miles away, where she had been found in a felled pine tree one New Year's Eve, spent her first

Ricky Raccoon is sound asleep on his towel-wrapped hot-water bottle in a glass aquarium.

weeks in a glass-walled tank—and they were literally her first weeks, for she came to us when she was only about a day old.

When we got Mischief, we had already raised five infants successfully, so we knew what to feed her and had the necessary equipment. Even for a day-old baby raccoon, a regular baby's bottle works well. I use Esbilac, a powdered formula made by the Borden Company for puppies, kittens, and many other small animals, as it is the nearest thing to mother's milk available for animals. Esbilac can be found at a veterinarian's or in many pet shops. I supplement it with Zymadrops, a multiple-vitamin preparation for human infants that is available in any drugstore. I mix my raccoon formula daily in my kitchen blender.

Infant Raccoon Formula

$\frac{2}{3}$ cup Esbilac
2 cups cool boiled water
16 drops Zymadrops vitamin supplement

Blend on medium speed for twenty seconds and store in refrigerator.

This makes enough formula for several feedings and is kept refrigerated in a sterile jar. I warm small amounts, as needed, and sterilize bottles and nipples after each use. If the baby is too weak to suck, it may take formula from a medicine dropper, but it should not be fed too fast.

An emergency-only formula can be made using evaporated milk. However, this is not nearly as nutritious or suitable as the Esbilac formula and should not be used over a long period of time.

Emergency Formula

⅓ cup evaporated milk
⅔ cup cool boiled water
8 drops Zymadrops vitamin supplement

Mix as for regular formula and store in refrigerator.

Tiny baby raccoons should be fed about every two hours, day and night, which means setting an alarm clock. A day-old raccoon will usually take barely a quarter of an ounce of formula at each feeding. By the end of the week it will often be up to half an ounce, gradually taking more and more as it grows.

I always burp my raccoon babies after feeding; they need it. I burp them just like a human baby—put a towel on my shoulder, hold the raccoon (tummy down) against me, and gently pat its back until it belches nicely. If this method doesn't produce a belch, I try rubbing gently in a circular motion between the shoulder blades.

The baby raccoon also must have a bowel and bladder action after feeding, but it can't do it alone. Mother raccoons take care of this by licking the little one. I do it by gently stroking the baby's tummy and groin until I get results. Without this

Mischief at five weeks, busy with her bottle. She drank from a standard baby bottle, sometimes holding it herself.

GEORGE R. COLLETT, JR.

aid, a baby raccoon will die of uremic poisoning or bowel blockage, so it is a vital part of the feeding procedure.

I find it advisable to keep a box of facial tissues handy for mopping up the baby *and* me. Placing the soft tissue on the genitals and gently jiggling (that's the only apt description of this action) seems to stimulate elimination extremely well, and the tissue keeps me drier and cleaner.

A raccoon baby opens its eyes at about three weeks. Within the next week, strained baby foods can be added to the diet. Raccoons like beef, chicken, and turkey and, for dessert, bananas, applesauce, and peaches. (My babies invariably prefer the chicken and bananas.) Cereal feedings can also begin at this time, using baby oatmeal mixed with a little formula into a thin gruel and fed by the bottle. I gradually increase the thickness of the mixture until I can feed it by spoon. Then I try some in a small dish. I always have tissues ready, for those first tries at a dish are pretty messy.

When they are old enough to develop teeth, small raccoons like bits of *lean* ground beef and, a little later, bones with bits of meat on them and hard dog biscuits. The raccoon will reject the bottle when it no longer needs or wants it and can then be given three meals a day of solid foods, eating as much as it wants at each feeding.

By this time, the babies should graduate to an indoor cage, as they are too large and active for a box or tank. I use a portable cage, made for dogs and cats and available at pet shops. This cage is about 40 inches long, 24 inches wide, and 24 inches high. It has a galvanized metal tray bottom which is removable. I cover this with newspapers. The top is made in one piece and is hinged, so that it is easy to clean the cage or lift out the baby. It also has 4-inch legs that hold it up off the floors, protecting against drafts. I like this type of cage at this stage, for it gives the baby raccoons room to climb, play, and get their exercise. I usually put in a towel, for a baby raccoon loves to roll up in it to doze or play at leisure.

A large, heavy water bowl is best for drinking water. As little raccoons like to use their water bowl for a potty (a natural evasive tactic in nature), the water bowl must be cleaned several times a day. In a way, this is a good thing, because it is no trouble to dump and rinse the bowl, and it saves a lot of mess on the floor of the cage.

I understand that in the wild a mother raccoon will nurse her young till they're about three months old, despite those tiny sharp teeth which must make it uncomfortable for her. My babies have refused the bottle as early as two months, while a few have clung to it until the thirteenth or fourteenth week. Mischief was one of those in no hurry to give it up. She always took her bottle in my lap, and she liked to be held and petted when she sucked her fingers too.

Raccoons have a very distinctive communicative sound, something like *churr-churr-churr*. This sound can indicate many things, depending on their mood. They can make it sound happy and contented, or angry and threatening, or even plaintive and pitiful. You soon learn to read it as you do a human baby's cry. Even day-old raccoons can *churr*. Some are more talkative than others, just as people are. Some of our baby raccoons never shut up but comment on everything, and some only talk when they have something to say.

Adult Diet and Housing

Although grown-up raccoons will eat almost anything, they should not be given greasy or spicy food. They like raw chicken necks, canned or dry dog food, cooked or raw lean meat, cooked or raw vegetables, and fruits. Their favorite of all foods is corn on the cob, and wild raccoons raid cornfields for this delicacy.

Marshmallows are a preferred dessert (although always eaten *first*) but should be given sparingly if at all, say, one or two a week. (Bear in mind that sweet people-foods of this kind are not found in the wild, as part of the raccoon's natural diet.) There is one sweet that raccoons love that is good for them—candy vitamins. I feed Pet Tabs, which are available from your veterinarian. I put them in their food dish, and they eagerly snatch them up with their hands and gobble them just like children. They are allowed just one a day.

Now, about raccoons needing water in which to "wash" their food: It has been my experience that a raccoon naturally loves to dabble in water and likes to feel things, especially in the water, just for the pleasure of feeling them and for fun and curiosity.

One of my charges, Ringer, learned to use the toilet like any human, a feat which we praised him for daily—but then he also loved to feel around in the toilet bowl and play with his production before dashing down the hall to throw his arms around my neck. One learned to flee when Ringer emerged from the bathroom.

If you are keeping a raccoon and have it in an outdoor cage, put in a small washtub of water on hot days for playing purposes. With some of our outdoor cages for raccoons, I use a drinking valve. The drinking valve is a small attachment that screws onto the end of a hose. The hose stays on at the spigot, but no water comes out until the valve is pressed. Then, *voilà!* Raccoons are very clever and learn the first time they press the valve that water will come out. They soon press it often, and with devilish precision, learning very quickly to squirt themselves in the eye, and then one another, and then you, just like a child playing with a hose. It isn't always fun for the victim, but it saves cleaning raccoon deposits out of drinking water bowls, so you might prefer the valve system. The valves are generally available at pet shops.

If you use an outdoor cage, make it large, at least 5 feet wide, 10 feet high, and 8 feet long. Build it of heavy galvanized welded wire. (See Cages and Housing at the end of the book.) If you raise the cage floor 2 feet above the ground, the droppings will fall through. The cage will stay cleaner and so will your raccoon.

The raccoon needs a nest box, in the upper cage corner, and a heavy tree limb or two for climbing purposes. Raccoons love to climb, which is why they are so hard on draperies, chandeliers, and other such home furnishings. Make sure the cage door is escape-proof—indoors or out—because raccoons can open almost anything, including your kitchen cabinets, bureau drawers, and clothes closets. When Mischief was allowed the freedom of the kitchen in our house, I had to make sure the cabinets were firmly latched. If not, she would open them and pull out all the pots and pans.

Rachel Raccoon, at eight weeks, is very playful.
Most raccoons love shiny objects, and curious Rachel is after
George's glasses.

If I seem to be giving the impression that raccoons do not make good house pets, I intend to. They are very curious, cunning, and charming, but they are also wild animals and can never be completely domesticated. They are temperamental and will bite easily if angered or crossed for a moment. Don't ever try to take food or anything else away from a raccoon.

If you are willing to endure all this to have a raccoon for a pet, never leave it alone loose in the house. Nothing is sacred with a raccoon around. I've known families who gave theirs the run of their homes. When it finally left them, just about everything—paint, draperies, wallpaper, slipcovers— had to be repaired or replaced. Cage the raccoon and take it out only at playtime.

In or out of the cage, make sure it has plenty of toys and amusing objects to play with. Raccoons love bright shiny things and will always reach for a watch, a ring, or a pen. They love balls, hard rubber ones that they can chase and chew on, and they like those rawhide bones made for dogs. They even like teddy bears, but they also like to dunk them in water. If you don't mind spending some time drying out soggy teddy bears, by all means provide one.

We see that all our raccoons receive rabies and distemper shots, whether or not we plan to release them right away. It protects the raccoon, and it could protect us from some very unpleasant consequences. The distemper shots, both canine and feline distemper vaccines of the killed virus variety, are given by the veterinarian at the age of three months. The rabies shots are given at six months. For further details on these diseases in small animals, see chapter 7, First Aid for Mammals.

Preparing the Raccoon for Release

Our friends Mary and Bill have a home in a wooded area not far from us, and they have been of great help to us in returning raccoons to the wild. For here, Mary and Bill also have the Coonrad Hilton, a raccoon halfway house constructed for just this purpose. Located in raccoon country yet not too far from civilization, the Coonrad Hilton has all the comforts of a raccoon home. Almost all our home-raised raccoons spend some time in it before returning to the woodlands, and we have found this is an excellent solution to the problem of releasing wildlife.

You cannot take a raccoon that has been raised on the bottle practically from birth and just drive out to the country, dump it, and drive off. It is something akin to dumping the family pet, only worse. The home-reared raccoon has come to depend on a supply of food, companionship, and the care of people. It does not immediately know how to find food or even how to exist in the wilderness and in all likelihood has never even seen another of its own species. A strange raccoon left in new territory might soon be attacked as an intruder by other raccoons.

At the Coonrad Hilton this problem is solved nicely by a period of reorientation with the environment. The C.H. is a large wire outdoor cage, 10 feet high, 8 feet long, and 5 feet wide, with a nice snug roof, three protected sides, big tree trunks for climbing, sleeping shelves, and an inner and an outer door with a safety corridor between.

When our raccoons are old enough to release, we take them there, and they live in the big cage, with three square meals a day, plenty of water, and human companionship. Mary often goes into the cage or sits on a stool in the entry corridor, playing and talking with the raccoon residents. Other raccoons who are native to the area, or former residents, come to visit, talk, and inspect the newcomers. When it is thought the residents are ready, both doors are left open at times, and they can go in and out as they please. Eventually they go out for good and return only as true native raccoons, to visit newcomers or to renew acquaintances with humans.

Sometimes it is hard for a released raccoon to leave. A funny case in point was that of four raccoon brothers who were thought to be ready at last for the outside world. Mary had been sitting in the corridor playing with them, and without their knowing it she left the outer door open, as well as the inner one. One by one, the raccoons wandered out into the open world.

Suddenly, one realized he was out in the open and, terrified, bolted back into the cage. His three brothers, looking up, bolted after him, and the last one in, Mary swears, slammed the door behind him with a horrified look on his face.

Eventually, though, they do adjust to their new surroundings and find homes in the woods. They gradually return to the wild state and usually do not encourage human petting, though a few have remained quite friendly and will still climb into Mary's lap on occasion.

Mary always keeps food and water out to feed the general wildlife population near her home, and we often see our "babies" among them. I see Mischief now and then, with her latest batch of children trailing along behind her. I can always recognize her because she is exceptionally tiny, has a very long, thin nose, and still responds to her name. Genghis Coon's left ear has a small notch in it, a reminder of a rough-and-tumble brawl with his brother Kubla, so he's always easy to spot. And Meeney, smallest of four brothers, still runs to Mary for protection when another raccoon gives him a hard time.

If you are planning to release a raccoon and have no Coon-rad Hilton, I can only suggest that you prevail on a friend in raccoon territory to take in a lodger for a while or, failing that, take your raccoon to the country for daily visits until it feels ready to strike out on its own. It may be that you can go to a nearby state park. In some of these, release of hand-raised animals is permitted. In others it is not, so check first with the park supervisor.

In any case, it seems advisable to release raccoons away from densely inhabited areas. Having no fear of man when first released, hand-reared animals can sometimes get into trouble with humans. I know of one gentle male raccoon that escaped from his owner in the city and was beaten to death with a shovel by a neighbor who was frightened when this docile creature approached him in friendliness.

Only the raccoon knows when it is ready for release, and no two are alike. Some mature early, and some are shy and retiring. Some are curious and aggressive, and some are home-loving and need longer periods of adjustment. A few of my babies have left home at the tender age of seven or eight months, and some, like Mischief, were not ready to face the world outside until they were well over a year old. There is no set time limit. In all releasing situations, observe your raccoon carefully, and use your own judgment and common sense.

Finally, when you have released it, make food and water available for some time. The raccoon will need this while adjusting to the wild, for it has been totally dependent on your supplying everything it requires to live. But the animal is intelligent and adaptable and will soon get along on its own.

2
READY, AIM, FIRE!
Skunks

STRIPED SKUNK

Every spring, usually in April or May, striped skunks are born throughout the United States and in parts of Canada. The mothers usually have from three to eight young ones. Blind, toothless, and hairless, the infants nevertheless show their distinctive black and white pattern on the skin at birth. They open their eyes at three weeks, are active at six weeks, and are weaned at two months. They are nearsighted animals, but they have a keen sense of smell and hearing. As they grow (full grown, they are about 25 inches long, including the tail and weigh 3½ to 10 pounds), they develop sharp teeth and claws—and, of course, the famous scent glands, one of the great defense weapons in nature.

The skunk's glands are located on each side of the anus, just under the tail. It only squirts them when very angry or frightened, and it always gives fair warning. The animal will stamp both front feet—that's the first warning. It may growl a little—the second warning. And it will lift its tail—the last call for your departure. The skunk can fire accurately (which it does by whirling and presenting its stern guns) at a distance of at least 12 feet. If it has a tail wind, it can squirt 20 feet. Five or six shots are the full magazine, and then it takes a while to summon up more firepower. Since it aims for the eyes, and is pretty accurate, keep the battle plan in mind.

Being squirted in the eyes by a skunk is very painful, but it is not blinding. The eyes can be washed out with water until they stop tearing.

None of my research tells me at precisely what age a skunk can begin firing, but the old saying that teaches "Pick up a skunk by the tail and it can't fire" is not so. If you do this, I suggest you point it in a safe direction. However, it is not right to pick up *any* animal by the tail.

We captured our wonderful striped skunk, Lovey, and took him home without ever once being sprayed. Lovey was living under a floor of a local lumberyard building, and we were asked to come and get him out. It was easier than I thought. We were shown a hole in the floor where Lovey had been seen. George stood at a distance with a long-handled dip net while I approached the hole with a bologna sandwich. I made coaxing noises, and the skunk finally came out, enticed by the smell

Lovey the striped skunk was aptly named.

ROSEMARY K. COLLETT

of the meat and bread. We popped the net over him. We judged him to be about four months old, since his mother had been in residence under the floor for about that length of time. He had not yet reached full growth, but he was old enough to use his scent glands. Yet he didn't spray. He didn't bite. He *never* did either, in all the time we had him, even before he was descented. He was always a perfect gentleman.

Skunks can be pets for years without ever being descented. The only reason I had Lovey's scent glands removed later was to use him in my school wildlife education programs; he made a wonderful example for the kids. Of course I knew he could never be released once this was done. A skunk is defenseless without scent glands.

Incidentally, when our vet descented Lovey (a very simple operation) he prudently did it outside his office building, making do with an orange crate for an operating table. He was wise enough to know that even with careful handling the scent glands can rupture when they are being removed, and his office was one of several in a large block of buildings. He was right—and even with the help of All Outdoors, the adjacent buildings emptied rapidly when the unexpected happened. "Just think," the doctor is fond of saying, "what would have happened if I'd done the operation in my office."

If descenting is required, it should be done if possible before the skunk is six weeks old, the age at which the glands are fully developed. In an older animal the procedure is a bit more difficult for both the skunk and the veterinarian.

Diet

I have never raised baby skunks from the hairless stage. Lovey was, of course, much older when we found him. I have since read that some infant skunks are allergic to milk. If so, they would probably do well on Soyalac, a soybean substitute formula for human babies, fed from a sterilized pet nurser bottle every two or three hours. The Esbilac formula suitable to infant raccoons (⅔ cup Esbilac mixed with 2 cups cool boiled water, plus 16 drops Zymadrops vitamin supplement) is probably all right for infant skunks too, unless they develop diarrhea from it.

In any case, I had not heard of the milk allergy when Lovey turned up, and I put him on a bread and milk mush which he ate off my fingers. He ate about two cups at a feeding, six times a day. He did beautifully on it.

When Lovey had been on milk and bread for a month, I tried him on Friskies canned cat food. He liked it and soon showed a preference for the chicken and kidney variety. In the wild, skunks eat all sorts of things—grubs and worms, insects, fruits of all kinds, and small animals such as meadow mice, pocket gophers, chipmunks, ground squirrels, and small cottontail rabbits. They have even been known to eat carrion. In his domesticated world, Lovey's diet grew to include fruit and vegetables such as apples, corn on the cob, and grapes, and sometimes stripped raw chicken necks. He also liked leftover roast beef.

This variety must have been good for him. He lived with us to the age of seven and a half years, when he finally died in his sleep of old age. He was always healthy. Zoo records I have seen say the average life span for their skunks is five and a half to six years.

Skunks as Pets

Although it has never been my purpose to recommend wildlife as pets, the striped skunk is probably the best species fitted for that role.

Of course, it depends on the skunk. Skunks vary widely in personality, as do all animals, but they are generally clean, affectionate, and intelligent. They can be easily trained to use a kitty litter box, but it is a good idea to clean it daily, because skunk droppings are very odoriferous.

Lovey was a shy, quiet, and retiring skunk, but always loving and gentle. I liked to use him in my school programs because he was so good with the children and did not mind being petted by many hands. I always told the children not to touch his tail, however. Most skunks dislike having their tails handled.

If you do plan to keep a skunk as a pet, be sure that it is inoculated for rabies and distemper. And if descenting is to be done, remember to do it early (preferably before the animal

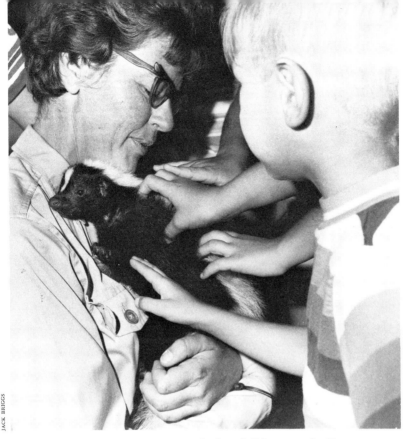

Lovey was a great favorite with the children and often accompanied me for our school programs.

is six weeks old) and remember that once descented your pet should never be released into the wild.

There are places that sell wild animals such as skunks for pets. You should always start with a very young one, six or eight weeks old, that has never been owned by anyone else, so you can train it to your own household. From living with former owners many older pets develop neuroses, or at least habits that can never be broken.

After Lovey died, we needed a replacement for him in our school lectures and made the mistake of buying Flower at a pet shop. She was a year old, and though she is descented, has had her shots, and is gentle enough after she is picked up, she has one strange habit. When she has not been handled for a while, she bites once at being picked up. After that she is all right. But whoever picks her up the *first* time is bitten. We don't know what started this habit, but there seems no cure.

Housing

Pet skunks can be kept in the house just like a house cat. We keep ours in outdoor cages, one to a cage, since we are not attempting to breed them. Young skunks can graduate at about five or six weeks from an infant cardboard box with heating pad.

Since young skunks are weaned at two months in the wild, and are pretty much on their own at three months, they could be moved from an indoor cage to an outdoor cage at the latter age, provided the weather is mild. We use welded wire cages with wire floors, 5 feet long, 4 feet wide, and 3 feet high, as striped skunks do not climb and do not need much headroom in their cages (see Cages and Housing section). We put in a box with soft bedding for a den—we use wooden boxes with burlap or old towels. They like to hole up in these to sleep, especially in cool weather. The cage is raised about 2 feet off the ground so droppings can fall through. On hot days, skunks need shade, so be sure there is a shady corner in the cage. Lovey liked to lie on his back with his feet in the air and snooze in the shade on hot days.

With skunks we use gravity-flow water bottles with plastic or metal tubes instead of water bowls. Skunks are not very fond of water and feel no need to dabble in it. To the water bottle we add one drop Zymadrops vitamins per ounce of water.

Our adult skunks eat one large meal a day, usually in the evening, containing a selection of whatever they like that is available at the moment. A salt-mineral block, like that used for rabbits and guinea pigs, is kept in the cage. Any uneaten food is removed in the morning.

SPOTTED SKUNK

The spotted skunk, sometimes incorrectly called "civet cat," lives in the mountainous areas of the southeastern and central United States and occurs as far west as British Columbia and as far south as Mexico and Guatemala.

Like the striped skunk, it is born hairless and blind. The eyes open at four weeks, in five weeks it is active, and by the age of five months it is full-grown. This is a smaller breed of skunk, however, and the adults are no larger than a kitten, about 14 to 22 inches long, including tail, and average 6 inches in height at the shoulder. Full adult weight for these little skunks is from 1 to 2 pounds.

The same feeding and care applies to infant spotted skunks as to striped skunks. The adults will eat anything, and in the wild eat approximately the same diet as the striped skunks. Our spotted skunk, Tabu, eats the same adult diet as our striped skunks. These skunks are climbers, however, and need a taller outdoor cage than the striped variety, with a branch or tree section for climbing.

Because spotted skunks are more nervous and high-strung than the striped variety, they do not make good pets. We bought Tabu from a roadside animal attraction to give him a better life than the one he was living. He is now almost seven years old—a ripe old age for a skunk—and in good health, but we don't handle him very much because of his nervous temperament. For the same reason, although he has been descented and has been with us for a long time, I don't use him in my school programs. He will simply live out his years in a large cage in our backyard, and he seems quite contented to do so.

Release

To repeat, a descented skunk should never be returned to the wild. It is a certain death sentence to turn any skunk loose in the woods and mountains without its weaponry intact. Although it has very sharp teeth and sharp claws, it cannot defend itself with these alone.

Unlike raccoons, skunks do not require a period of preparation and adjustment to release. It is a one-shot procedure, luckily, because whoever transports them—preferably to a nice skunky-type environment, with woodlands or mountains, depending on their original home—can expect to get sprayed.

I released three young skunks from the same litter at the age of four months. They had been kept at my home and I had been feeding them for two months, just to be certain they were old enough to make it on their own. They had never offered to spray me—of course, they were striped skunks with gentlemanly qualities—but when I put them in a cardboard box to drive them out to the country, they were frightened and all three of them fired at will.

I drove them out to the country, released them, wished them well, and then came home and took a bath in tomato juice. It was a while before my clothes and the car lost the aromatic reminders of that good deed.

3
PABLUM TO PECANS
Squirrels, Chipmunks, and Other Rodents

Over the years we have raised several dozen squirrels, many of them from infancy. Like infant raccoons, they are raised on a bottle and kept in the same warm cozy surroundings—on soft bedding in a box or fish tank with heating pad under it.

While most of our experience has been with flying squirrels and gray squirrels, which are native to Florida, we have also raised ground squirrels and chipmunks, which are not native to this state, and white-tailed antelope squirrels—but more about them later.

GRAY SQUIRREL

The gray squirrel ranges the eastern United States, parts of the Midwest, the extreme western United States, and from Baja California to the state of Washington. There are two species, the eastern gray squirrel and the western gray squirrel. The color varies from grayish to brownish, with light underparts. They average in size from 17 to 23 inches, including their long bushy tails, and weigh from 1 to 1½ pounds. There are occasional albino squirrels and melanistic (black) squirrels. A few scattered colonies of white squirrels have black eyes.

Baby squirrels are usually born in late winter or spring, but they can be born any time of year. The gestation period is about forty-four days. Two to six are born in a litter. Their eyes open at five weeks, but they often stay with the mother throughout the first winter.

These squirrels, a great favorite of hunters, are most active in their playing and feeding times at early morning and at dusk. Their natural food is nuts and large seeds, acorns, fruits and berries, mushrooms, and the larvae and cocoons of insects.

FLYING SQUIRREL

The unique little flying squirrel also occurs in two species, the eastern and the northern. It has a flattened, bushy tail and folds of skin between the fore and hind legs, which it can spread to sail through the air from tree to tree. It does not actually "fly," but it appears to when it glides through the air. This squirrel comes in varying shades of brown, with buffy underparts, and has large eyes with good night vision,

A young flying squirrel is very small.

ROSEMARY K. COLLETT

as it is primarily a nocturnal animal. The adult averages from 9 to 14 inches in length, including tail, and weighs from 1½ to 5¾ ounces.

The northern species breeds once a year, in February or March. The southern variety may have two litters a year. The gestation period is forty days. These little squirrels open their eyes at about twenty-six days and are nursed by the mother every hour or two for a full five weeks. Then they can start nibbling soft foods.

The natural food of the flying squirrel includes nuts and seeds, mushrooms, persimmons, apples, wild grapes and other fruits, beetles and insects, and the eggs and nestlings of birds.

Flying squirrels have been known to live as long as five years.

EASTERN CHIPMUNK

The eastern chipmunk, distinguished by its facial stripes in its particular range, is about 5 to 6 inches in length, not counting the tail, which can be 3 to 4 inches long. Average weight for the adult is about 2¼ ounces. April birthdays are the rule for young eastern chipmunks, which are usually born four to five in a litter after a gestation period of thirty-two days. Naked at birth, they have a light coat of hair at two weeks, and their eyes open at about one month. They leave their mother and their underground burrow when they are three months old. Their adult food is berries, nuts, acorns, mushrooms, seeds, grain, and insects.

The eastern chipmunk is found in most of the eastern United States and in southeastern Canada.

LEAST CHIPMUNK

The least chipmunk is the smallest of the chipmunk family. Average adult size is about 3 to 4½ inches in length, plus a 3- to 4-inch tail. This little fellow only weighs 1 to 2 ounces at maturity. Underground burrows are the home of this species, which is a hibernating creature. Food for the adult least chipmunk is seeds, fruit, nuts, and insects.

THIRTEEN-LINED GROUND SQUIRREL

The thirteen-lined ground squirrel, at maturity, is 4½ to 6½ inches long, with a tail that may range from 2½ to 5 inches. The adult can weigh from 5 to 9 ounces. As the name implies, they have—usually but not always—thirteen markings formed by spots or lines on the body.

These striking little fellows favor the shortgrass prairies and are found in the Great Plains and also the prairie regions of the central United States and southern Canada. They can have seven to ten young in a litter, generally born in May after a gestation period of twenty-eight days. A hibernating creature which lives in underground burrows, this ground squirrel feeds mostly on seeds and insects.

WHITE-TAILED ANTELOPE SQUIRREL

The white-tailed antelope squirrel is native to the American West and Southwest. This species somewhat resembles the chipmunk, with a single stripe pattern, but the stripes are only on the body, not on the face. The adult grows to 5½ to 6½ inches in length and has a 2- to 3-inch tail. Weight varies from 3 to 5½ ounces. These squirrels do not hibernate. The eight to nine young are usually born in April or May.

Our first pair came from a pet dealer some years ago. We were told they would not breed in captivity—a point on which most authorities agree—but within a year after we acquired them the female gave birth to twelve young. They were all immediately trampled to death by the father, who was still in an amorous mood.

We were too ignorant to know that we should have re-

Wiggles, a white-tailed antelope squirrel, sits in her food dish.

ROSEMARY K. COLLETT

moved the father from the cage a week before birth, a fact we found out later from Ivan Sanderson, the noted zoologist and author. We had learned by this time that the gestation period was thirty-one days, and we watched the pair for the next event.

The summer of the same year, they bred again, and this time we removed the father a week before the birth. We put him in a cage nearby where he and the mother could "talk" and visit, and they were very well satisfied. Mama had ten babies this time and raised them all successfully.

This is, to our knowledge, the first known breeding in captivity of the white-tailed antelope squirrel. At least, that's what zoologists and mammologists tell us. The little pair hadn't read the book, I guess, because they continued to reproduce regularly. They raised four more litters, and the first generation is now producing litters of its own. We are now conducting longevity and behavioral studies on the white-tailed antelope squirrel.

We can only attribute our success (or their success) to the fact that they have a secure, happy home and a very good diet. They get the same basic food as all our squirrels. (In the wild this species eats leaves, twigs, and plant buds, the fruit of cactus, insects, and seeds, grains, and cultivated fruits. They rarely drink water in their natural habitat, but ours, raised in captivity, drink quite a lot of water, perhaps because their diet is different.) Although we have them in relatively small cages, some only 22 inches square, they are active and happy little animals. Needless to say, we will never release them.

Infant Diet and Care

The same diet and care will work with all varieties of baby squirrels and chipmunks.

Bottles for them should be the pet nurser type, available at your pet shop. If the animals are very small, we find the little doll bottles from the dime store are useful. You can also use a medicine dropper. Keep a good supply of nipples on hand if using bottles, for these babies have very sharp little teeth and can chew through a nipple pretty fast.

The formula for baby squirrels, chipmunks, ground squirrels, et al., is similar to the raccoon formula.

Baby Squirrel Formula

⅓ cup Esbilac
1 cup cool boiled water

Blend on medium speed for twenty seconds and store in refrigerator.

We do *not* use the vitamin drops with this formula; it seems to cause diarrhea in baby squirrels and chipmunks. We warm small amounts as needed, always sterilizing bottles or droppers.

An infant gray squirrel and its doll bottle.

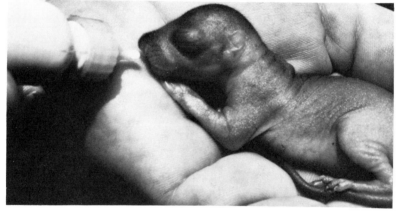

Sebastian Squirrel takes his Esbilac formula from a pet nurser bottle. At six weeks he began to scamper across the sofa and explore.

Very tiny babies need to be fed every two hours day and night. Young gray squirrels may take only ⅛ ounce at a time. Flying squirrels and chipmunks may take even less.

The grays have their eyes open at five weeks, and the flying squirrels open their eyes at twenty-six to twenty-eight days. Two weeks after their eyes open, we make a thin gruel, by adding baby oatmeal cereal to the formula, and feed it three times a day with the bottle. We also continue the regular formula bottle feedings, however, at the more frequent intervals.

We gradually thicken the oatmeal mix, and after three to four weeks we try feeding it with a spoon, so the baby can learn to lap it, still continuing with the formula bottle feedings. The tummy and groin must be stroked after feeding to encourage elimination, as with baby raccoons.

As the babies take more formula at a time, the time between feedings can be lengthened, for by the time they are six or seven weeks old they can take ½ ounce or better at a feeding. Then we drop the night feedings. We feed them just before we retire, and as soon as we get up in the morning.

First solid foods are given when the babies start nibbling— on their towel, on their cereal spoon, and on us. Such treats as small slices of apple, dry toast, and dog biscuits are good starters.

When they eat these well, we add sunflower seeds. As baby raccoons do, squirrels will refuse the bottle when they adapt to a solid diet and no longer need the formula.

Adult Diet and Housing

When they become self-feeders, a good diet is a mixture of sunflower seeds, wild birdseed, nonsweetened puffed-wheat cereal, and unsweetened wheat germ.

To this mixture can be added dry dog kibbles and Granola, a cereal product.

All the "squirrel people"—and in this category I include the squirrels mentioned, the ground squirrel and chipmunk, and some other varieties—like many kinds of fruits, vegetables, and nuts. We give them a choice of cherries, lettuce, apples, oranges, grapes, raisins, carrots, raw sweet potatoes, corn on the cob, and, if available, the fruit of the prickly pear cactus. White-tailed antelope squirrels love the prickly pear cactus fruit, as they come from the desert Southwest. Thirteen-lined ground squirrels like meat as well—occasional grasshoppers and insects. Some favorite nuts are raw peanuts (but not too many), pecans (shelled or unshelled), walnuts, hickory nuts, and acorns. If raw peanuts are unavailable, roasted *unsalted* peanuts can be given.

When squirrels are big enough to be very active, if they are going to be indoors for a while they should be moved to a cage at least 2 to 3 feet square. (See Cages and Housing section.) The cage should have in it an exercise wheel, small branches (nonpoisonous) * for climbing, and a clean pine cone for chewing. These animals need chewing material or their teeth get too long.

We use cedar chips on the floor of the cage. They are available at pet shops or feedstores. They smell good, are absorbent, and will last about a week before they need changing. We use parakeet nesting boxes for "beds," because these creatures love to curl up in something cozy when they sleep. Half a dozen flying squirrels or chipmunks will crowd into one box together. A cockatiel nestbox, available in many pet stores, works well for the larger gray squirrels.

We put a salt-mineral block in their cage and supply water to cages in water bottles, the self-feeding gravity-flow bottles made of glass or plastic with a stopper and glass or metal tube. To their water we add one drop of Zymadrops liquid vitamins per ounce. We change the water daily and keep the water bottle and tube clean, using a bottle brush and pipe cleaners.

We never put the cage near a wall, as these animals have a habit of urinating and defecating through the wire without inhibition. And we don't put the cage near our draperies,

* Examples of nonpoisonous branches would be pine, fir, oak, and cypress. So many plants in our tropical Florida climate are poisonous in some respect, such as sap, root, or fruit. These may be poisonous only to humans and not to other mammals and birds, but I prefer to play it safe. Some poisonous exotics found in Florida are tung oil tree, wax-leaf ligustrum, chinaberry, and oleander. Interestingly, squirrels sometimes eat mushrooms that would be poisonous to man, but the squirrels are not affected.

either, for they are fond of chewing anything they can reach.

Handling Squirrels

If you are handling any of these small animals, be careful because you may get bitten. These are nervous little creatures, and you should never pounce on them from above when picking them up. Lift them by sliding a hand underneath and picking them up gently. They do like to bite, and they *are* wild animals, so they may bite you anyway if they just don't want to be picked up, or if they are interrupted in their play and don't want to be bothered.

Pontius and Tallulah were two thirteen-lined ground squirrels we raised. Pontius was always washing his hands, and Tallulah had a very throaty voice. Tallulah bit me.

Don't, as I did when bitten, playfully call the doctor's office and tell the nurse, "I've just been bitten by a *Citellus tridecemlineatus*. Do I need a tetanus shot?" You will get a cool reception from the nurse, who doesn't think such jokes are funny, especially when she finds out you're talking about a thirteen-lined ground squirrel. (Yes, I got a tetanus shot.)

Preparing for Release

Sister and Brother were two gray squirrels of the same litter. They were the first we raised from infancy. When they were old enough to need more exercise, we let them out of their cage and they played in the house, getting ready for the day of their release. The young gray squirrel is two months old before it is strong enough to climb trees.

Their favorite game was "Tree," a game which involved their getting a running start across the living room and climbing—me! I soon learned to wear slacks and long sleeves, because they climbed me with great glee. If George happened to be standing nearby, they made great leaps to his head. The landings were slippery, because George is bald as an egg.

When Christmas came along, they discovered with delight the joy of romping among the gift packages and rolling themselves up in ribbon—not to mention the wonder of the Christmas tree. They wrought havoc playing "Tree" with a real tree, and the Christmas ornaments suffered miniature earthquakes daily. They liked the tree so much that when Christmas was over we just took off the decorations and lights and left it there for them to climb. They loved it, and so did we, even if it did look rather odd to have a bare Christmas tree in the living room long after the holidays.

If you plan to do this, make sure your Christmas tree is not a chemically treated tree that might be poisonous to small animals.

Releasing squirrels and chipmunks is rather like releasing raccoons, only squirrels seem to adapt much more easily. When Sister and Brother began to bite when we took them down from the Christmas tree skeleton, we moved them to an outdoor cage much like the Coonrad Hilton. After several weeks, we left the cage door open and let them go.

When first released, they would come to us, but after two or three weeks they would not come at all and quickly reverted to the wild state.

RATS AND MICE

Rats and mice, we have found, both domestic and wild varieties, can be raised in the same manner as squirrels. There is really not much point in raising baby field mice and wild rats—they are too high-strung to be good pets and never really settle down to a people-oriented environment as squirrels and raccoons do—but when they are brought to you by a tearful little boy, it is hard to say no. We have raised the black rat (*Rattus rattus*), the hispid cotton rat, and several field mice from infancy. We did it as an experiment, to see if we could, and we successfully used the squirrel bottle formula and dry diet.

There are, of course, no problems involved in releasing wild rats and mice—except that they may not leave, preferring to become permanent tenants somewhere in or under your house. It's a good idea to take them a safe distance away when you let them go. Domestic varieties, such as white mice or rats, are another matter. They are not equipped to survive in a natural environment and should never be released in the wild.

4
ODDBALLS
Opossums and Armadillos

OPOSSUM

The opossum, with its long, naked prehensile tail, is the only marsupial (pouched mammal) in North America. Opossums have been found as far north as New Hampshire, Vermont, New York, Michigan, and Wisconsin. They are also found in the Pacific coast states of California, Oregon, and Washington and in many parts of the South.

The babies are born after only a thirteen-day gestation period and are still almost in the embryonic state, weighing $\frac{1}{15}$ ounce. They crawl into the mother's pouch and attach themselves to a nipple, and there they stay off and on for several months. They begin leaving the pouch to ride their mother's back at about two months. They go off on their own at around three months.

Infant Care

It is almost impossible to hand-raise a baby opossum that is so young as to be blind and hairless. If they are well haired and their eyes are open, you can use a bottle-fed Esbilac formula.

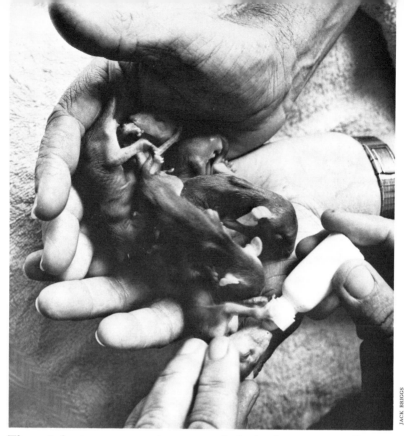

These infant opossums, just recently haired, are so small they can only manage a doll bottle nurser.

Infant Formula

⅓ cup Esbilac
1 cup cool boiled water
2 to 3 drops Zymadrops vitamin supplement

Mix the formula in a blender and store in the refrigerator.

A pet nurser bottle or doll bottle, sterilized, is good for very small opossums. Small amounts of the formula are warmed as needed and given every two hours day and night.

The young opossum is kept in a box with soft bedding and a heating pad on low under the box. Elimination is encouraged after each feeding by stroking the belly and groin.

Possum Personalities

The opossum, I am sorry to say, is the stupidest animal

alive. It is dumb, dumb, dumb; most zoologists with whom I have talked agree with me. Ask any of them what is the dumbest animal alive, and they will answer immediately, "The opossum."

It is also, however, one of the most ancient orders of animals on our planet. Extremely adaptable to changes in both environment and diet, it has survived a very long time.

The adult opossum is omnivorous. It will eat anything: meat, vegetables, fruits—and your hand. It will also eat carrion, insects, worms, mice, and birds and their eggs.

The adult opossum has fifty very sharp teeth and knows how to use them. I do not believe much in their "playing possum," since all the opossums I have raised charge, snarling, with fangs bared, when they are angry. Once they take hold, they do not always let go. Whether they think they are eating dinner or forget what they are doing, I don't know.

George was bitten this way just by reaching into the cage to pet Peter, one of our possum patients. Peter hung in there; we had to tap him smartly on the head to make him let go. George applied antiseptic to his hand and gave up possum petting.

There is nothing quite as mad as a mad opossum. I once had an experience with a rogue opossum that was invading our yard, teasing our crippled gulls and pelicans regularly. It was the only time in my life I ever picked up an opossum —or any animal—by the tail, but I grabbed this one just as it was coming over our back fence on its nightly foray. If I hadn't had it by the tail, I wouldn't have had much hand left, because it snarled and snapped in a fury. But I plopped it into a box and we hauled it off to the country for release. I hope it didn't find more mischief to get into in the wild.

Opossums like to use their "hands" when they eat, as a raccoon does. Peter was a terrible slob—he was really mad about overripe bananas, and he would take a whole one, literally mash it into his face with a dreadful slurp, and then, chewing, with ripe banana squirting out both sides of his jaws, he would grin—like a possum. His other favorite was ripe mangoes. In general, we have found opossums like ripe fruit of all kinds.

Peter developed a lesion on his hand which turned out to be a cancer. A vet, after doing a biopsy and determining it was malignant, operated on the hand, but it was too late. Peter died at the age of two and a half years.

Here in Florida, as elsewhere, many opossums are hit by cars, and many babies still in the pouch or clinging to their mother's back are orphaned and usually die. Some of the opossums we have raised from infancy were such victims. Sometimes we could save them if they were old enough, hadn't been injured, and didn't get too cold before we got them home.

One of our girl opossums, Blossom, was such an orphan. (The female, incidentally, can easily be determined by the semicircular pouch opening on the lower abdomen.) Blossom was raised successfully and released.

Two other highway orphans, Skinny and Fat Stuff, arrived one Mother's Day. Returning home that evening, I found a large cardboard box beside the door. It contained a dead opossum. Since it hardly seemed a suitable Mother's Day gift, I took a closer look. Suddenly it moved—or rather, a portion of its anatomy moved. It proved to be a female with two

This baby opossum, less than two months old, arrived in its dead mother's pouch. It was haired and its eyes were open, so we were able to raise it successfully.

ROSEMARY K. COLLETT

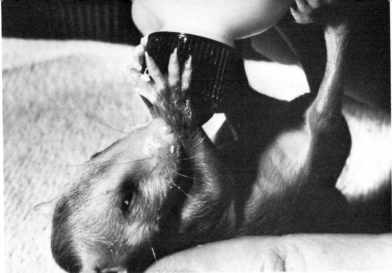

*At this size the baby can take its formula from a pet nurser
bottle. Though raising opossums is unrewarding, it is
certainly a challenge.*

young in her pouch. She had obviously been struck and killed
by a car, but the two youngsters were still alive.

They were completely haired and their eyes were open. I
rushed the box inside to an aquarium tank, set the heating
pad beneath it on low, and popped the youngsters in. The
Esbilac formula was quickly prepared, and within twenty
minutes the infants were fed and sound asleep.

Skinny and Fat Stuff are still here, having more than
doubled in size. They graduated from the Esbilac to strained
baby foods and are now eating canned cat food. They defi-
nitely prefer chicken and kidney, and they like ripe bananas
for dessert. They will be released soon.

Adult Diet and Care

Opossums are ready to go on solid foods as soon as they
refuse the bottle. Then we put them on a diet which may include any one or a variety of these: lean ground beef, canned
cat or dog food, raw eggs, fruits of all kinds, and vegetables.
They are very fond of such vegetables as raw sweet potatoes
and corn on the cob. Skinny and Fat Stuff adore unseasoned
scrambled eggs, their first solid food.

When first put on a solid diet, our young opossums get two
to three meals daily. But by the time they are ready to be
released, they are eating only one large meal a day, in the

morning. They must have fresh water in their cage at all times.

We put opossums in a wire-bottomed cage as soon as they are too active for a small box or tank, because their droppings are very smelly and messy. We always move them to an outdoor cage as soon as we can. We put a tray under the wire floor when the cage is indoors and cover the tray bottom with absorbent cedar chips or kitty litter. We change it often. When the cage is outdoors, we raise it on legs or blocks so the droppings can fall through the wire floor.

Adults and nonrelated young opossums must be housed one to a cage. They are solitary creatures and may fight if caged together.

Release

There is not much problem to releasing an opossum when it is adult and self-feeding. In fact, it need not be fully adult. Half-grown opossums can get along just fine. We simply take the cage out to some nice wooded area and open it. It will walk out snarling, without a word of thanks, and depart without a backward glance. Opossums seem to adapt well and easily return to the wild.

There are few rewards in raising opossums. However, they are certainly a real challenge, and if you like challenges, there is something to be said for that. Just remember that opossums are not affectionate or loyal or trustworthy. They are true only to their own nature. It does not include charm, so don't expect it of them.

ARMADILLO

The armadillo has to be seen to be believed. It is surely the oddest of all oddballs in our area. Armadillos are plentiful here in Florida, where they snoofle about the lawns at early dawn and dusk, digging for grubs and insects. They are extremely shy and very nearsighted, and many are killed by cars on our highways. They are also hunted by dogs and man, because they are considered as tasty as pork.

We have the nine-banded variety in the United States, which cannot curl up into a tight ball as some of the South

JACK BRIGGS

A local boy "rescued" this armadillo, which immediately became camera-shy. Since it was unhurt and old enough to take care of itself, we released it.

American varieties do. It can only run, dig a hole and curl up as best it can to protect its soft belly, which is not armored like the back.

The armadillo ranges in Texas, Oklahoma, Louisiana, Arkansas, Mississippi, and Florida on our continent, because it likes warmer climes and cannot live or feed in cold weather.

It is a good pest controller, eating sugar-cane borers, termites, wireworms, centipedes, grasshoppers, fire ants, scorpions, tarantulas, roaches, and the eggs and larvae of many insects.

At maturity it is 2½ feet long and weighs from 12 to 15 pounds. It has funny little muley ears but doesn't hear well. It has lovely long eyelashes, scaly legs like a dragon, with long talons for digging, and a light growth of hair on its armored back and unprotected belly.

Armadillos are odd in so many ways. They always have four young, always the same sex. Appropriately, the mother has four nipples for nursing. The babies are identical, even to the number of hairs and scales, say the experts. They are born in February, March, or April, with their eyes open, and are able to move about with the mother, like young guinea pigs, within a few hours of birth. Their armor is soft as fine leather at birth, and lightly haired, but grows harder as they mature. They can outrun a man and outdodge many dogs, and they can swim. They have been known to walk across short waterways on the bottom, holding their breath, as the hippopotamus does.

The babies nurse for about two months but begin eating insects before they are weaned. They eat, like an anteater, with a long, sticky tongue, which sucks up insects and larvae. They have no canine or incisor teeth, only back molars.

Infant Diet and Care

Armand, the youngest armadillo we ever had, was brought to us with a gash behind his ear—probably he had been attacked by a dog. After a visit to the vet, who treated his wounds, we put him in a warm box to recover, since he was obviously very young. His shell was still soft, and we estimated his age at six to eight weeks.

*Armand Armadillo, at the age of eight weeks, fit in Jan's
cupped hands.*

He did well on a diet of a *sloppy* mixture of ground chuck,
Esbilac, raw egg, several drops of Zymadrops vitamins, and
several drops of cod liver oil.

Very tiny baby armadillos can be given the same Esbilac
formula as opossums. They need to be fed every three hours,
using a sterilized pet nurser bottle.

At six weeks, bottle-fed armadillos can be started on the
meat-milk-egg mix. We use a wide-mouthed plastic medicine
dropper until they can learn to eat from a dish.

When armadillos are kept in a larger cage than the infant
box they are given a dish of water—a heavy dish that cannot
be turned over easily. Armadillos are clumsy and awkward
when moving about and turn things over without half trying.

Baby armadillos can be housed in heavy cardboard cartons,
but a large metal washtub is best, lined with newspapers.

They are great diggers and can dig their way out of a flimsy box.

It is necessary to put a wire cover, securely fastened, over the top, because they are also jumpers. In fact, the funny little jump an armadillo gives when it is startled is peculiar to its personality.

One summer evening, George and I were standing barefoot on our lawn quietly watching five or six armadillos rooting about, completely unaware of our presence. (They are so nearsighted and their hearing is so poor that they are almost totally dependent on their noses and sense of smell to warn them of danger.) One of them came busily rooting along right up to George's foot, and suddenly its snout touched a human toe. The armadillo leaped straight up in the air just like a cartoon character and was gone like a shot. These animals can move very fast, despite their bulk.

The armadillo will often sit on its hind legs, bracing itself with its tail, and sniff the air for danger or for food. They are gregarious creatures—as many as fifty have been seen, feeding quietly together.

Adults

In spite of the fact that armadillos are numerous here in Florida, we have not had many for patients. They are often too severely injured to recover by the time we get them.

I have not discussed the adult diet and care of these animals, because the majority of our patients were infants which we released as soon as they were self-feeding and large enough.

Adult armadillos could probably eat the same sloppy mixture prepared for Armand, with the addition of grubs and insects when available. They should always have fresh water available.

Release

Releasing armadillos has always been easy. We carry them out to the woods in their washtub with its screened lid. We lift the screen, and they leap straight out of the tub and are off like a shot into the woodland home they love so well.

5
PETER WHO?
Rabbits

There are many species of wild rabbits, and they are found in almost every part of the United States. We have worked only with the cottontail and the swamp rabbit, but the diet and methods described in this chapter would probably suit all the rabbit clan, including the domestic rabbit.

COTTONTAIL RABBIT

The cottontail consists of several subspecies found throughout the United States and Central and South America. Their fur color differs in various areas, but the white "cottontail" is their distinguishing characteristic. Rabbits in this family may vary in weight from 4 to 11 pounds, and their length ranges from 11 to 22 inches. Cottontails are smaller than jackrabbits and other hares, and their ears are shorter.

Cottontails can and do breed any month of the year. Their gestation period is twenty-eight days. The mother makes a carefully concealed nest, often in high grass or brush, and lines it with fur pulled from her own body. This cozy lining makes a warm soft bed, for it is 3 to 4 inches deep when the nest is finished.

Litters generally range from one to eight bunnies. The tiny

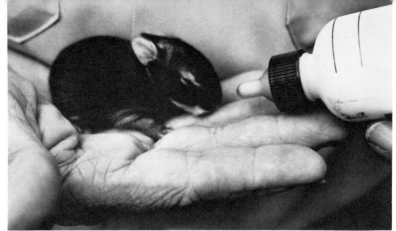

This tiny cottontail rabbit, eyes still closed, is less than a week old; it is fed the Esbilac formula with a pet nurser bottle.

babies are 4 inches long, born with their eyes closed and their little ears flat against their heads. They are not born with fur, but within a week they have a full rabbit coat. The eyes open as early as the sixth day after birth. They grow rapidly, nursing the mother at night. She feeds on green shoots and vegetable growth in the interim.

Baby cottontails leave the nest at two weeks, but they don't range far at first. They learn to nibble tender green shoots, under their mother's tutelage, and finally leave the nest for good when they are about three weeks old.

At that age, though they are still hardly more than babies, they are self-sufficient and do not need "rescuing" if found alone. They mature rapidly, too, and are full grown at five or six months. They can start producing babies of their own before they are a year old.

This species generally rests during the day and feeds from dusk to dawn. When living out a full span, they generally live about two years.

SWAMP RABBIT

The swamp rabbit is found in marshy wetland areas from the southeastern Atlantic to the Gulf coasts. Swamp rabbits range inland also in southern Illinois and Oklahoma, and from Mexico to parts of South America.

The swamp rabbit is a dark rabbit. Its fur is short and coarse, and it does not have the startling white undertail of its cottontail cousins.

Its breeding and feeding habits are similar to the cottontail.

Rabbit Rescues

Remember the early self-sufficiency of young rabbits, and don't rescue them if they don't need it and are minding their own business. To illustrate: The day after one of my lectures at a junior high school, a teacher telephoned to tell me of a rabbit "rescue." One of her young students, an aspiring track star, had spotted a half-grown cottontail on the school campus. Off went the youngster, determined to rescue the unfortunate animal. The rabbit had other ideas. Boy and rabbit tore around the school grounds as though it were a Marine Corps obstacle course. Over, under, and around trees, bushes, bicycle racks, basketball courts, football field, and grandstands they went, dodging, twisting, and turning.

The poor rabbit was no match for the speed and endurance of his rescuer and at last, exhausted, was caught. The triumphant youngster, clutching the now almost prostrate rabbit, appeared before his teacher. "Mrs. Stuart, I rescued a rabbit for Mrs. Collett."

The teacher examined the rabbit and then gently explained to the boy that it was hale and hearty, though totally exhausted, and didn't really need rescuing. At her suggestion, the boy returned the rabbit to a small plot of grass on the corner of the school yard. It was last seen hurrying to the safety of the woods beyond.

Even young rabbits of two weeks may be feeding under the watchful eye of their mother, so don't be too eager to save them. But if the mother is nowhere in sight, and the baby rabbit is in an abandoned nest or in the open, and if it has closed eyes and ears flat against the head, it is probably an orphan.

Rabbits, even when tiny, are extremely shy and nervous, so pick them up carefully and handle them gently. Wrap them in a sweater or put them in a shoebox for transport.

Diet

Our infant cottontail and swamp rabbits do well on the same Esbilac formula we use for other small mammals (⅓ cup Esbilac and 1 cup cool boiled water), but we do not use the Zymadrops with this formula. We store the formula in the refrigerator, as usual, and warm the bottles before feeding. For baby rabbits we use a sterilized doll bottle or pet nurser bottle or medicine dropper. (Don't feed too fast with the dropper.)

If you have no Esbilac, here is an emergency-only infant formula:

> ⅓ cup evaporated milk
> ⅔ cup cool boiled water
> 2 drops Zymadrops vitamin supplement

Blend on medium speed for twenty seconds.

This formula is also stored in the refrigerator and warmed only when used. The Esbilac formula should be used as soon as you can get it—it is a far superior diet.

Tiny baby rabbits are fed every hour. I do not burp my rabbit babies. We find that baby rabbits do not want to be burped. As soon as they are full, they get very squirmy, and all they want to do is get down and hop off their energy. They know best.

Since in the wild baby rabbits are accustomed to nursing at night, they take their bottle better at night. However, for our sakes, we try to convert them to a daytime schedule.

At two weeks, baby rabbits are quite active and like a supplement to the bottle, such as strained carrots (we use baby food) and bits of clean, washed lettuce. They also enjoy rolled

Little Peter Cottontail, age four weeks, still likes to take his oatmeal and formula mixture from a spoon. He soon graduated to solid foods and was finally released on our acre.

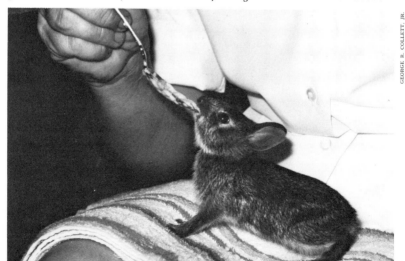

GEORGE R. COLLETT, JR.

oats, which they will eat from a dish. A substitute for the rolled oats is oatmeal baby cereal, made into a thin gruel with the Esbilac formula. The strained carrots and gruel are fed with a medicine dropper or from a small spoon.

Injuries

We have dealt mostly with infant rabbits in our work, so only the rearing and release of young rabbits will be covered in this chapter. We have had a few injured adult rabbits, but rabbits are so prone to instant death from shock, heart attack, and injuries that we have had very few recoveries. Smashed bones or internal injuries are usually fatal. Rabbits that have been mauled by dogs and cats can sometimes be helped if they do not die instantly of shock, but they usually do.

Bite wounds can be treated with Panalog ointment (see Veterinary Reference), and the victim can be kept quiet and warm in a box with a heating pad, if it is a young rabbit, or in an outdoor cage with a den box, if it is an adult. However, even with these cases we have had a very high death rate.

Housing and Release

We house our baby rabbits in a ten-gallon glass tank, which gives them room to be active and gives us the fun of watching them. We keep a heating pad on low setting under one end of the tank so they can move to it when they need warmth or move away when they are active.

When they are very active and self-feeding (at about three weeks) we move them to an outdoor cage of welded wire set about 2 feet off the ground, with a wire floor. The droppings fall through, so the cage is self-cleaning. The cage is protected from wind and rain. We also put a little wooden house or box inside with soft towel bedding. This provides a den environment when needed for rest or privacy. Since rabbits at this stage are self-feeding, they get a diet of medicated rabbit pellets, with supplements of lettuce, young carrots, and apple bits. They also like fresh green grass when available. (Be sure the grass has not been sprayed with a pesticide, and wash all fruits and vegetables carefully.) Fresh water and a salt-mineral block (as used for guinea pigs) are kept in the cage at all times. Fresh food is supplied daily.

Rabbits mature so early that we seldom keep them once they have reached this stage. They may be released at any age from four to six weeks.

Elvis, a rabbit orphan we received when he was two days old, stayed with us longer than most of our young rabbits. He was not released until he was eight weeks old, because he did not seem to be ready.

We took him to a field next to a wooded area which looked like nice rabbit country. To make sure he didn't feel immediately abandoned, we took along a supply of rabbit pellets to leave with him.

He made the trip in a cardboard box, and when we arrived at the area we put his box on the ground and opened it. Then we waited. We make it a practice not to force shy animals such as rabbits to leave their shelter right away.

It was about fifteen minutes before Elvis decided to hop out. His supply of rabbit pellets was waiting on the ground in front of his box. However, after a few twitches of the nose, Elvis evidently decided he liked natural food best and hopped off toward the tall grass, where he began nibbling happily. He finally disappeared from view in his green pastures, and we counted him as another successful release.

We release some cottontail rabbits here on our acre of ground, as there is plenty of natural cover and food for them. They can also be returned to where they were found for release.

Swamp rabbits should be released in a marshy area, for this is their natural environment. For cottontails, any country with fields, brush, and open country will do.

DOMESTIC RABBITS

Although this is a wildlife book, a note on domestic rabbits might be useful, since they often seem to be abandoned by their owners or have strayed and become lost. In Florida it is against the law to release a non-native species into the environment. Unfortunately, people do release and abandon domestic rabbits; we have treated a few that have been hit by cars or mauled by dogs. Domestic rabbits should never be released anywhere. They are not equipped to survive in the wild, and release is a certain death sentence.

Our method of care, diet, and housing for wild rabbits will work well for domestic rabbits. Domestic rabbit babies can also be bottle-fed with the Esbilac formula; we have done so in the case of the loss of the mother, or when the mother refuses to nurse her young.

Domestic rabbits live longer than wild rabbits. We have a domestic rabbit named Brownie, whom we inherited when a new housing development here forced several children to give up their pets. Brownie was fortunate in that she was not dumped by the roadside to fend for herself. She became the star of our school programs and even performed in the Turnau opera company production of *Susannah* at Sarasota's Asolo Theatre. Brownie is retired now, at the ripe age of four years. She is a good-natured animal, but in her old age, as occurs with many rabbits, her temper has developed. When she began to kick and bite if I removed her from her cage, I followed my Golden Rule: "Never force an animal to do something it doesn't want to do." So Brownie is now spending her declining years in her backyard cage, sunbathing, eating, and enjoying her life of leisure.

6
PIPPA
Otters

Note: I have never had the good fortune to have an otter as a houseguest, so I cannot speak from experience about these marvelous mammals. However, my good friend Charlie Briggs was so honored. This chapter is her own story of Pippa the otter.

R. K. C.

The otter is, to me, the most enthusiastic and charming of the wild creatures, and the only wild animal I know with a bona fide sense of humor.

Pippa came to us in the spring of 1965 quite by accident. We—me, my husband, Jack, and our sons, Clark and Tony— spotted her one spring evening racing across the fields behind our house and thought at first she was a black cat. But the undulating way she ran quickly told us she was an otter. My son Clark, then a teen-ager, ran across the field to confirm our identification and soon came back carrying Pippa.

Kitten-size, she couldn't have been more than just past weaning age. She was terribly frightened and sopping wet. Clark reported that she had been heading toward the dead end of the canal on our street, and, thinking she wanted to go in the water, he had caught her and thrown her in. Somehow she had managed to struggle back to the shore, piping pitifully and shivering.

We were totally ignorant about otters, at that time, and had no idea that baby otters cannot swim and are terrified of the water. They must be taught to swim, and she was not old enough to have had any training.

When Clark had first picked her up she'd bitten him, but not severely, and he carried her home. Since she seemed to be alone, frightened, and lost, we assumed she had come from an otter colony in the swampy land west of our house. We lived in a small "undeveloped" development which was open country and grassy lots, cut by manmade canals connecting to the Gulf of Mexico. She could have come from anywhere.

We put her in an old vacant rabbit cage outdoors and gave her a tub of water and a dish of canned cat food. We had no idea what she ate, besides fish, and didn't even know if she had been weaned.

We were so ignorant we didn't even know that otters must have something on which to dry themselves or they will get sick. Their beautiful outer coat of dark brown is waterproof hair, but their undercoat is soft and woolly and soaks up water like a sponge. So there she sat in that empty cage with a bare wire floor, piping unhappily.

That night a cold northwest wind came up and blew all night, and we could hear poor Pippa piping in her lost wailing way all night long. We decided we would release her the next day. The next morning, she had turned over her water tub, was soaked and chilled, and was plainly very sick.

We took her in the house and I put her on a foam rubber pillow on the couch with a hot-water bottle under it and dried her off with a towel. That was the first intelligent thing we did, I think. Our next move was to call the vet. He knew nothing about otters, but by good luck he had a vet visiting him who knew something about mink. The mink vet asked about her symptoms, and we told him she was shivering and chilled, could not stand, and was trying to drag herself along on her belly.

He said he was sure she had a disease common to mink called hard-pad disease. He said it was almost always fatal. The only treatment was to keep her warm, dry, and quiet,

Pippa Otter when very young, recovering from her near-fatal illness on her pillow.

and three times a day rub her foot pads with lanolin. The disease hardens the pads on the feet, he said, and makes them so tender and painful the animal cannot walk or bear any weight.

We started treating Pippa, and for days she lay on the couch, sleeping most of the time, only waking to call to be let outside, as we discovered—just like a house-trained dog. I would carry her out and put her on the grass, and she would drag herself around until she found a satisfactory place. When she had completed her business, I would carry her back into the house.

This went on for about a week. After that she began to improve rapidly. We put a dish for her with the family dog and cat arrangement by the refrigerator, and she soon learned to drag herself off the couch and go for food and water. She enjoyed canned cat food but would fight for table scraps too, especially fried eggs and fried chicken. Our dog Brownie and our tomcat Higgins soon learned to eat after Pippa finished.

Otters, we quickly discovered, will not tolerate any interference with their feeding. *Never* attempt to take food away from an otter. They have jaws which are long and flat, like a nutcracker, and very strong. Their teeth are razor sharp, and they go absolutely mad if you bother them when they are eating. Pippa would warn us first, with a high-pitched whine which became louder and more ominous, and then she would attack.

I learned this first hand, so to speak, when Pippa snatched a cupcake out of my hand one night at dinner. I tried to snatch it back and just missed losing several fingers in the process.

Pippa recovered rapidly from her illness, but her feet healed slowly. Three times a day we had an otter session on the living room floor, oiling Pippa's feet. She thought it was a grand game, for her feet were ticklish. She would roll over and over in that great flipping motion otters have, giggling madly, while I tried to hold her and Jack applied the lanolin. All the skin peeled off her pads and then rehealed, and soon she could walk and then run, with no sign of a limp. She was completely well in a month.

Once Pippa was well, our education in otterdom really began. We already knew all her otter noises. Otters will pipe and whistle like a bird, usually when they are unhappy, frightened, or uncomfortable. They can grunt, like a frog, usually a conversational sound. And they can literally chuckle and giggle almost like a human, as Pippa did when she was tickled or feeling happy. When her foot pads were healed her other talents got full play.

Pippa still stayed outside in her rabbit cage at night, which by this time we had learned to fill with fresh hay or dried grass from the meadows. She liked to burrow in it, practice "drying" herself, and sleep in it. She had a crockery nontippable water bowl and a heavy dish for her cat food, though by now she was eating anything, including all the fresh fish she could get. She ate them whole, like stick candy, holding them in her webbed front paws and starting at either end. Sometimes when eating them in the kitchen, she would take a fish head or tail into the living room and stow it under the television set for a later snack.

She was brought inside first thing in the morning, stayed there all day, and was the delight of the household and the constant tormentor of the dog and cat. She lived in the house much in the same manner as they did—she napped, usually on the couch or under the television set, she ate, and she played with her toys and with members of the family. She liked to sit on our laps. She had a squeaky rubber mouse on which she liked to pounce heartily for the squeaking sound. Then she would pick it up and drop it in the water bowl or carry it about the house until she tired of it or decided to hide it. She liked to catch the dog or cat napping, whereupon she would slip up behind them and nip them sharply in the posterior. The yelp of dismay from the dog and the explosion of hissing from the cat afforded her great satisfaction. Sometimes she and Brownie played tag all over the house, under the beds and chairs and across the couch. The game usually ended, however, when Pippa's sharp teeth scored once too often.

We put her in her cage only at night or during the day when we had to go away and the house was shut up. She didn't like to be alone in the house but seemed to like the outdoor cage and considered it her own personal den. She could open the button latch whenever it suited her, but she seldom left the cage once she was put in until we came for her.

Pippa loved to play all sorts of games, of her own invention. We had a coffee table with a raised rim around it, and on it she found some marbles one day that the boys had left there. She discovered that by standing on her hind legs and holding on with her forepaws, she could pad around the table, "shooting" the marbles with her nose and banking them off the rim, in a game we called "otter billiards." This was one of her favorites, and held her attention longer than anything else when she was very small, so I kept the coffee table cleared and the marbles on it just for her.

She was always getting into things when she was bored, seemed to need constant activity, and was never still except when she was asleep. She slept on her back, feet in the air, paws crossed on her chest, in a liquid S-curve, as if she were drifting on the water.

One day I found an entire roll of toilet paper trailing down the hallway from the bathroom, and I went to look for Pippa, for she loved to play in the toilet bowl if we forgot to close the lid. The toilet paper trail led rather soggily down the hall to the hall storage closet, which had sliding doors. I opened the doors and found Pippa peacefully asleep on her back, wound in yards of toilet paper, holding my bathroom sponge on her chest like a lily.

When playing outside, she gravitated toward the dog's water bowl, which sat under a spigot in the carport. She carried seagrape leaves, which she seemed to favor because they are round and flat like a wafer, and twigs of assorted sizes, dropped them in the bowl, and stirred thoroughly with great concentration. The neighborhood children loved this game— they called it "making otter soup." She loved to show off for the children, or anybody else who came by.

Pippa could also go in and out of our house whenever she pleased. To make this possible, we had built a screened enclosure—a small porch—around the front door and had put a swinging doggie door in the outer screen door for her. With the front door into the living room left open all summer, she went back and forth at will, taking a special joy in working the swinging door. But this suggested another game to her which turned into a bad habit. When visitors came to the house, she would watch their approach from inside through the full-length living room windows and then slink Indian fashion out across the little porch and pop through her swinging door to land directly at their feet. Since some of our visitors were unaware both of the swinging door and an otter on the premises, they got quite a jolt. But she never tried to bite or attack anyone and even learned to temper her own natural "biting play" when wrestling with the dog, the cat, or the family.

At first, she was a little rough. She liked to take a "running shoot" down the long living room couch, clearing dogs, cats, and people out of her path. If I stayed, she leaped in my lap, flipped over on her back, and began biting and giggling, panting all the while in a funny way much like a dog. During these bouts she loved to have her whiskers pulled and her belly tickled. When she bit too much I rapped her muzzle and said, "No bite!" and she simmered down immediately. When she was tired of playing she liked to slide down my legs to the floor, head first, like a child going down a park slide.

As she grew older, she settled on a regular diet of raw chicken necks and raw fish, plus table scraps which might include corn, green beans, tomatoes, chili, vegetable soup, and perhaps pork chops and roast beef. She loved all kinds of seafood.

She became very fond of my husband, Jack, and decided he was her favorite. Her pet game with him was to pounce into his lap when he came home from work and sat down in his armchair. She would get that "I'm going to do something devastatingly funny" look in her eye and start to push between his back and the chair. The game was for Jack to lean very hard against the chair and try to prevent her passage behind his back. She was very strong, and she always won, coming out giggling on the other side. She always urinated in little dribbles during this hilarious test of strength—somehow it seemed to her funnier and more exciting than any game she could play—but Jack never minded a few dribbles on his pants.

When she seemed old enough to learn to swim, Jack "taught" her. We took her to the canal across the street, where she liked to wade in the shallows and play with stones and fiddler crabs, but she showed no interest in swimming or hunting. Chubs and minnows of all kinds did not even attract her notice.

Jack waded in deep enough to start swimming, and she began to chirp with great anxiety. She became so worried about him, as he ignored her and frolicked in the water, that she edged farther and farther out, her feet left the bottom, and suddenly she was swimming!

Pippa, now a lovely adolescent, has just had a "drying" after her afternoon swim.

JACK BRIGGS

The grassy canal banks were Pippa's favorite romping grounds.

From then on, she went to the canal every day by herself and began to spend more and more time there, though we never saw her catch anything. When I would hear her coming through her door from the canal I always ran to fetch her towel, to dry her as much as I could before she got on the rugs; she "dried" on the canal banks, but not very well.

Sometimes, if she caught the tomcat napping, she liked to dry out on *him*, which usually sent poor Higgins into a state of shock but delighted Pippa.

Her old ragged towel had a fist-sized hole in it, and she would run toward me when I held it up and leap through the hole, then twist and roll until she rolled herself up in the towel. This was her favorite drying technique.

As the summer wore on, she began to spend entire days at the canal and would not answer a call, seeming to be invisible, until Jack went over and called her name late in the evening. Then she would appear from the water, or from one of the many "nests" she had made in the tall grass along the bank, and frolic madly around his legs. We all knew she would be ready to go off on her own soon, but we assumed only she would know when she was ready.

She was ready that August, when we had to go away on a trip and leave her for ten days. Worried about leaving her alone in the neighborhood, we made arrangements to board her at a kennel in the country. We took her cage out there first, put a new lock on the door, and set it in a wooded area behind the keeper's home. We stocked up several cartons of frozen fish and chicken necks. The day we were ready to take. her there, we also packed up her ragged towel, her water bowl, a mattress tick of her dried grass, and several of her rubber squeaky toys which she liked to carry in her mouth.

She had never ridden in the car, and we coaxed her into a laundry basket with chicken necks and put her in the car with great trepidation.

The whole family, including the dog, went along. As soon as the engine started, she began to chirp with anxiety; then a mounting fearful piping began, as she broke loose from the basket. We hastily rolled up all the windows, for fear she would escape the car—it was ten miles to the kennel—and then we discovered something new about otters. The car began to fill with a musky choking scent almost as bad as that given off by a skunk. The more frightened she grew, the more powerful the miasma became. We turned on the air conditioning. Brownie fell over the front seat and stuck his head in an air conditioner vent, his eyes watering. We all gasped for air, but there was nothing for it but to press on.

We all survived, reached the kennel, still gasping, and put Pippa in her old familiar cage with all her things and a large fresh fish. She immediately became calm and began eating her fish, not minding at all the barking of the kennel dogs. We stood around woefully, hating to leave, but finally we did, with many instructions to her keepers. That was the last time we ever saw her.

While we were gone—the third day, in fact—she gnawed through the cage wire and headed for the kennel keeper's house. When he trapped her in the utility room and grabbed her, she bit him and escaped out the back door and into the surrounding saw grass and swamps.

"It was like trying to hold a wet noodle," the keeper complained when he told us about it on our return.

We went out to that place every evening for a week, calling Pippa's name and searching the ditches and canals for a trace or a footprint, but we never found any.

I was glad, in a way. It was time for her to leave us, and we had left her first, after all. We had always worried that when she grew more mature she might become aggressive, and trouble would have been the result in our "civilized" neighborhood.

I like to think that she never went too far away, but only back to her native territory where she was born, and that she produced many little otters to populate the weedy streams she loved so well.

7
FIRST AID FOR MAMMALS

In our work of providing a temporary home for sick and injured native wildlife, we have cared for many small mammals that have been traffic casualties. The recovery rate for animals struck by cars traveling at high speeds is not good, and most of the animals we take to the vet for injuries of this type don't live long. Bones are not just broken, they are smashed; internal injuries are usually not visible but nearly always fatal. Shock takes a high toll, too. We and the veterinarian do what we can for them.

Rescue and Transport

In picking up an injured animal, use heavy leather gloves. If you get bitten, call your doctor about a tetanus shot. If the animal seems sick instead of hurt, rabies may be the problem. You should let the official agency handle it.

Hurt animals can be transported in a cardboard box lined with newspapers. We always carry such a box in the car so we will be prepared for roadside victims which need transporting to the vet or to our home for care. Wooden dog crates, as used on airlines, are also very useful for transporting mammals.

After handling any sick or injured animal, I always wash

my hands with an antiseptic soap. I use one called Septisol, but there are others available in drugstores.

Rabies

Rabies is a dangerous disease to both humans and wildlife, and no discussion of this terrible malady can overstress the care you must use in approaching any animal suspected of being rabid. All warm-blooded creatures are vulnerable to rabies, including bats (probably the prime carriers of the virus, according to vets), with raccoons, skunks, and foxes, in that order, also highly susceptible. Don't forget that rabies can infect rats, mice, chipmunks, and the smaller mammals, too. Size is no protection. Even very young animals are susceptible.

There is no cure for rabies, only a preventive vaccine. For humans, the preventive is a painful series of injections after exposure.

Any wild animal acting in an unusual manner is suspect; a normally shy creature, for instance, may attack and attempt to bite anyone or anything when it is rabid. That is not normal behavior for a healthy animal.

Symptomatic signs are lack of coordination, especially in the hindquarters, convulsions and thirst—with the inability to drink water.

Never approach an animal exhibiting any of these signs. You do not have to be bitten to get the disease from a rabid animal. Saliva from a rabid creature can get into a tiny scratch or sore and infect you. Even when handling "normally" sick animals, we generally use heavy leather welder's gloves. If you see what seems to be a rabid animal, *stay away from it.* Call the sheriff's office, the city police, the animal control officer, or the health department. They will take care of it.

If a rabid animal is shot, it should *never* be shot in the head. The head is needed for laboratory analysis to determine if rabies is present. If someone has been bitten by the animal, this evidence is vital.

If the animal can be captured alive by authorities, it is often quarantined for fourteen days to see if the disease develops.

An animal control officer once brought us a half-grown

raccoon which was found lying beside the road on Casey Key, a beach-front residential area near our town. The officer thought the animal might have a broken leg from a traffic encounter. The raccoon was in a control cage and looked sick. I put on disposable gloves, loaded the cage in the car, and took it to the vet. He, also, did not feel rabies was the problem but, to play it safe, advised me to take the animal home, quarantine it for fourteen days, give it food and water but not touch it, and tend the cage only when wearing disposable plastic gloves which could be discarded immediately after each use.

I took the raccoon home, bought a case of disposable gloves, and dumped the poor fellow into a clean cage, well isolated from all my other patients. Every day I donned gloves, fed the raccoon, and then immediately stripped off the gloves and put them in the garbage. The raccoon ate very little and died on the tenth day. I called the health department, and they picked up the body and took it to a lab. It did not have rabies. If it had, I discovered later, the health department would have routinely urged rabies shots for me, despite the precautions I had taken.

In all the years we have handled all kinds of wild mammals and birds, I have never "caught" any disease from them, but I always take precautions and, above all, use common sense.

Our pet skunk, Lovey, whom we kept to use in our school programs, received yearly rabies shots just as a dog does. Any wild animal which cannot be released and becomes a permanent patient or pet in your home should have rabies shots. Check with your vet. Raccoons and skunks should be inoculated at six months. We even inoculate our hand-raised babies before release, hoping to give them a better chance for survival, at least in their first year.

Distemper

Distemper is a viral disease which is highly contagious to animals (but not to man) and is often fatal. We have all our resident raccoons and skunks inoculated against distemper at three months of age, even when we plan to release them. Raccoons, skunks, foxes, and some other mammals should receive the inactivated nervous tissue vaccine (phenolized). Check with your veterinarian.

Distemper outbreaks occasionally occur in certain groups of mammals, perhaps due to overcrowding or poor living conditions. It might be nature's way of thinning out animal populations. Some animals survive it—the fittest ones. An outbreak of what one conservation officer termed feline distemper swept Casey Key in August and September of 1972 and wiped out probably about 75 percent of the raccoon population there before it ended.

Injuries

The point has already been made that there is not much you can do for a small animal that has been hit by a speeding car. However, there are exceptions.

We had a gray squirrel patient which was found on the main street in the city. Its hindquarters seemed to be paralyzed, but in this case injury instead of illness was indicated. It had a skinned, bruised haunch, suggesting that it had probably been struck by a car.

We donned heavy leather gloves, popped the squirrel into a cardboard box, and took it to the veterinarian. The vet thought it was possibly a car victim and was perhaps suffering from a pinched nerve. There were no broken bones.

We brought it home and kept it indoors in a large cardboard box lined with newspapers, in which we put a soft towel for bedding. We put sulfamethazine (see Veterinary Reference) in the water bowl for five days; this is always one of our methods to guard against possible infection. It doesn't hurt anything, and it might help. We dressed its scrapes and bruises with Panalog ointment once a day for a week.

We had to place food on the floor of the box, as it couldn't get up, even to eat. We used our regular squirrel diet of sunflower seeds, wild bird seed, apples, unpeeled oranges cut into quarters, and raw unshelled peanuts. The squirrel ate well from the beginning, and we did not attempt to handle it but left it alone and quiet as much as possible.

The second week, it began to regain the use of its hind legs. After a month, it was walking with a limp. We moved it to a

ROSEMARY K. COLLETT

Some dietary needs: vitamin B$_1$ tablets (50 mg.); mortar and pestle for crushing tablets; Vionate powdered vitamins; Esbilac formula for infant mammals; baby bottle, used for baby raccoons as young as one day; pet nurser bottle, used for rabbits, squirrels, opossums, etc.; and swab sticks for feeding infant birds.

large outdoor cage fitted out for squirrels with a tree limb for climbing exercise and a den box for snuggling. At the end of two months our squirrel was scampering all over the cage, and we opened the cage door and released it.

This was a happy story. Another gray squirrel we treated with a similar problem died within the week, presumably from more serious internal injuries.

I have already mentioned car-struck mother opossums with young ones still in their pouch. One of these brought to us had nine babies. The vet treated the mother, but she was too badly injured and died within two hours. The young were too small. They were blind and hairless, almost embryonic. We tried, but they all died within forty-eight hours. Another opossum, however, had young which were haired and had their eyes open. They survived.

Car-struck armadillos are often brought to us from the highways. They usually do not recover well from injuries of this type, either. We had one with a cracked shell—it died within two days, probably of internal injuries.

If a small animal such as a raccoon, skunk, squirrel, or opossum is badly hurt, the only care you can give it (after treatment by a vet) is to keep it quiet, with sulfamethazine water and food available. If you live in the north, keep it warm with a heating pad on low under half the cardboard box. Our climate is so mild the year round we seldom need heat in these cases, but we do use it if the weather is chilly or if the animal seems to be cold, in shock, or losing body heat.

Surface wounds, scrapes, and bruises can be treated with Panalog ointment once or twice daily.

General Care of Sick or Injured Animals

Any animal, whether injured or ill, should be handled with care, immediately isolated, and kept quiet. To repeat—in dealing with any apparently sick animals, we use extreme caution.

If a baby animal is so weak it cannot swallow or eat at all, ask your veterinarian about teaching you how to tube-feed it. This procedure is not complicated, but it cannot be described well in words. A demonstration is the best way to learn how to do it properly. We do not feel an animal should be tube-fed over a long period of time. An animal, especially if it is small, needs companionship, holding, and cuddling. In its need for love and affection, it is no different from humans.

I, personally, do not approve of de-clawing or de-fanging wild creatures. If an animal is so dangerous that such procedures must be followed, that animal should not be kept in captivity in the first place, and certainly not in a home. And since our aim is to cure or to hand-raise wild creatures for release, to remove their claws or fangs is out of the question.

If you have mistakenly used such procedures on any wild creature, such as a raccoon, bobcat, cougar, or bear, be sure that animal is *never* released to the wild. It will no longer have any defense against its enemies, will be unable to climb or dig, and may be unable to hunt successfully. Release of such an animal would be a death sentence. Remember, too, never to release a skunk that has been descented. The scent glands are its only means of defense.

Treating Animals in the Wild

We have had some experience with treating animals in nature, either after they have been released or as backyard visitors.

Two large male raccoons which we released from the Coonrad Hilton, Genghis and Kubla, were brothers, but they were so rough-and-tumble in their play that even after they moved to the Hilton we wore long pants, heavy jackets, and gloves to play with them. Also a bandanna on the head, for they loved to pull hair. They even hurt each other in their rough play after they were released and would return for treatment of scrapes and bruises.

Another male, Meeney, often came back for treatment after he had tangled with another raccoon. He would climb into the nearest lap, crying and begging for help. Panalog ointment would be applied to his minor wounds. He was gentle, and never tired of being petted.

I noticed in the yard one day a skinny gray squirrel that looked poorly. Its coat was rough, and it appeared sleepy and seemed to have a runny nose. I saw it eating sunflower seeds that had fallen from a feeder and licking water from the dripping hose.

I put out a dish of sunflower seeds just for this squirrel, and a bowl of sulfamethazine drinking water. It came every day and helped itself. After four days it showed definite improvement. It began to fatten, and its eyes began to brighten. It is frisking around my yard today, looking bright-eyed and bushy-tailed as a squirrel should.

It may have been just a runt, or it may have been only hungry or slightly ill. All I know is, our efforts seemed to help, and it was an easy matter to do.

Any help you can give animals in the wild in this way is really better for them, if they are self-sufficient, than capturing them and taking them into isolation. I feel that many small animals could be helped in this way by backyard Good Samaritans.

8
GARDEN SONGSTERS
Song and Garden Birds

Every spring, as sure as the vernal equinox arrives, my dining room table is covered with cages of baby birds. The high influx of babies is a normal spring event for us, because many young birds are blown down from their nests by high winds or storms and many parents are killed or frightened away during the nesting season.

Often, too, these "orphans" are the victims of well-meaning people who assume that because they find them on the ground they are lost or in need of help. If you will wait before rushing in to pick up a baby bird, you may see the mother come for it. She may be teaching it to fly and has gone to get it food in the interim, or she may be watching it from a distance. It is a good idea always to wait and observe quietly for a while before "rescuing" a baby bird you find apparently alone. If its nest is in sight you may return the baby to it. Contrary to what you may have heard, it is not necessarily true that the mother bird will no longer care for it if it has been handled by a human.

Infant Care

Raising baby birds is a chore, because they must be fed very frequently—every fifteen minutes, more or less—during the

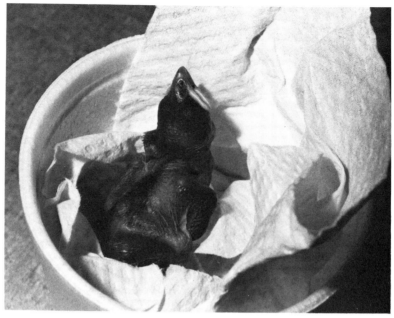

This naked baby sparrow still has its eyes closed.

daylight hours. The primary concerns for a baby bird are, of course, warmth and food. I keep our baby birds—especially the very tiny unfeathered ones—in a kitchen mixing bowl, with a light bulb clipped on the side for warmth. I use a standard 7½-watt bulb and the sort of clamp used on the headboard of a bed for a reading light. The bowl is lined with paper towels (not cotton, for it clings to the birds).

Before feeding, it is useful to determine, if possible, what kind of bird you are dealing with. Some birds eat only insects. Some eat insects, fruit, and seeds. The chart at the back of the book tells what diet is natural to a number of common species in the United States.

Very tiny baby birds look almost alike to the layman, but we can identify some of them by observing their open mouths (and they are always open for many weeks). The mouth of a baby blue jay is bright red inside, and its dark bill is fairly long and sturdy (two or three times longer than that of a sparrow). The mockingbird also has a fairly long bill, but a wider mouth than a jay. Its bill is slender, and bordered in bright yellow, and the inside of the mouth is yellow also.

The starling has a rather long and slender bill, as does the mockingbird, but the inside of its mouth is pink. The sparrow has a small bill and a yellow mouth.

A featherless baby sparrow may be barely an inch long. A jay or mockingbird without feathers will be two or three times the size of a featherless sparrow.

As another means of identifying an infant bird, it is a good idea, if you know where the bird came from, to look the place over. What birds inhabit the area? Look for their nests. The sparrow often builds in the eaves, the mockingbird in a bushy tree or shrub. Cardinals are shy; their nests are hard to find.

If the bird has feathers, it is relatively easy to figure out its ancestry.

Infant Diet

If the identity is confused, this is a good basic diet, we have found, for most young song and garden birds, such as sparrows, blue jays, cardinals, and mockingbirds:

$\frac{1}{2}$ cup medicated turkey starter
1 drop Zymadrops vitamin supplement
1 25-mg. tablet vitamin B_1, crushed

Moisten with warm water.

Vitamin B_1 (thiamine hydrochloride) is important, particularly in the diet of baby mockers. Without this ingredient they often develop a condition similar to rickets and lose the use of their legs. They can die without B_1. This is available at drugstores.

The medicated turkey starter is available through feedstores. Our local store does not stock it but orders it for me when needed. The brand I use is Red Rose, simply because this is what my feedstore handles. Other brands would probably work as well. Turkey starter is used, rather than chicken starter, because it is a higher protein food, and the natural diet of wild birds is higher in protein than domestic fowl. Turkey starter generally comes in 50-pound bags.

Zymadrops are a liquid vitamin supplement for human

babies, available at a drugstore. I have used other brands but have had the best results with Zymadrops.

Mix the ingredients to a moist consistency sticky enough to be picked up on the end of a swab stick (without the cotton swab). The mixture should be neither too dry nor too soupy. If it is too dry and crumbly, you cannot pick it up on the stick. If it is too soupy, you have the same problem. Very small birds need a moister mixture to avoid dehydration.

Put the food stick well back in the baby's throat to trigger the swallowing reflex, just as the mother bird does with her bill. If the birds are very small, I sometimes use a No. 4 sable watercolor brush, with the food on the tip.

Do not try to feed the bird with a medicine dropper—it may strangle or drown or get pneumonia. And do not give it milk or any other liquids. It gets its water from its food mixture.

If you have a weak baby which does not open its mouth, tap the edge of the bowl several times with your finger and make kissing noises. It may think it is its mother, landing on the edge of the nest, and will usually open wide. If you have to force-feed it, gently pry open the bill with a thumbnail and carefully hold the mouth open at the corners while feeding a bite or two. It will soon get the idea.

A tiny sparrow fledging, left on my doorstep by a Good Samaritan. I get dozens of little ones like this in the springtime.
JACK BRIGGS

Very tiny babies, like sparrows, should be fed every ten minutes, all day long. Slightly larger babies like blue jays and mockingbirds, can be fed every twenty minutes. Feeding can gradually be done at thirty-minute intervals as the baby progresses.

If turkey starter is not available, an emergency mixture can be made with Gaines Meal dog food. I suggest this be used only until turkey starter can be obtained. I have never raised infant birds to maturity on this diet, so I am not sure if it can be used successfully for them in place of turkey starter.

Emergency Infant Bird Diet

$\frac{1}{4}$ cup Gaines Meal dry dog food
2 drops Zymadrops vitamin supplement
1 25-mg. tablet vitamin B_1, crushed

Soak the Gaines Meal in lukewarm water for about ten minutes. Drain off excess liquid. Mix in Zymadrops and B_1. Feed as directed for turkey starter mixture.

Intermediate Diet and Care

When the young bird begins to hop to the edge of its bowl, it is time to move to a cage. This can happen after two to three weeks in the bowl, depending how young it was when originally found. A standard canary or parakeet cage, found at pet shops, is fine for a starter. Line the cage tray with paper towels or newspaper cut to size, and change them at least once a day.

At this point, the bird should be quite well feathered and will not need further heat. Soon it will begin to peck at the food stick. When it does this, we put a small jar lid of the turkey starter mix in the cage, along with a shallow lid of water. The bird will soon begin to eat and drink on its own, but we keep up the hand-feeding until we are sure it is completely self-feeding.

When, at last, the bird is feeding itself, we change to a mixture of soaked Gaines Meal with chopped fruit added:

Soak Gaines Meal in water for ten minutes, as in making

emergency infant formula. Drain off excess water. Sprinkle liberally with Vionate, a vitamin-mineral supplement sold in pet shops. Add finely chopped apple and soaked raisins. (Soak dark raisins in cold water overnight and drain them before using.) Mix well. This is our standard basic diet for most adult song and garden birds. For variety we add chopped banana or grapes. Some birds enjoy bits of orange.

When it is eating well on its own, if it is a blue jay, cardinal, or other seed-eater, we add wild bird seed with sunflower seeds to the diet.

Keep fresh food before birds at all times. Unlike mammals, birds must have food available at any hour, since the expression "eat like a bird" literally means that they peck a little here and there, all day long, generally never gorging at any one feeding. We prepare the Gaines Meal and fruit mixture in the morning and put a bowlful in each cage. Unless it is very hot weather, this food will stay fresh all day. If the food sours during the day, as it might in extremely hot weather, it should be replaced. Many of the birds also enjoy mynah pellets (available at pet shops). These are expensive, however, and we do not feed them except as special treats. Since they are a dry food, they keep better than a moist mixture and can be left in the feed bowl for long periods. Even when feeding mynah pellets, we keep the Gaines Meal and fruit mixture in the cage.

When our young birds are completely self-feeding—after one or two months in the small cage—we move them to a large outdoor cage, at least 4 feet long, 4 feet high, and 2 feet wide. We make these cages as per the instructions in the section on Cages and Housing. If possible, we put the birds into a large walk-in flight (also described there). This really gives them room to exercise and practice flying.

After that, it may be another one or two months before they are ready for release, the time depending on the individual bird's readiness.

Do's and Don'ts

If you know your bird eats insects as well as fruits, you can give it *lean* ground beef (chuck or round) when it is well feathered. This is fed in small bites on the stick in the same manner as the starter mix.

Do not give baby birds water with a medicine dropper, keeping always in mind that they can handle water only when they are old enough to drink from a jar lid or shallow dish by themselves. Did you ever see a mother bird give her youngsters a drink of water? The moisture in the food is enough.

Do not give them milk, either. The same goes for bread soaked in milk. Many people think this is good for baby birds, but it is not their natural diet, and their digestive system is not made to take it.

Don't feed fish to seed-eating birds, and don't feed seeds to fish-eaters or meat-eaters.

If you cannot identify your bird by the time it is well feathered, check your reference books, your veterinarian, or your Audubon Society. Someone can help you figure out what you have, and you need to know this for later diet supplements.

Keep your bird bowl or cage clean. Change paper towels in the bowl several times a day, and change cage paper for caged birds at least once a day.

Remember, you do not need to feed baby birds at night. Mother bird broods her babies at night to keep them warm. She only works at feeding them in the daytime—and believe me, she works, because they are hungry constantly.

When feeding infant birds, use your common sense about how much to feed them, because they will often keep yelling and opening their mouths long after they have had more than is good for them. The mother has to fly off and bring more food, but you can keep stuffing it in, so watch it. Some babies will stop eating after four to eight mouthfuls, but I had one baby sparrow an inch long which did not know when it was full. After it took twenty-two mouthfuls, I wouldn't give it any more. Heaven knows how long it would have gone on, and if I'd let it, it might have killed itself.

When making either the turkey starter or Gaines Meal mixture, do so in small amounts, or throw away leftovers, and make it two or three times daily for freshness. It has a tendency to sour. Your nose will tell you if it has gone sour. Don't feed any animal or bird anything old, sour, stale, or moldy that you wouldn't want to eat yourself.

If you live in a "buggy" climate, store dry ingredients such as turkey starter in the refrigerator or freezer until you need them. This is the best way to keep the bugs out.

If someone brings us baby birds in their nest, we get rid of the nest fast! It is probably full of mites. Many baby birds have mites, tiny bugs that crawl all over them—and *you*. These mites can sap the strength of a young bird.

To remove mites, if you see your bird has them, use a light dusting of mite powder, available at pet shops or dime stores. I use Hartz Mountain brand. Try not to get it in the baby's eyes, but dust the bird lightly, and don't forget *underneath* the wings.

Releasing Your Bird

When our birds fly and eat well on their own in an outdoor cage, our releasing procedure is simply to leave the cage door open. The bird will leave when it is ready. Some of our birds wait several days. In this case, we make sure we have closed the cage door at night to protect it from marauders. Some of our birds go and come back a few times, not sure they are ready to leave "home." We always keep fresh food and water in the cage for these undecided releasees. We also have feeders placed around the yard for these fellows, and for the wild birds, too.

After you have released your bird, see to it that food and water are left in the vicinity where you freed it. It can always come back if it needs to.

Remember, don't (if you can help it) make too much of a pet of your bird patient—this only makes it harder for it (and for you) to readjust when releasing time comes.

If you have a bird that doesn't want to readjust, you are stuck with a permanent resident—and sometimes that happens.

Tinker Too, a blue jay we raised from infancy, is one of those. He is five years old and still lives in our backyard, where he has his own cage home. Sparky the starling is another of our permanent residents. He lives in a cage in our family room and doesn't want to live anywhere else.

Many of the birds we have released in our backyard acre are still around. They visit our feeders and sometimes bring

Tinker Too, the blue jay, is too people-oriented to release.

their little ones for the free lunch. Our city, Venice, is a bird sanctuary and provides a protected environment for them. One of the rewards of raising and releasing birds is seeing them come back with the next generation to visit the backyard feeder.

The song and garden birds we have discussed in this chapter are the birds of our experience, birds who winter or spend their entire lives in Florida. They include mockingbirds, catbirds, blue jays, scrub jays, sparrows, cardinals, brown thrashers, towhees, grackles, and blackbirds. Other U.S. song and garden birds, such as robins, cedar waxwings, painted buntings, indigo buntings, certain chickadees, finches, and nuthatches, we see occasionally.

I see no reason why many of these and other song and garden birds cannot be raised successfully on the diet and in the manner described here.

9
THE FARMER'S FRIENDS
Insectivorous Birds

The insectivorous birds that we have raised or treated include purple martins, chimney swifts, nighthawks, chuck-will's-widows, meadowlarks, flycatchers, woodpeckers, swallows, shrikes, warblers, and ovenbirds. We have only had mature swallows, warblers, and ovenbirds. We have had both infant and mature birds of the other species.

Some of these birds do eat fruits, seeds, and wild berries occasionally, but their diet is a little different from that of the song and garden birds, and they differ in other ways too.

Care of Infants

The methods of caring for and feeding these infant birds are the same as for song and garden birds. We keep them in a mixing bowl lined with paper towels, with a 7½-watt light bulb clipped on the side for warmth. We feed them every thirty minutes with a bare swab stick—very tiny birds, every fifteen minutes. We tap the bowl or make kissing noises to encourage open mouths, and we put the food stick far back in the throat to trigger the swallowing reflex. If force-feeding is necessary at first, we open the bill by pressing gently with thumb and forefinger at the base of the beak.

Infant Diet

The basic diet for these baby birds (except very young infant woodpeckers) is:

½ cup medicated turkey starter
1 drop Zymadrops vitamin supplement
1 25-mg. tablet vitamin B_1, crushed
¼ lb. lean ground beef (chuck or round)

Combine starter and vitamins with water to a sticky consistency, add beef, and mix well.

This formula must be kept refrigerated, as the meat will spoil easily. It can be warmed in the hand before feeding, or a small amount of hot water can be added. We never feed any mixture that is sour, stale, moldy, or icy cold.

The meat mixture is formed into tiny moist balls, and placed on the end of the swab stick for feeding. The addition of meat to the diet is necessary for these insectivorous birds.

WOODPECKERS

The diet for tiny baby woodpeckers is the same as above, only without the meat at first, and the consistency should be soupy, not sticky. This formula is fed with a wide-mouthed plastic medicine dropper, with the tip cut off so it is straight and wide. Baby woodpeckers will suck up the mixture from the end of the tube at their own pace. A gentle pressure on the bulb will keep food at the end of the tube. It should not be squirted or squeezed out.

Older woodpecker babies, which have begun to feather and have their eyes open, may have the meat added to their diet and can then be fed with the swab stick.

Mature woodpeckers, when self-feeding, often like the Gaines Meal mixture as prepared for song and garden birds— dog kibbles moistened with a little warm water, with the addition of chopped apples and soaked raisins.

Our adult woodpeckers often like a little peanut butter. (I

use the smooth type, because it doesn't choke them or stick to their beaks.) I put the peanut butter in a dish in their cage, and sometimes I give them sunflower seeds and raw peanuts. Adult warblers are also fond of peanut butter.

Woodpeckers are climbers—they have two toes pointing forward and two toes pointing backward instead of the normal three toes in front and one in back such as other birds have. We have raised yellow-shafted flickers, redheaded woodpeckers, and red-bellied woodpeckers, all from infancy, and have had adult yellow-bellied sapsuckers, pileated woodpeckers, and downy woodpeckers as patients.

When the woodpecker baby can climb to the edge of its mixing bowl nest, it is time to put it in a cage.

Woodpeckers like a few small branches in their cage, so they can climb, and a small wooden chunk or log for pecking. The baby woodpeckers start pecking on their cage bars in the birdcage stage, and sometimes when they all get going at different tempos it sounds like the "Anvil Chorus" at our house.

NIGHTHAWKS AND CHUCK-WILL'S-WIDOWS

None of our nighthawks or chuck-will's-widows ever became self-feeding, even when adult. They are birds which feed by swooping through the air at dusk or dawn, scooping insects into their cavernous mouths in flight. They cannot stand for long, as they have weak legs and feet, and ours never learned how to peck or pick up food from the ground or a dish. We had to hand-feed them as long as we kept them in captivity. When they graduated from the bowl, we housed them in small cages indoors, without perches, but allowed them flight time on the screened porch once a day for exercise and to prepare them for release.

Our only hope is that those we released knew instinctively how to feed themselves in flight, because they are gone so quickly when you release them that there is no time to observe them. These problems would probably also apply to the northern version of the chuck-will's-widow, the whippoorwill.

The nighthawk is strictly insectivorous. It feeds in flight and rarely learns to take food from a dish in captivity.

CHIMNEY SWIFTS

Chimney swifts generally nest in dark chimneys, and it has been our observation that the babies take much longer to open their eyes than other birds. For some reason these infants do not seem to respond to bowl tapping or kissing sounds with open mouths, but I find that tapping their bill with the food stick soon gives them the cue.

The babies will start trying to climb and cling at an early stage in the mixing bowl, because this is what they instinctively do inside chimneys. When mine start this, I move them to a glass fish tank with a few rough-barked (nonpoisonous) branches inside for them to climb and a brick standing on end. It seems to make them feel quite at home. I keep a screen lid on top of the tank, so they can't pop out.

I used to carry four little ones around the house with me while wearing a sweater—they clung to my sweater just like little bats and were very decorative. This little quartet of clingers I acquired from an irate lady who said they were making too much noise in her chimney, and she evicted them with a broom. They are indeed probably the most raucous and homely of all infant birds. But I raised them all successfully and released them—near a house with a chimney. I should hasten to add that the house and chimney belonged to my friend Mary, of Coonrad Hilton fame.

PURPLE MARTINS

We have had purple martins as patients and successfully raised and released them. There are never enough purple martins, because they eat lots of mosquitoes and insects to pay their way.

Most of our adult patients of this type are brought in after swooping into power lines or plate-glass windows or being hit by cars or shot.

We have raised purple martins on the meat mixture, moving them from the mixing bowl to a cage when they began hopping out of the bowl. When grown, we let them fly about the screened porch to exercise their wings and prepare them for release.

It is our understanding that purple martins drink by swooping and drinking on the fly, but we find they can drink from a dish in captivity. Purple martins have a strict insect diet and to our knowledge do not eat fruit or seeds.

MEADOWLARKS

In the field of feeding problems, we have had one baby meadowlark, which I called Dum-Dum because I could never teach him to eat properly. He would retreat from the food stick to the farthest corner of his cage and finally, twisting his head to one side, open his mouth and accept the food, wagging his head all the time and making my aim difficult. He took more time than he did food, so I boarded him out to my friend Ruth, who has helped me on other occasions with bird patients.

Ruth raised him and then released him in her backyard garden, but he wouldn't go away. He still lives there, running under her feet every time she goes to the garden, so she must be careful not to step on him. He also flies down from the trees to perch on her shoulder or head, when he's not in a hiking mood, and even follows her into the house. Ruth insists he's not stupid, and maybe he's not, at that. At least he knows a good thing when he's found it.

SHRIKES

The shrike is another odd one. In nature it has a habit of impaling its prey on a thornbush or a barbed-wire fence until it has finished the day's hunting and can come back and eat at its leisure.

Our adult shrike patient approximated this practice by planting mouthfuls of food mixture on its cage wire mesh. This certainly made for a messy cage, but at least the shrike hadn't forgotten its upbringing. We did not have this bird very long. It suffered from a minor wing injury, and it quickly recovered and returned to nature.

FLYCATCHERS

We received one infant great crested flycatcher which had been evicted from its nest in a newspaper box when the irate homeowner, tired of having his morning paper thrown on the damp grass, decided to reclaim the box.

The little flycatcher had a few feathers, and its eyes were just barely open. We housed it in the usual mixing bowl with 7½-watt light for warmth. Its diet was the infant one with ground beef given earlier in this chapter. It thrived and soon was flying about the porch, snapping up flies, true to its name. Since most Florida homes are "buggy," I was tempted to keep it, but one day, when we felt the time had come, we opened the porch door and let it go. There is a family of flycatchers nesting in our yard now, and I can't help but wonder if one of the pair is my little friend.

Cages

When these young birds have outgrown the bowl and are in small indoor cages, we continue to hand-feed them till we are sure they can feed themselves from the small dishes of food and water that we place in the cages. (The nighthawks and chuck-will's-widows only get water, since a food dish would be useless to them.) The cage papers are changed at least once a day, and more often when needed.

Later some of the birds are moved into large outdoor cages, at least 4 feet long, 4 feet high, and 2 feet wide. These cages are fitted with perches, and food and water are available at all times.

We do not provide the larger outdoor cages for every species. Till their release, the nighthawks and chuck-will's-widows either fly freely about on our screened porch, for exercise, or remain in the small cages, and the purple martins stay indoors too, simply because they are a lot of fun to have in the house.

We generally house one bird in each cage unless there are several young from a single nest. We have found that often if we mix young of one nest with young of another, even the infants will squabble.

This little warbler suffered from exhaustion from its long migration. After a short rest, however, it was up and on its way.

ROSEMARY K. COLLETT

Release

We have had a very good rate of success with raising, treating, and releasing insectivorous birds, so we can recommend these techniques and diets. Most of these birds can be released from our backyard, and though some, like Dum-Dum, never go away, many of them are migrating birds and leave us when the time comes.

10
NATURE'S MIMICS
Talking Birds

We have raised infant starlings and crows but have had only adult magpies and ravens, as they do not breed in this area and are not native to Florida.

Sparky, our resident starling, is now a talkative five-year-old. He was a fallen nestling brought in by a child, and we raised him from blind naked babyhood. We have never released Sparky, as he is entirely people-oriented. He began to talk at an early age, babbles constantly when he feels like it, and has a vocabulary of phrases, to the surprise of visitors who do not know that starlings can talk at all.

Sparky can say, "Sparky's pretty," "Funny fellow," "Hi, cutie!" and he has recently learned to call loudly the name of our Afghan hound, "Rhani!" The first time she heard it, Rhani came running, but Rhani is smart and quickly learned she was being had. Sparky is also fond of saying "Kiss me, baby!" followed by loud kissing noises.

Snowflake, our crow, is another permanent resident, but he lives outdoors instead of in the house. He has a large flight (a walk-in cage, or aviary) by the back door.

Snowflake came to us from Sarasota, where he had fallen from the nest. Baby crows are very big, and this one was easy to identify as a crow, because he had a few black feathers, and no other ordinary baby bird could have been *that* big.

Snowflake is a talker too, now that he is nearly full grown. Until recently, crows were not protected in Florida, so he has stayed on. He still uses a baby voice to call to me when I approach his cage.

He is a great help to us in our children's programs at schools, where he sits on my finger and poses prettily.

Infant Care and Diet

The diet for infant crows and starlings is:

$\frac{1}{2}$ cup medicated turkey starter
1 drop Zymadrops vitamin supplement
1 25-mg. tablet vitamin B_1, crushed

Mix with warm water to a sticky consistency.

Snowflake the crow is getting a special treat, a tidbit of lean meat. Feeding with a swab stick in this manner is necessary for many of our baby bird patients, but Snowflake is really big enough to feed himself.
JACK BRIGGS

To this turkey-starter mixture we add about a quarter pound of *lean* ground beef (such as chuck or round) for at least every other feeding. This may seem a lot of meat, but the turkey starter swells as it absorbs water and increases in volume.

If a baby won't eat the mixture without the added meat, we add the ground beef at every feeding. Our crow Snowflake insisted on it.

When meat is mixed with the turkey starter formula, we are careful to keep it refrigerated to avoid the possibility of botulism. We warm small amounts in the hand for each feeding or add hot water to the cold meat mixture.

The infant birds are fed this mixture with a bare swab stick every thirty minutes, except for very tiny birds (eyes not open, featherless), which are fed every fifteen minutes from about 7 A.M. to 7 P.M. The food stick is put far back in the throat to trigger the swallowing reflex. This diet would probably work well also for infant magpies and ravens.

We always keep infant birds in a kitchen mixing bowl lined with paper towels and with a 7½-watt light bulb clipped on the side for warmth. We change the papers two or three times a day. Baby birds can stay in this environment until they are big enough to hop to the edge of the bowl.

Cages

We keep Sparky, now an adult starling, in a relatively small cage in the house. It is 3 feet long, 2 feet high, and 1½ feet wide, and sits by a sunny window.

Older crows, magpies, and ravens need a larger cage, preferably outside, because they grow up to be larger birds and need room in which to exercise. Generally speaking we house them singly, since some are inclined to be aggressive. But occasionally, if two or three from a single nest are raised together, they can be housed together.

Our adults live in flights 6 to 8 feet long, 6 feet tall, and at least 4 feet wide. These cages are big enough for us to walk inside and are constructed with safety entries to prevent accidental escapes. (The Cages and Housing section gives details on how to build flights for large birds.) Their floors—

Large walk-in flights are excellent for recuperating birds such as crows, magpies, and ravens. Note the safety door to prevent accidental escape of the bird before it is fully ready for release.

the ground they stand on—are covered with clean builder's sand. This needs to be raked twice weekly to remove the droppings, and the sand should be completely changed at least every six months.

These large flights are furnished with perches, rocks, and small stumps for a variety of perching tastes. We also provide them with very large water containers, such as birdbaths, because these birds love to bathe.

Even small Sparky, in his indoor cage, bathes so vigorously and with such enthusiasm that I never change his cage papers until after he has had his bath. Indoor cages need a sheet of clear plastic around three sides to confine the splashing. Sparky has one and it helps some, though I still usually have to mop the floor around his cage after bathing time.

The bird housed outdoors always must have protection from sun and bad weather. Here in Florida, the weather is never too cold, but the summer sun gets very hot. Birds can get heatstroke, just like people.

All our flights have a portion of the cage roofed over, usually at the rear of the flight, which has a closed back wall and partial walls on two sides. This protects the birds from sun, blowing rain, and chilly winds.

These birds *do* like to sun themselves, however. The first time I saw Sparky doing this I was afraid that he had had a heatstroke and was dying. He was lying on his cage floor in a spot of sunlight, half turned onto his side with his eyes closed and one wing spread out. I rushed over, screaming "Sparky!" and scared him almost out of his wits. He leaped up, looking extremely startled, and I realized he was only having a peaceful sunbathing session. So remember that birds do like to sprawl out in the sun, just like people, and you don't need to go screaming for the vet if it looks as if your bird has passed out on the floor.

These birds love shiny objects, such as aluminum pie tins and spoons. We put these things in their cages for their entertainment. Crows given the freedom of the house have been known to steal jewelry or any other shiny object and hide it in their favorite cache.

Adult Diet

When these birds are old enough to be self-feeding (we know they are approaching this stage when they begin to peck at the food on the food stick) we make an adult diet available to them in a dish but continue feeding them the infant diet mixture until we are sure they are getting enough to eat by themselves.

For these adult birds—starlings, crows, magpies, and ravens—we feed the Gaines Meal and fruit mixture so favored by most song and garden birds and woodpeckers:

Soak Gaines Meal in water for about ten minutes. Drain off excess water. Add finely chopped apples and soaked raisins or chopped banana and grapes when available. Sprinkle Vionate powdered vitamins over the mixture.

All these birds, when adult, also get lean ground beef tidbits (chuck or round). Feeding this by hand daily helps keep the bird tame. The Vionate may be sprinkled on the meat bits instead of on the formula.

A bowl of dry Gaines Meal dog food is also kept in the cage of adult birds for their own feeding whenever they want it. (Our raven, Edgar, however, prefers Purina Dog Chow. He also likes raw chicken necks. We strip off the fatty skin before giving these. In the wild, crows, magpies, and ravens sometimes raid other birds' nests and will eat their eggs and young in search of a high-protein diet.) These birds also like grasshoppers, crickets, and little green frogs.

Adult crows, magpies, and ravens like a varied menu, and we have found they relish corn on the cob, fresh orange sections, peaches, strawberries, cherries, cantaloupe, and cottage cheese. Remember that birds, unlike mammals, must have food kept before them at all times.

Teaching the Bird to Talk

Teaching these birds to talk is just like working with a parakeet, cockatiel, or parrot. We speak a simple word or phrase clearly, over and over, working on only one at a time until they learn it, and then move on to another word or phrase. Some of our birds have learned to talk by themselves, but they do better if they are not around other birds and have no one to imitate except people.

Our resident magpie, Fella, came from Wyoming. We ordered him several years ago from a lady who hand-raises magpies for pets. He learned how to talk from Edgar, our raven, and is almost unintelligible, because in imitating an imitator he lost much of the voice quality he would have had if he had learned from people directly.

Edgar is one of our most fascinating birds. He is enormous and very, very black. He has a massive, powerful beak and speaks all sorts of words and phrases. He was raised by a friend of ours in Tampa who had to move and asked us to take Edgar in as a permanent resident.

Edgar learned to talk after we took him and put his cage outside our back door. I have a habit of sticking my head out the back door and calling "Hey, George!" when there is a phone call for my husband. It wasn't long before Edgar was calling, "Hey, George!" He does a perfect imitation of my voice. Once, when George was away, I heard Edgar call "Hey, George!" and I called to him, "George isn't here, Edgar. He's gone." (Sounds a little weird, holding conversations with a raven, but I get that way sometimes.) Edgar presumably gave my answer some thought and then answered himself, in George's voice, "Hello, Edgar." However, since that time he has learned to say "George is gone" when George doesn't answer his call.

Edgar also calls poor Rhani and another of our pets, Janice's rabbit, Snowball, who isn't very bright. Snowball comes every time she hears "Hi, Snowball!"

Edgar seems especially fond of men. He does a sort of courting dance with George, although at first we didn't know that's what it was. When George is visiting him, Edgar will sometimes crouch low on his perch, raising his tail in the air and spreading it as his head goes down and his wings spread and tremble.

Ravens make good watchdogs. Edgar will always give his special warning call when a cat or other strange animal approaches the backyard where so many of our charges live.

He is friendly with other bird creatures, though. We had a pet chicken, Baby, who liked to make a little nest next to Edgar's cage. It was odd to see the dappled gray chicken listening carefully to big, black Edgar muttering and babbling in his own conversational tone.

Releasing the Bird

If you have any of these birds—the starling, crow, magpie, or raven—ready for release, remember to check with your game warden on the rules in your state. In Florida, it is not legal to release non-native species. So be sure your bird is within the law when you decide to let it go.

These birds can be released from your backyard but will probably hang around for a while before leaving you for good. Keep food available to them until they readapt to the wild. They are so easy to tame, and communicate so well with people, that sometimes they are almost too friendly to release without a long adaptation period to the world of nature.

11
BOBWHITE AND HIS BROTHERS
Quail, Partridges, and Pheasants

Our experience with game birds has differed from our work with other patients in that we have raised some of them from the egg, presented to us by a mother in residence, hatching them with the aid of an incubator—our work does *not* include sitting on eggs—of which, more later.

We have cared for the eastern bobwhite, the Coturnix quail, the chukar, the ring-necked pheasant, the Reeves's pheasant, and the silver pheasant. Several of the birds discussed in this chapter are native to this country, and some were introduced years ago and are now considered native species.

All these birds are gallinaceous birds—relatively heavy-bodied and short-legged types that scratch in the ground for their food, like a chicken. They leave the nest almost immediately after hatching, follow the parents, and are self-feeding and active. They are not fed by the parents in the nest.

Because they are game birds, their chief enemy is man, though they are preyed on by other species.

EASTERN BOBWHITE

The eastern bobwhite is the most familiar species of quail. It is widely distributed in the Eastern United States (where it is the *only* native quail), the South, and on through the West. This familiar little fellow is found in Texas, Colorado, the Dakotas, and has been introduced in the northwestern United States and Southern Ontario.

Taking its name from its cheery call, the bobwhite is a fat reddish-brown bird about 8 inches long. The male is identified by his white throat and white eyeline. The female is plain, buffy brownish. The quail family, seen in the countryside or in quiet city residential districts, crossing the street in dignified single file, is always a charming sight.

Though this quail is a popular game bird with hunters, it is also the farmer's friend, as it eats weed seeds, grasshoppers, potato beetles, locusts, and many other insect raiders of crop fields. Its nest is a simple one, usually well hidden in the tall grass, and the female will stay on it until flushed. The dull white eggs number from twelve to twenty and hatch in twenty-three to twenty-four days. Sometimes more than one brood is hatched in a season. If anything happens to the female, the male will incubate the eggs in her place.

Coturnix Quail

The Coturnix quail is not a native species, though it has been introduced in some areas of the United States; it is found in Europe and the warmer areas of the Old World. Somewhat smaller than the well-known American bobwhite, this bird differs in coloration between the male and female but not as markedly as the American bobwhite. Habits, however, are similar. The female lays two or more eggs, white, with brownish splotches, which take eighteen days to hatch. The birds feed on insects, seeds, and grain.

CHUKAR

The chukar is a European partridge which is now established in the Western United States and parts of Canada. It is a handsome bird, as large as a small chicken, with a white face and barred wings. This species ranges in size from 12 to 18 inches long and is probably the "partridge in the pear tree" of caroling fame.

A swift flyer, with a fast takeoff and erratic flight, it is highly prized by game bird hunters. It feeds on insects, seeds, and grain and likes a bushy grasslands habitat. It is a buffy-grayish in color, and the normal hatch for a pair is three to seven eggs.

RING-NECKED PHEASANT

The ring-necked pheasant was introduced in this country from China in 1881. Although it has done well in some areas, principally in the northern United States and southern Canada, it has not done very well in Florida.

A hardy prolific bird, the ring-necked pheasant is distinctive for its handsome markings. Though the female is plain and mousy, the male sports an orange-green face, a red eye ring, and the white and black collar which gives the breed its name.

This bird usually nests on the ground and hatches six to fourteen eggs in twenty-three to twenty-five days. The diet is varied. They eat acorns, wild seeds, wild fruits, and berries and are also fond of cultivated grain and vegetable crops. On the insect bill of fare, they eat such things as grasshoppers, crickets, and potato beetles, and they also eat small rodents.

REEVES'S AND SILVER PHEASANTS

Although we have had brief experience with two other species of pheasants, the Reeves's pheasant and the silver pheasant, our background information on them is sketchy. They are natives of Asia and are beautifully marked.

The main thing to remember about them, aside from the fact that we raised them in the same manner as native pheasants, is that these two species are not native to this country, and cannot be released here.

Incubation

Some of our game bird patients have presented us with eggs at various times—notably quail, chukar, and pheasant varieties. Of course, if you plan to incubate eggs, there must be a male on the scene when the female produces the eggs. A

Pheasant eggs hatch in the incubator as I watch.

female can lay eggs if no male is present, but they will not be fertile.

When we started incubating eggs, some years ago, we ordered our incubator by mail from GQF Company in Savannah, Georgia. This is a quail farm which sells incubation equipment, and as I recall we paid $24.95 for the incubator at that time. It has been worth it many times over for the hours of learning and pleasure it has brought to our household and to visiting children.

A small bird egg incubator is an amazingly compact machine. Ours has a round styrofoam body, is about 15 inches in diameter, and is 4 to 6 inches tall. The bottom has wells for water, for the humidity must be kept right for the eggs to hatch. An electric thermostat controls the temperature.

The eggs are placed on a wire screen, which sits above the water wells. Our model has a plastic window in the top for observation, which is a "must" as far as I am concerned, for it is a wonderful experience watching the baby birds hatch.

Game birds like tall grass to nest in, so we don't mow or trim the grass in their part of the yard. They just drop the eggs here and there, and we gather them daily. We put the eggs in a box of bran—to cushion them—on our kitchen counter for three to four days. This keeps them safe in storage for the time when we put them all in the incubator at one time.

We learned to keep our hands off once the eggs were inside, except to turn them at least twice daily, rolling each egg one quarter turn. The last three days we do not turn them at all. The temperature is kept at 97 to 103 degrees. If it falls below 97 degrees, the eggs will not hatch. If the temperature is too high, the eggs cook and the embryo dies. If you use an incubator, you should follow the instructions that come with it, but these are general rules we have used.

The required hatching time may be checked with bird manuals. For our quail, it is twenty-three to twenty-four days. When the baby is ready to come out of the shell, it makes a small hole with its egg tooth, a little projection on the bird's beak which enables it to crack the shell. The egg tooth disappears shortly after birth. When the baby bird is finally free of the shell—a process which seems to take an agonizingly long time and actually varies from minutes to many hours—it is wet and naked-looking, but the fluff dries out very rapidly.

There is nothing more beguiling in this world than a bumblebee-sized baby quail with that delightful Mohawk haircut. (Baby chukars and pheasants are buffy in color and proportionately larger than quail.) The babies may be left in the incubator for two or three hours, until they are very fluffy and well dried, and then they should be moved to a brooder.

We use homemade brooders—tall cardboard boxes lined with newspapers, paper towels, or sand. The boxes are heated with a 25-watt bulb hung in one corner. The chicks can move under the light bulb if they need heat and move away when they wish.

Infant Diet

The first twenty-four hours, these babies do not eat much. They have been feeding on the embryo yolk in the egg and do not need anything the first day.

When the chicks are ready for food, we give them medicated turkey starter or game-bird starter. We have used both with equal success. Both are high-protein foods.

In nature, the parents teach the chicks how to scratch for food and find it. We have to teach our incubated birds to eat and drink.

We use a chick water jar (available at feedstores), which is simply an inverted glass jar with a screw-on metal base that has a narrow rim around the edges. When it is filled with water and inverted, it supplies just enough water to fill the rim until the jar is empty. We use 6 drops of Zymadrops to a pint of water. To teach the babies to drink, we dip their beaks gently a few times into the water. If you must use an ordinary jar lid or dish for the chick's drinking supply, put in enough pebbles so the chick cannot possibly drown itself.

In nature, the chicks follow their parents and learn to peck from watching them. We have several methods of teaching little ones to peck. We peck with a sharpened pencil tip in the food, and the babies will get curious and come over to watch. They will peck at the pencil, then the food, and so discover how to eat.

Pecking sounds, such as the pencil tapping the lid jar, encourage them. We have also used a small flat square of aluminum foil, on which we sprinkle the food. The rattle of feed falling on the foil brings them on the run, and they will start pecking at the feed right away.

Baby game birds are very nervous, shy little fellows. They are difficult to hand-raise, so be patient and quiet with them.

Young and Adult Diet and Care

After about six weeks on the starter feed, we put the young chicks on adult game bird or turkey food "crumbles," a coarser version of the starter. The birds eat this diet until they are ready to be released.

Both adult and young game birds enjoy insects and mealworms. If we feed mealworms (we use very small ones available at pet shops) we don't give too many. Young birds should not get more than two a day. They are hard to digest because they have a tough outer skin or shell. Larger birds also like crickets and grasshoppers, usually available in plentiful supply in anyone's yard in the summertime.

We add red mineral grit to the floor of the brooder box at two or three weeks. This helps the grinding and digesting of the food in the bird's crop. Grit for bird feeding is available at pet shops.

We have received young quail patients and raised them on the above diets and care, but some of them died. Game birds hatched in the wild are very hard to raise in captivity, much harder than those hatched from the egg in your own home.

Once the birds are adult enough to eat crumbles, you can add intermediate chicken scratch feed and some greens, such as washed lettuce, carrot peelings, and seedy weeds, but be sure they have not been sprayed with pesticides. Ground beef can be fed to some game birds.

Our Coturnix quail was absolutely mad about lean ground beef. Her name was Anna (after Pavlova), and for her first birthday we gave her a cake—a walnut-sized patty of ground beef with a candle in the center, surrounded with lettuce bits. The birthday party was held on the dining room table, and after performing a few ballet steps, Anna ate the whole thing—except the candle. She would have eaten that too, if we'd let her. Anna was a great dancer and leaper. She could leap into our cupped hands from the tabletop, but it was such an exhausting performance she often fell asleep there for a tiny nap.

Quail are relatively easy to tame. Anna and Bobby, an eastern bobwhite, lived on our screened porch and were allowed the freedom of our house. We had to be careful not to step on them, because they walked a lot and seldom flew. They preferred to follow us about the house, always very curious about our destination. Bobby loved to ride on someone's shoulder and found washing dishes an especially fascinating show. He was also a household help, as he liked to catch flies off the window from the sofa back. He and Anna enjoyed sitting on the screened porch because, when Bobby whistled, wild quail often came by to talk and visit.

Bobby and Anna lived to the very old age of four and a half and five years. We never released them because they

Bobby Quail loved to ride around on Jan's shoulder. Hand-raised from infancy, he was a people-oriented bird and spent his whole life with us.

were so tame. Game birds in the wild generally do not live this long, even if they get the chance.

Housing

We house most of our friendly pet and nonreleasable birds in large outdoor flights when they reach adulthood. When startled, these birds fly straight up, as any hunter will tell you, and they need at least 6 feet of headroom. These cages are made of welded wire and are at least 8 feet long and 4 to 6 feet wide. (See Cages and Housing for building instructions.) We keep clean builder's sand on the floors. Game birds like dust baths—in the wild they do not bathe in water.

The flight cages are supplied with drinking water in large poultry waterers available at feedstores. These are larger versions of the waterer described for infants.

Feed is kept in chicken feeders—enclosed troughs with head-sized holes in the top to permit the bird to eat but not to scatter or dirty the food. A large bowl of mineral grit is kept in the cage so the birds can take it when they want it.

We keep potted flowering bushes in our quail cages. Our quail like to hop up and perch in them, partly because they just like it and partly because the blooms attract insects. Quail also like to eat the leaves (we are talking about non-poisonous plants, of course), so you may have to keep rotating the pots to keep the supply growing.

Chukars and pheasants need perches in their cages because they roost after sundown. Roofs and back walls provide shelter in these cages, so our perches are always placed under the roof in the back of the cage.

If you should by any chance be keeping a Reeves's pheasant, please allow for its very long tail in planning cage room. This bird has a five-foot tail.

Release

Convalescing birds can be kept in the yard by clipping their wings; the feathers will grow back by the time they are ready to fly away. Unless you clip the wings, it would probably be better to keep such patients in flight cages.

Bobwhites can be taken back where they came from, for there they will find available food and cover and suitable company. The same goes for the ring-necked pheasant, a native of northern states, and the chukar, a western bird. Our acre is home to a number of wild quail, so we release some of our quail patients right in our own backyard.

I have not discussed injuries to these birds, because treatment is covered in chapter 23 on First Aid for Birds. However, most of the adult game birds we have treated were suffering from concussion and had relatively simple recoveries.

12
SYMBOLS OF PEACE?
Doves and Pigeons

The dove—that well-known symbol of peace—is an exceptionally aggressive bird. Doves fight so much they must be housed in separate cages, unless in mating pairs. They like to make war as well as love.

We have worked with the mourning dove, the ground dove, and the ringed turtledove. We have also handled several varieties of domestic pigeons.

There are only three native species of pigeon, and none live in our area. The band-tailed pigeon frequents the western coast of the United States and Mexico, as well as parts of the American Southwest. The white-crowned pigeon is limited to the Florida Keys. The red-billed pigeon is found in parts of southern Texas. We have handled none of these but have worked with some of the other varieties of domestic pigeons.

As any urban citizen can tell you, although scientists only recognize three native breeds of pigeons, there are many "native" pigeon flocks of great variety in towns and cities. Like the dove, they are prolific breeders. Scientifically, however, the "city" pigeon is not considered native wildlife.

The mourning dove builds a sloppy nest and often loses her babies, but she never seems to miss them.

MOURNING DOVE

The mourning dove is a chubby little buffy brown and grayish bird, about 10½ inches long. When the light is right, its feathers show rosy iridescent tinges. The mourning dove is greatly sought by hunters in season. The species is a fast and erratic flyer and the breed is prolific, so luckily the hunters never manage to reduce their numbers seriously.

This is the most common native dove, found throughout the United States and in southern Canada. Doves are sloppy nest builders. They just throw a few twigs in a loose platform on boughs, the ground, in shrubs, or on top of the deserted nests of other birds. They are forever losing their babies. Their white eggs number two and incubate in about fifteen days.

The baby doves are hatched blind and naked. They are fed "pigeon milk," a liquid food produced and regurgitated by the mother. The babies stick their bills into her throat and suck the fluid. Solid foods such as insects and seeds are gradually added by the parents. By the time the babies leave the nest, well feathered at two or three weeks, they are on a solid diet.

Their natural food is principally seeds; they like buckwheat and wheat, weed seeds, and cultivated grain. Sometimes they flock to pine woods when the pine cones are producing seeds —they are very fond of pine seeds.

Their call is the soft liquid *coo* that is so often heard from fields and hedgerows in the summertime.

GROUND DOVE

The ground dove is a small bird, only 5½ inches long, but similar in coloration to the mourning dove, with rusty red wing patches. This species is found in the extreme southern United States and into Mexico. The ground dove is also a sloppy, loose nest builder, like its larger cousin, but generally confines its nest making to low bushes or to the ground. There are two white eggs, which incubate in twelve to fourteen days. They breed from February to November and can raise several broods in a season. Their babies are also fed pigeon milk and leave the nest at about two weeks.

Their natural food is weed and grass seeds, insects, and wild berries. These little doves are often seen resting on the ground, sometimes in the center of a country road, and will fly up very fast when disturbed. They are really too small for hunting purposes. Their call is a low soft whistle.

RINGED TURTLEDOVE

This dove is not native. It is an introduced species, originally a cage bird, now found in Los Angeles, California; Tampa, Florida; and Miami, Florida. It is a soft buffy bird with a black ring around the neck, though there is a variation in the species which is totally white, with an indistinct ring around the neck. The adult ringed turtledove is about 10 inches long.

There are two white eggs to a nest, and the babies hatch in two weeks, blind and naked. They, too, are fed on pigeon milk and in two to three weeks are fully feathered and ready to leave the nest.

The adult call is a lovely soft *coo*. These are the popular "turtledoves" often found in caged pairs in pet shops.

In nature, their food is seeds, grain, and insects.

PIGEONS

I will not attempt to discuss the many varieties of domestic pigeons in this chapter. They are raised widely as pets and racing pigeons and, of course, are abundant in flocks in many cities and on farmlands. Pigeons may be hand-raised in the same manner as our native doves, and their general habits are much the same.

Homing pigeons, which are used in pigeon long-distance events by pigeon fanciers, are sometimes found downed along their route, either injured or exhausted. Such pigeons are always banded. Usually, pigeon racers can help you locate the owner or the club where the pigeon belongs. If you happen to find an exhausted racing pigeon, pen it and feed and water it until it is rested. Whether or not you can locate the owner, if the bird can be released rested and strong, it will probably find its own way home. That's its business.

Infant Diet and Care

I have raised both baby doves and pigeons. Baby doves come in often; they fall out of the nest and their mother never seems to miss them. Dove babies are tiny, homely, blind, and naked. I keep them in the old standby mixing bowl nursery, with the 7½-watt bulb clipped on the side for warmth and the paper towel bedding.

The diet for infant doves and pigeons is the same as for infant song and garden birds (½ cup medicated turkey starter, 1 drop Zymadrops, and 1 25-mg. vitamin B_1 tablet, crushed, mixed with lukewarm water); the main differences are in the consistency, which should be *soupy*, and the method of feeding. Instead of a food stick, we use the modified plastic dropper that I make by cutting the end off a plastic medicine dropper with a sharp kitchen knife on the cutting board. The resulting wide-mouth dropper is easy to fill with the soupy mixture.

The baby's bill is gently poked into the end of the dropper. Keeping a gentle pressure on the dropper bulb pushes the food at the baby's bill. The baby will suck the food as it does the "pigeon milk" from its mother's throat. I keep the gentle pressure up so the food will stay constant in the end of the dropper, but I don't rush the baby or drown it in food until it gets the idea.

This is a very messy procedure, rather like feeding a human baby pureed baby food for the first time. I need plenty of paper towels on hand for mopping up both me and the baby bird. The baby usually gets food all over its face, body, and feet during the learning process.

Tiny baby doves and pigeons are fed every twenty minutes during the daylight hours. As they grow larger, the time between feedings can be lengthened.

When they can hop to the edge of their mixing bowl and are well feathered, I move them to a small indoor birdcage. At this point, I put some of the food in a jar lid and put it in the cage, dipping their bill in to show them what it is. However, I continue the hand-feeding until they are self-feeding. Although these birds are self-feeding at two weeks in the wild, it takes longer in captivity—three weeks or a little longer, depending on the development of the individual bird—for them to give up sucking.

I gradually add less water to the formula in the jar lid, thickening it so they will learn to eat more solid food. Finally, I put dry turkey starter in another jar lid.

When the baby is eating the dry food well, I add wild birdseed and fine chicken scratch (available at feedstores). When it is eating this well, I move the bird to a large outdoor cage (at least 4 feet long, 4 feet tall, and 2 feet wide). After becoming accustomed to the outdoors, it can be released— that is, the cage door is opened for the bird to leave when it likes.

Adult Diet and Care

The diet for adult doves and pigeons can include wild bird-seed, fine or intermediate chicken scratch, and commercial pigeon feed. Pigeon feed is more expensive than other feeds and is usually sold in 50-pound bags. Chicken scratch is cheaper, comes in smaller amounts, and can be bought in various grinds from fine to coarse. It is simply corn. The wild birdseed is a mixture of millet and other seeds and is cheaper when you buy it without the sunflower seeds. The sunflower seeds are too big for these small birds, anyway. Wild birdseed can be bought in small 2- or 3-pound bags at supermarkets, hardware stores, and drugstores, as well as pet shops and feedstores.

To the above diet I add, for greens and variety, washed lettuce, washed broad-leafed weeds (from my yard), and little bits of lean ground beef.

Both doves and pigeons like to bathe. I put their drinking water in a large clean pan, so they have plenty for both purposes.

Housing

We have found we usually must house these birds in separate cages or they will fight. This is true of both doves and pigeons.

The bird is kept in a large cage, with a roof shelter and back and partial side protection. Perches are placed under the roof. I usually cut small rough branches of the right diameter for their feet, rather than use manufactured perches.

We keep these cages raised 2 feet above the ground, so the droppings can fall through the wire floor. These birds are messy and prone to some infections, and they need to be kept as clean as possible.

We have a little different cage arrangement for nesting birds.

Nesting

Both doves and pigeons are extremely prolific. If you ever start breeding them, be prepared to be up to your elbows in baby birds. We have worked with nesting pigeons and turtledoves, but our native doves are released, as soon as they are able to be gone, to do their multiplying in the wild.

We were given a pair of fantailed pigeons, a pair of Jacobin pigeons, and a pair of ringed turtledoves. Needless to say, it did not stop there.

They raised babies with the greatest enthusiasm. We put each pair of birds in a large walk-in flight cage, 6 feet long, 6 feet high, and 4 feet wide, made of welded wire and floored with clean builder's sand. Nesting boxes were made of plywood (Cages and Housing section), and we lined them with dry pine needles. Each cage had a shelf for roosting, a perch, and was roofed, backed, and partially sided for shelter.

These birds did not waste much time on nest building. They just kicked a hollow in the pine needles and started laying eggs. We had to check the boxes daily, for if their eggs rolled into the corners the mothers were either too lazy or too stupid to gather them back under their warmth, but with our help they hatched many babies. We took the babies out of the cage as soon as they were self-feeding and found homes for them.

Our two fantails, Sally and Randy, were a most loving pair. They had many, many babies. It was fun to watch their court-ship—the way Randy would puff his chest and spread his wings, and the cooing and dancing they did together! Randy grabbed Sally by the head so often she was half bald. But this was all for love. They were a very compatible pair.

We had one pair of pigeons, Muffin and Puffin, who were brought in separately. We housed them in the same cage and found out they weren't a pair at all, because they were immediately at each other's throats. After we separated them, they were quite tame and biddable. They took turns par-ticipating in our children's programs, and both were noted for the fact that they would take off and fly to the highest bookshelf in the schoolroom, where, much to the children's delight, I had to climb up and capture them.

Injuries and Illness

Most of our dove patients were brought to us suffering from concussion, broken wings and legs, or gunshot wounds.

This mourning dove was shot; half its wing is gone.

The treatment for concussion is quiet and rest, the vet can set bones not broken in the joint, and gunshot wounds can be treated if the wound is not in a vital spot. Remedial treatment after the shot is removed is usually Panalog ointment. (See chapter 23, First Aid for Birds.)

We had one dove with a wing shot completely off, but it had survived somehow and escaped. We had to put it to sleep, as it was horribly mangled.

Sometimes a gunshot will only knock off a few feathers or stun a bird. In this case, all that is needed is quiet and rest with food and water until the broken feathers regrow.

Canker is a common and highly contagious disease occurring in doves and pigeons. (You will find more details on this ailment in chapter 23.) The main thing to remember is that it is spotted by a swelling of the throat and mouth. It is very infectious and is spread via drinking water and fecal deposits. Birds with canker should be kept isolated from all other birdlife. Canker can be treated in the early stages, but if it is in the advanced stages the bird must be destroyed.

We have treated several domestic pigeons with mysterious injuries. One, Pudgy, was found in the middle of the highway by a schoolchild. He was a banded bird, but we never found the owner. He had a swollen wing, and after food, rest, and the sulfamethazine-water treatment, he recovered. He became a popular star in our school programs and was noted for his tap dance on top of my safari hat. (It was actually a courtship dance.) Pudgy lived to a very old age for a pigeon.

Pudgy Pigeon does a tap dance on my hat for a group of schoolchildren.

CHARLES PATTON

Capture and Release

I have not discussed "capture" for doves and pigeons, because usually you can just pick them up when they have been hurt or downed for some other reason. Sometimes a long-handled net is needed to catch a crippled one.

A local boy who was caddying on the golf course found an unconscious dove which had been struck by a driven golf ball. He put it in his shirt and bicycled home with it. The dove made a good recovery in a few days, living in a shoebox with seed and water available. It was released in the boy's backyard and flew away, but it still returns every spring and pecks about busily on the sidewalk as if in annual remembrance of its benefactor.

Native doves can be released from the yard if there are lots of doves in the area, but if not, they should be taken to a field or meadow where they can rejoin their kind.

We often release doves in our backyard and they stay around for a while, returning occasionally for visits, even months after they have departed. They are not hard to recognize. One may have a slightly droopy wing from its original injury, or a perpetually stiff leg. Another may have a particularly dark spot on its head which we remember. Beyond these physical features, many of them have remained fairly friendly and trusting toward us and permit us to approach them with a closeness other birds will not tolerate. It is a combination of a lot of little things that tells us that the visiting dove is an old friend.

It is unlawful in our state to release domestic pigeons or such imported species as the ringed turtledove, as they are not native. However, a good home can usually be found for such birds with bird lovers. Pigeons and turtledoves are popular pets, easily tamed, and are very responsive to human company and care.

13
HIS BELLY HOLDS MORE THAN HIS BILL
Pelicans

Pelicans are our favorite patients; they are such clowns. Pelicans are friendly, curious, gregarious birds. In the past eight years we have treated and worked with over fifty of them. Some have not recovered from wounds or illness. Some have been released. Several have been donated to zoos, because they were not releasable. It gets a little crowded in our backyard sometimes, because off and on we usually have about a dozen pelicans in residence.

BROWN PELICAN

In our work we have dealt mostly with the eastern brown pelican, the species which frequents our shores. There is also a California brown pelican. Like the bald eagle, the brown pelican is diminishing in numbers. In California, brown pelicans raised only one young in the year 1970 and only a handful in the years following. Though the pelican is the state bird of Louisiana, it disappeared entirely from that state. Experts there tried to reestablish the brown pelican by importing birds from Florida in the late sixties and early seventies. Results are as yet unknown. Large colonies of pelicans were once found on the Carolina coasts, but these have all but disappeared. Only in Florida are these birds found in large numbers, and even here they have decreased to some extent. Major reasons for the decline of the brown pelican appear to be destruction of habitat and use of hard pesticides, such as DDT. Both the eastern and the California are now classed as endangered species.

Our familiar local eastern brown pelican can be seen flying and diving for food on our coastal waters and bays. It skims across the top of the water or a wave, its wing tips almost touching the water, watching for fish. Sometimes it will dive from a height of 50 feet for its prey. It plummets into the water and emerges, gulping a fish and dodging the gulls who often hang around, hoping for a bite.

The adult pelican can most easily be distinguished from the younger birds by its white head, which turns yellowish near the mating season. The young birds have plain brownish heads. The adult pelican is dark brown underneath and has silvery gray wings and gray eyes. The yellow forehead and breast patch is a sure sign of breeding season, but in the summer the back of the neck is chocolate brown.

The young pelican does not come into adult plumage until it is around four or five years old. The color of the immature bird is light brown on the upper parts and still lighter below. Their eyes are dark brown.

The eastern brown pelican is a very large bird, with a body about 41 inches long and a wingspan of around 90 inches. However, in spite of its size, it only averages 4 to 6 pounds in weight. This is because its bones are hollow, and the air sacs in its skin tissue and body make it extremely light and buoyant. It is amazing to lift such a large bird and find it so light in weight. Its waterproofing comes from an oil gland at the base of the tail, as does that of most birds, and it preens its feathers often, keeping itself so sleek that both fresh and salt water slide right off. The bird often rests on the water, bobbing lightly on the waves like a cork, even in a pouring rain, seemingly very comfortable. Experts say that pelicans eat about 4 pounds of fish a day, but it may be more in the wild. My resident pelicans eat less, but they lead a protected life in the backyard. Somebody has figured out that baby pelicans need about 150 pounds of fish to grow to fledgling size, ready to leave the nest. After hearing such news, I rejoiced that I had never had to raise one from babyhood!

Our local pelicans nest on mangrove islands, one of them located in the city of Venice, near the golf course. They lay two to three white eggs, which incubate in about four weeks. The father builds the nest, rather untidily, out of twigs and sticks. The nests are built very close together on the rookery islands, and sometimes the male pelicans steal sticks from each other's nests while nobody's looking.

Both male and female incubate the eggs, very formally exchanging places with bobs and curtsies. The babies are born blind, naked, and homely, and only a mother—or me—could love them.

When Mama or Papa comes home with a pouch full of semidigested fish, the babies puff and huff as they stick their heads into the pouch for a meal. The young birds are covered with white down in about two weeks and soon are as large as their parents, but they stay in the nest until almost ready to fly. I have watched and photographed them in the rookery many times and have noticed that parents will feed only their own babies, though other babies besiege them when they return from a fishing expedition. Sometimes a baby gets a bigger piece of fish than it can handle, and if its mother or father doesn't take it away, the baby just goes around with a large portion of its dinner hanging out of its mouth until it slowly digests and descends.

Pelicans, by the way, rarely make any sound but a huffing noise. I'll never forget the movie *Father Goose* in which Cary Grant watches a pelican land atop a palm tree with a terrible screech. Hollywood just can't resist those good old sound effects in this case probably borrowed from a bald eagle.

Pelican Personalities

Some of our pelicans are permanent residents: Pedro, Patch, Caddy, José, Dandy, Merry, Tony, Rod, and Poopsie are among these.

Pedro was less than two years old when he was brought to us. Now he is a mature male. In the early days, I discovered he liked to play a game which I called Huff-Huff. This game began with Pedro arching his neck, spreading his wings, and coming at me, going *huff-huff,* the closest equivalent I can give of the sound. I learned to get down on all fours, bend my head, wave my "wings," and *huff-huff* right back at him. He loved it. It was two years before I learned this was a part of the mating ritual, and I had ruined Pedro forever for girl pelicans. He likes me best. He pays no attention to the females in our yard.

Our fenced backyard must be a perfect environment for pelicans, because our permanent ones thrive here and seem to be very happy. We have many shade trees, with low hanging branches. There are small shrubs and grass and plenty of sunshine and shade. In the center of the backyard I keep several six-foot-wide plastic wading pools filled with fresh water from our garden hose. The pelicans do not seem to need salt water. They love baths and rush into a pool after a feeding.

Algae forms quickly in our climate, and our pools have to be scrubbed out at least once a week, more often when we have the time. Daily they are filled and overflowed to keep the water fresh. Around the yard we have short tree stumps, which resemble dock pilings. The pelicans love to sit on these and sun after they have had their bath.

Our pelicans have many games they like to play. One is "Mangrove"—they perch in the low branches of our trees just as they would if they were living in their rookery on a natural island.

Their favorite toys are rubber and plastic balls of various

George plays ball at the backyard pool with Pedro. No, Pedro never swallows the ball, he throws it back.

sizes, from baseball to soccer size. They do *not* swallow them. They like to bump and toss the soccer balls around the yard, and they like to toss the little balls, sometimes to each other, sometimes to me or George. Pedro likes me to toss a small rubber ball to him, which he catches and rolls back.

They also like to play with leaves, sticks, and feathers. Our yard is not manicured for a good reason. Some of our pelican couples have shown an interest in courting and have built nests. Though no pelicans have, to our knowledge, ever been known to hatch and raise young in captivity, we keep hoping, and we leave fallen twigs and branches all about the yard for them to use in nest building. We only mow when absolutely necessary, so as not to upset them.

Rain is a special delight to the pelicans in our yard. They like to play in it if it is a soft shower and not a blinding rainstorm. They will jump in their pool and splash around, while the raindrops shower them, and stand with their heads up trying to catch the raindrops. They become very playful during a shower and chase each other all over the yard, in a pelican game of tag.

Capture and Transport

If you live in pelican country, the time may come when you will find a hurt or ill pelican on the beach. These pointers will help in capture, treatment, care, and release of your patient.

When approaching a pelican on the beach, always stay between the bird and the water. It is smart, so don't arouse its suspicions by moving in too fast. Just saunter along the beach as if you are looking for shells at the water's edge and act as if you don't even know the bird is there. We use our long-handled dip net and usually work in pairs, George or Janice and I, to make a capture.

Once you have the net over the pelican, move in and seize it firmly. Tuck the bird under one arm, holding the bill in one hand so it cannot bite or snap.

Remember when capturing pelicans, even birds too weak to move away but still strong enough to snap, to wear light-weight plastic garden gloves. It saves you from a few

Jan brings an injured young brown pelican in from the Gulf of Mexico. It was wrapped in yards of monofilament line and had fishhooks embedded in both wings. It recovered and was released.

scratches. If you move your hand up and down in front of a pelican, it will snap, with a noise like a .22 rifle shot. The time to grab the bill is just after a snap, because it takes a few seconds for the bird to rear back and snap again. Once you have a firm hold on the bill, the battle is won.

The pelican can be transported in a cardboard carton with plenty of airholes and a lid secured with masking tape. If you must carry it on your lap in the car, take along an old sheet or towel and wrap the bird securely, as this keeps it from flapping around and keeps you clean. Pelicans should always be wrapped when hand-carried, because they are worse than geese about firing at will, and their droppings are very odoriferous.

Pelicans are easily upset and will throw up a fish from their stomachs at the slightest scare. Some say this is also an instinct to "lighten the load" before an emergency take-off. At any rate, be prepared for it. Fishitosis is one of the few unfortunate things about pelicans, but they can't help it if they have bad breath. They don't eat anything but fish.

Injuries

Some of our pelicans are amputees, some are suffering with healed but permanently crippled wings, one has an eye missing (which makes diving for fish impossible), and one is partially blind. José lost his right eye to a fishhook. Caddy, our partially blind female, took off over the back fence one day but was found within an hour two blocks away in a neighboring yard, peering nearsightedly at her surroundings. We now clip her wings, and those of the other resident pelicans who cannot survive in the wild.

Caddy Pelican, our partially blind adult, plays ball with one of her young friends.

ROSEMARY K. COLLETT

Our newest young resident is Rod (named after my teen-aged daughter Janice's idol, Rod McKuen). He is healthy now but was hurt by fishhooks embedded in his wing. He is too friendly and follows me everywhere. I am afraid that if he is released some stupid human may hurt him.

Pelicans are easily tamed, and there are many friendly ones in Florida that hang around fishing docks and piers for free fish handouts. They are all affectionately called "Pete" by those who love them—but there are people who will injure a pelican just for the fun of it. We have received pelicans who have been run over deliberately by motorboats, whose operators think it is great sport to go full speed through a flock of pelicans resting on the water. One of these pelicans who didn't get out of the way in time lost a wing. Another was literally scalped. We managed to save the first—Pedro—and he became a permanent ward. The second one died. Sometimes irate fishermen will club a pelican because it is hanging around their boat. We had one of those, too.

When Pedro spreads his wings, you can see he has only one and a half. The left wing was shattered and had to be amputated. He will spend the rest of his thirty- to thirty-five-year life with us.

ROSEMARY K. COLLETT

Treatment of most pelican wounds and injuries is covered in chapter 23.

Diet and Care

Pelicans eat only fish—lots of them. Ours consume 2 to 3 pounds of fish daily in captivity. They like small mullet, pinfish, whiting, trout, Spanish sardines, and smelts. (We never feed our birds catfish. I am always afraid the spines will cause injuries.) We use several hundred pounds of fish monthly, so we buy whatever is cheapest and most plentiful. We usually go to a commercial fish house, where we can get fish at wholesale prices. We buy 300 to 500 pounds at a time and store it in our freezer, contributed—bless them—by the Venice Area Audubon Society to help with our work.

Vitamin B_1 (thiamine hydrochloride) is part of the diet we feed to pelicans and all other fish-eating birds. It is easy to insert a 50-milligram vitamin tablet in the gill or mouth of the fish, or you can cut a slit in the fish and tuck in the tablet. B_1 is an important part of the diet for all fish-eating species because in captivity these birds get a limited variety of fish, and in some fish there is an enzyme called thiaminase which destroys vitamin B_1 in the system. In the wild fish-eating birds eat such a wide variety of fish that they automatically compensate for this vitamin lack, but in captivity it is necessary always to add B_1 to their fish diet.

When pelicans first arrive as patients, they are often frightened and upset, and for the first few days, until they become acclimated to their surroundings, they must usually be force-fed.

Force-feeding a pelican is a very important procedure, which must be done right or you will kill the bird. *Always* put a fish down a pelican's throat on the *right* side—that is, the bird's right side. *Never* put it down the left. If you do, you will choke it to death. The pelican is so constructed that its esophagus, which leads to the stomach, is on the right side of the throat; the trachea, through which it breathes, is on the left. So remember, the *bird's right side* is the only side on which to feed fish.

When you are ready to force-feed a pelican, grasp the bill

JACK BRIGGS

Force-feeding a pelican patient. Note that the bill is held firmly while the neck is stroked gently.

in one hand, gently stretching the neck upward, and open the bill. The fish should be moistened in water to make it go down easily. Put the fish far back in the throat on the bird's right side and slide it down as far as possible. Then close the bill, keeping the head up and the neck gently stretched. Gently jiggle the bill, and the fish will slide farther down the throat. Then stroke the throat softly, as when giving a dog a pill. If the fish seems to have gone pretty far down (you can see its progress by the bulge in the throat and neck) let go the bill and leave *immediately*. The pelican will throw up the fish if disturbed in any way. If left alone and quiet, it will usually complete the swallowing process.

You may have to force-feed a pelican several times before it will accept fish from you and swallow them by itself. If the pelican throws up the fish, wait a few minutes and quietly try again. It may take several tries before the fish stays down.

Incidentally, we never mow just after feeding the pelicans. They will always throw up their fish—which makes for a very smelly yard.

While acclimating pelicans to our backyard, we keep them in a pen, if they are well enough to stay outside, until the home bunch knows them. We have enclosures made of welded wire placed around the edge of the yard. These pens are 8 feet long, 4 feet wide, and 4 feet high. We use clean builder's sand on the bottom of the pens and add clean sand when necessary. We keep the newcomers penned about two weeks before releasing them into the yard. There they can exercise, bathe, and get to know the other pelicans while regaining their strength.

Although pelicans enjoy each other's company, we have learned not to introduce a new one into the backyard colony without this careful orientation. The old gang will fuss and snap at the newcomer. While the new pelican stays in the wire pen, it and they get acquainted. By the end of this period, they have met through the wire, "talked," and visited. Just before releasing the new one into the gang, we throw a big fish dinner and all the old pelicans get so stuffed they can't move—then we release the newcomer, and all is serene.

A group of our adult brown pelicans have a tête-à-tête in the fenced backyard. Left to right: Caddy, Patch, Merry, and Pedro.

If a pelican is sick or recovering from surgery or wounds, we don't put it outside; we put it in the bathroom. There it can be kept warm and dry and free from flies.

My bathroom (fortunately George has another one) is the hospital ward, because it has a tub which is just right for a sick pelican. The tile and porcelain are easy to clean. I place newspapers on the floor to save on mopping, and also because pelican droppings are like concrete and don't come off easily. The pelican in the bathtub doesn't need water to drink for a few days, as it gets enough moisture from its fish. (In-

We use our bathroom as a hospital ward; it is relatively easy to keep clean.

ROSEMARY K. COLLETT

cidentally, *never* attempt to pour water down a pelican's throat. You would doubtless kill it.)

After surgery, or with an open wound, I give pelicans sulfamethazine orally. I use a hypodermic syringe without a needle, open the pelican's bill, squirt 1 cc. of the medication down its throat—the *right* side—and pop in a fish quickly so it will swallow.

When we have houseguests, at some point I usually have to say to them, "The bathroom is down the hall, first door on the left, and be careful not to upset the pelican, please." I lose a few houseguests this way. And I must admit, even I

It's wise to keep a wary eye on a recovering patient.

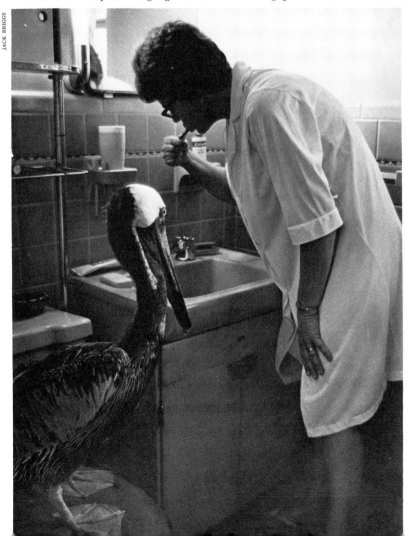

find it alarming to be nipped from behind by a playful pelican when I am brushing my teeth. But that's all right. It means the patient is feeling better. It also means it's just about time for a move to a pen in the yard.

Release

Sometimes we take a pelican that is ready for release back to the beach from which it came, but sometimes our backyard pelicans which are ready to go back to nature just take off over the fence and head for the Gulf of Mexico.

The Gulf is only three blocks west of our yard, so when a pelican is airborne it can see the water and head for it. If a pelican can clear the fence, the tall trees, hedges and house roof, we know it is strong enough to be on its own again. Only permanently disabled birds stay on with us, and we even try to thin out our permanent pelican population every now and then when it gets too crowded.

We donated two crippled brown pelicans to the San Diego Zoo in 1971 when I flew to Hollywood to appear on a television show. Sam and Casey, two young pelicans, had come to us with permanent injuries. Sam had a deformed wing, and Casey was picked up with a smashed wing which had to be amputated. San Diego was glad to give them a home, since they had no eastern brown pelicans, only the California ones.

The two birds were crated and shipped by air, with copies of their state and federal permits and health certificates attached. The zoo picked them up in Los Angeles on a Monday, and after I did the TV show we went out on Wednesday to see how they were faring in their new home. The zoo keeper reported that they threw up all their fish, and he was really worried about them.

I went to their pen, calling, "Sam! Casey!" and they came running. It had been four days since they had kept down any food, because I had deliberately withheld food from them before their flight, knowing they would regurgitate half-digested fish in their crates during the flight and probably asphyxiate everyone aboard the aircraft.

The keeper let me offer them some fish which I selected from the hospital kitchen. They gulped them down and squatted there with fat necks and happy looks just as if they were in my backyard in Venice.

The zoo keeper couldn't understand it.

"They're my babies," was the only explanation I could give him.

We called the zoo the following Saturday before we left for Florida, and the keeper said, "You sure broke the ice. We haven't had a bit of trouble since you were here. I just call their names, and they come running and take their fish. I never saw anything like it in my life!"

We have also donated pelicans to the Crandon Park Zoo in Miami, Florida. There they have a lovely home in their natural climate, with a big lake to swim in.

WHITE PELICAN

We have also worked with white pelicans and have had three as patients. The white pelican is larger than the brown and differs in other ways. It does not dive for fish as the brown does. White pelicans gather in groups or pairs on the water and herd small fish ahead of them, scooping them up into their pouches. Our white pelicans prefer smaller fish such as sardines or smelts. The pouch of the white pelican is not as expandable as that of the brown (the brown pelican can swallow a foot-long mullet), so that it really cannot eat larger fish comfortably. Other than the size of the fish we feed, housing and care for our white pelicans is the same as for brown.

The story of Luv, our white pelican star patient, is worth telling here to show what can be done when all seems lost with a bird patient.

Luv was picked up in Sarasota, where she came down in a canal, very thin and extremely weak. She could not even stand. We thought she would die the first night we had her. Her left eye appeared sightless, and her appetite was poor. We force-fed her, gave her B_{12} as an appetite stimulant, and the B_1 that is routine for fish-eating birds. In three days she was taking fish from my hand but still could not stand. We started physical therapy in a plastic wading pool with lukewarm water, massaging her legs twice daily. On the tenth day, a pelican expert came to the house and told us there was little hope. He said he had seen similar cases, and our efforts were probably wasted, because she would surely die.

On the fourteenth day, Luv stood up, wobbly and weak. That was the beginning. By the end of the month, she was waddling around the "isolation ward" in the patio. We finally moved her into the backyard with the brown pelicans. Her left eye cleared up and her vision returned. She was with us from October until the day she left in February, a period of four months. On that day she took off from the backyard, flying strongly, heading for the Everglades to rejoin her cousins before the return flight north.

We still think of her with great pride and fondness, as one of our most heartwarming experiences.

14
GRACEFUL FLYERS
Gulls

Gulls of many varieties are found throughout the United States. Most are scavengers. They are gregarious birds and are usually found in large groups. They like to steal food from each other and from other birds and are a cocky, raucous, freewheeling family.

Gulls are often hard to identify by species because their plumage changes periodically from infancy until adulthood. The laughing gull, for instance, goes through a series of several plumage changes until the age of three years, when full maturity is reached.

Here on the west coast of Florida, we have worked mostly with the laughing gull, ring-billed gull, and herring gull. All have been immature or adult birds. We have raised none from infancy. There are so many species of gulls throughout the world, it would take volumes to list them all and describe their diets and habitats. However, I am sure any gull species would do well on the diet and care we practice here in working with our gull patients.

LAUGHING GULL

The laughing gull is so-called because of its raucous call,

which resembles a wild laugh. Year-round residents in Florida, these birds are found also on the Atlantic and Gulf coasts of the United States. The laughing gull has white underparts and a soft gray back and wings. The wings are tipped in black. When in breeding plumage it has a handsome black head, and its legs and bill are deep red. The adult averages 13 inches in length and has a wingspan of 41 inches.

It lays three eggs, buffy colored, with brownish splotches, and the young are hatched in twenty days. They are fed at first on soft semidigested food from the parents' beaks. They leave the nest within a few days but are fed by the parents until they can fly, and sometimes for a while after that.

Laughing gulls feed mostly on small fish or minnows caught from the surface of the water in swooping dives. In our area you often see "every pelican with his own sea gull," meaning that a freeloading gull picks out a pelican which is a good fisherman and follows it around, waiting for the pelican to make a catch so the gull can steal it. I have seen them land on a pelican's head and steal the fish from its pouch before the pelican can swallow it.

Gulls also steal and eat eggs from other species. They scavenge the beach, pecking out the eyes of dead fish and looking for tidbits wherever they can find them.

People love to feed the gulls on our beaches here. It is a fact that they will eat anything. I have seen laughing gulls eat bread, popcorn, spaghetti, pizza, and even lemon meringue pie!

HERRING GULL

The herring gull is the most widely distributed gull in the Northern Hemisphere. It may be found on all coasts and inland, especially around lakes and rivers. Its head and body are white. The upper parts of the wings are light gray, the tips black. It has a yellow bill and pinkish legs.

I don't know why this bird is called a herring gull, because it eats a lot more than just herring. Its wingspan averages 55 inches and its body 20 inches.

It too lays three eggs, which may be pale bluish, greenish,

or buffy, with brownish markings. The young hatch in about twenty-six days, and they are fed semidigested food. The parents often drop the food at their feet, and the young will pick it up. They are fed for at least five weeks or until they can fly, sometimes longer. Young herring gulls swim well.

Their natural food is fish, squid, crabs, mollusks, and insects of all kinds. These gulls have learned to carry oysters or clams high in the air, drop them on hard rocks or a paved street to open them, and then descend to feast on the half shell.

RING-BILLED GULL

The ring-billed gull was called by Audubon the "Common American Gull," and it certainly is. Found on all coasts of the United States and inland, it is generally seen here in Florida in the winter.

This gull is so named because of its yellow bill with the black ring around it near the tip. It has white undersides, with wings topped by gray and tipped in black. Its legs are greenish-yellow in color. The adult is about 16 inches long and has a 49-inch wingspan.

This gull also lays three eggs—buff with brownish splotches—and its young hatch in about twenty-one days. They are fed semidigested food by the parents until they can fly and become self-feeding. They leave the nest after a few days and learn to swim at an early age.

In the wild they eat fish, large insects such as grasshoppers, and worms and grubs. They will also catch and eat field mice and other small rodents. They eat the eggs of other birds, and like most gulls they are scavengers, even eating garbage if it is available.

Capture and Transport

Gulls on land may be captured in the same way as pelicans, with a long-handled net or by throwing a large beach towel or sheet over them. Sometimes you can just pick them up if they are very sick or crippled. They may peck and pinch, and they can give you a nasty scratch with their razor-sharp bills if you have no light gloves. Put them into a cardboard box or wrap them in a towel for transport. The box is better, because it quiets them, and they travel well in a box. But such things are not always available at the beach when you find a crippled bird, and you must make do with what you have.

I once rescued a gull from the water, but it was a close call. On a cold windy day in January, I had a call from the city beach. A boy throwing rocks at a gull had broken its wing, and it had gone down in the Gulf of Mexico. I went to the beach and saw the gull bobbing off toward Yucatan at a rapid rate. The lifeguard made me use an air mattress, but I paddled out to the gull as fast as I could get there. The bird passed out, about the time I reached it, and didn't seem to be breathing as I grabbed it out of the water. The little boy was on shore, crying and hoping, or I (and the gull too, probably) would have been tempted to forget the whole thing.

I started back, giving "gull respiration" (I devoutly hoped it was, anyway), but it didn't work, so on a pure stroke of genius I administered mouth-to-mouth resuscitation. It worked, and the gull was breathing and conscious when I reached the beach. The first one to help me out of the water was the boy who had thrown the rock.

However, I do not recommend trying to rescue any of these birds from the water unless you have a boat and a long-handled net. Even then, the odds are pretty bad, unless the bird just cannot make any effort to get away. Once these birds are in the water, they are very hard to rescue, unless they are unconscious or badly hurt.

Diet

Although gulls will eat almost anything, ours get a varied high-protein diet: fish, soaked Gaines Meal dog kibbles, canned mackerel, cat-food tuna, bread scraps, lean ground beef, and assorted tidbits.

The gulls adore small fish, such as they catch in the Gulf, and since many people seine for minnows and baitfish here daily, sometimes fresh minnows are available. If not, we chop larger fish into smaller pieces. Smaller frozen smelts are a nice size for gull feeding and are usually easy to find at any super-market. They are thawed before feeding, of course.

If we are feeding the dog kibbles, we soak them in water for about ten minutes, drain off the excess liquid, and sprinkle with Vionate vitamins and a crushed 25-mg. B_1 tablet.

We feed fish twice a day and keep the soaked kibbles in dishes for the gulls to eat whenever they want it. We alter-nate the fresh or frozen fish with canned mackerel or canned tuna cat food.

Two of our resident gulls have developed an absolute pas-sion for Kennel Ration Cheeseburger dog food, which comes in ground beef form in little packets. It needs no soaking and is moist and easy to feed.

Force-feeding

The gull has a sharp-tipped, razor-edged bill. Plastic garden gloves can be worn when force-feeding, to avoid cuts and scrapes, although I am experienced enough not to need them with gulls—and they *are* awkward when trying to force-feed a small bird.

I gently open the bill by holding the base of the bill be-tween thumb and forefinger and, prying with a thumb slipped between the upper and lower bill, I pop in a piece of fish, pushing it as far back in the throat as I can. Then I close the bill and stroke the throat to encourage swallowing. I feed as much as possible, but if the bird starts getting too nervous, I leave it alone immediately. Like the pelicans and many other water and shore birds, the gull will regurgitate its food if it becomes too excited or nervous.

Force-feeding a laughing gull.

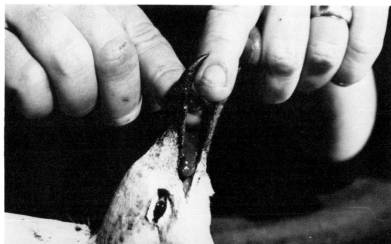

Our gulls generally learn to eat from a dish in a day or so. We have found a good way to get them started on the Gaines Meal diet is to put small fish on top of a dish of soaked kibbles. The gull will eat the fish and then start on the kibbles. From that point on, it eats easily from a dish.

Injuries and Illness

Occasionally we get gulls which have no visible injuries but are sick. These birds may be thin and weak, and sometimes they have convulsions. Their droppings may be the wrong color. Droppings from a healthy gull are gray and white. Greenish droppings may mean intestinal problems, poisoning, or the first stages of starvation. Brown droppings often indicate near-starvation, and it is not always possible to save a bird that is badly malnourished. We have found, however, that our gulls on the dog kibble diet also develop brownish droppings—this is all right; it is just the result of the diet residue. Black droppings may mean that the gull is bleeding internally.

In some cases of extreme emaciation and dehydration, we give the gull Gatorade to drink. Gatorade, usually found in the fruit juice section of the supermarket, was developed at the University of Florida for the football team, as a quick refreshing drink to replenish lost body fluids and provide glucose. It is now produced nationally, and we use it with many of our dehydration patients.

In these cases we also give a high dose of vitamin B_1 daily, as much as 50 mg. tucked into a fish. Sometimes, when gulls are very thin, we force-feed them on slender strips of raw beef liver. This supplement is an excellent body builder.

We treat many gulls of all types with broken wings. These injuries occur from flying or being blown by storms into power lines and TV antennas or by people deliberately injuring the birds.

If the wing is broken at the joint or at the body, chances for good recovery are very slim. Joint wounds seldom heal so that the bird can fly again.

A clean bone break not occurring in the joint can be set successfully. Our vet has devised a lightweight aluminum splint to set such breaks. Sometimes he binds them instead with paper tape, effectively holding the wing in its natural folded position. The splint or tape usually stays on two to three weeks, depending on the type of break. If any flight feathers must be clipped or damaged in the setting, the bird must be kept until the feathers regrow, sometimes a period of several months.

Broken legs also can heal well if they are not joint breaks. And even if amputation is necessary, gulls can get along on one leg, so long as they can fly. Some of our gulls have amputated wings, but a gull with one wing is grounded. We generally have about a dozen in the yard—the children love to see them, when they visit, and learn to identify the different species. The gulls live a relatively happy and peaceful life in our backyard.

Following surgery or bonesetting, we keep the gulls in large cardboard boxes lined with newspapers. They stay indoors or on our screened porch until they are healed. They drink a sulfamethazine solution (as described in Veterinary Reference at the end of this book) instead of water, for five days. We use a small bowl that they cannot bathe in or tip over. After these birds are healed, they have a large bath pan or wading pool filled with fresh water. They love to bathe and do not need salt water.

Smiley, a young laughing gull, lived in the bathroom hospital ward for five weeks. His favorite resting spot was the johnny lid, which we always remembered to close.

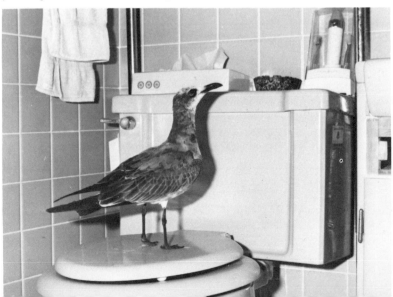

ROSEMARY K. COLLETT

One of our gulls makes use of a birdbath.

Housing and Release

We put our recovering gull patients in outdoor pens made of welded wire. Clean builder's sand covers the bottom of the pen. A portion of the pen is roofed, and an easily cleaned aluminum doghouse is in each pen for further protection from bad weather.

When the recovering gulls need more exercise, we release them to the freedom of the backyard and the wading pool, where they circulate with the other patients, including the permanent gull residents such as the amputees. This is possible because the yard is fenced and we have no problem with marauding dogs, cats, raccoons, opossums, or rats, rogue raiders that can make short work of a crippled bird.

Since we live so near the Gulf, our gulls, like many of our other water and shore bird patients, can take off over the back fence when they feel the call of the wild. If we did not live near a gull's habitat, we would simply put it in a cardboard box and return it to its home beach, where it would not hesitate to join its raucous cousins.

Sometimes our previous gull patients return for a visit or a quick meal. But whether or not we ever see them again, one of the greatest rewards we have found in working with gulls is seeing them return to the sky, soaring and turning in the sun, back in their real element.

15

AERIAL ACROBATS
Terns and Skimmers

Terns are famous for their aerial displays of fancy flying. They move through the sky on graceful tapered wings, twisting, turning, and diving with lightning speed and amazing agility.

Skimmers, in their striking black and white plumage, accented by brilliant red bills, fly just above the water searching for small fish. They scoop their catch from the water with their bill, which is especially designed for this purpose.

We have worked with the least tern, common tern, sooty tern, and royal tern, and the black skimmer. Some background information on these species may be helpful in identifying and caring for them.

LEAST TERN

The least tern, as the name implies, is the smallest of the terns in the United States. This bird is white below, gray on top of the wings, with black accents. It has a white face and a black cap. A yellow-pointed bill is tipped with black. Yellowish legs complete the ensemble.

The least tern is found along sandy beaches and sometimes, but rarely, in inland areas. The eggs of these birds (they lay two, buff colored with dark brown markings) hatch in about fifteen days, and the young are fed small fish. The fledglings only stay in the nest a few days before they become active.

Least terns live on fish but do eat some insects. They hunt by flying just over the surface of the water until they spot a fish and then diving into the water for it. Sometimes they just snatch it up with their bill.

The adult least tern is only 8½ inches long and has a 20-inch wingspan.

COMMON TERN

The common tern—again aptly named—is the most abundantly found tern in the United States. It can be seen along the Atlantic seaboard and Gulf coast, and also at inland lakes. This bird averages 14 inches in length and has a 31-inch wingspan. The common tern has white undersides, soft gray wings, a black cap, and a red-orange bill. The female lays two or three eggs which are colored buff to cinnamon with dark brown spots.

Common tern babies, hatch in twenty-one days. They are out of the nest and active in two or three days. They are generally spotted or speckled and are thus very hard to see on the rocky beaches. They are fed by the parents until they can fly well. Their main food is small fish, not more than 4 inches long. These birds also eat some shrimp, aquatic insects, and sand eels. They fish by diving as well as by snatching their food from the water.

We have a nesting area on Casey Key nearby, which has developed on the white sand and shell dug out to form the Intracoastal Waterway. On this "created" land are hundreds of tern nests. You must be careful not to step on them when walking there, because they are no more than hollow depressions in the sand, high enough upland to be out of reach of tides and high water. The mottled eggs blend perfectly with sand and shell. The mother birds will fly up from these nests and dive-bomb intruders. We try never to disturb the nests. In this climate the mother needs to stay on the nest not so much to keep the eggs warm as to shield them from the fierce sun. Even after the young are hatched, she will spread her wings to shade them.

SOOTY TERN

The sooty tern does not properly belong in our area. The one we treated was blown from the south by Hurricane Agnes. They nest in the Dry Tortugas, a string of islands off the southern west coast of the Florida peninsula. This is the only tern that is entirely black above and white underneath. It has a sharp black bill and a forked tail, very much like a swallow's.

Incubation time for the cream buff brown-spotted eggs is twenty-six days. The babies are active in two or three days. They are greedy and eat as many as twenty to forty small minnows a day. The diet of these birds is almost entirely fish.

ROYAL TERN

The royal tern, as befits royalty, is one of the larger terns. It is as big as a gull, 18 inches long with a 43-inch wingspan. It lives in saltwater areas, such as the lower east coast and Gulf coast of the United States, as well as the lower Pacific coast and south to Baja California. This is a large white bird with a black crest. It has a yellow-orange bill and dark legs. Its food is principally small fish up to 4 inches in length, which it plunges into the water to catch. It also eats shrimp and crabs.

BLACK SKIMMERS

The black skimmer is a large bird, about 17 inches in length. It is found on the lower Atlantic and Gulf coasts, but there is an African counterpart, similar to our native species, which I have seen in Kenya.

The unique feature of the black skimmer is its bill. Besides being a vivid orange-red, the bill is constructed with the lower bill much longer than the upper. With this lower bill, the bird can scoop fish from the surface of the water as it flies above the sea.

Black skimmers in flight are beautiful examples of birds in motion. "Parked" on the beach for their sunning session, they always face the same way, into the wind. We have had several of these birds for patients.

The black skimmer's eggs are bluish white marked in shades of brown. The downy infants are fed regurgitated fish, dropped in front of them by the parents. Sometimes, though, they are so eager they snatch the food before it drops. When feathers begin to show, the young are fed whole fish. These fish are presented to them crosswise by the parent. Oddly enough, these baby birds do not develop the unequal bill until they learn to fly and hunt on their own. Until that time, their upper and lower bills are of equal length.

These birds feed mostly on small fish, but also eat shrimp and other small crustaceans.

Diet

For all terns and skimmers small whole fish (3 to 4 inches) are best. If no small fish such as minnows or very small smelts are available, the larger frozen smelts, available at the super-market, may be thawed and cut into bite-sized pieces. Whole fish are easier because these birds recognize it as their nat-ural food. I add a 25-mg. vitamin B_1 tablet by putting it in the fish's mouth. When feeding cut pieces, I crush the tablet and sprinkle it on the bites. These birds need a daily B_1 ration in this amount to supplement their all-fish diet.

If a bird is very weak and is too sick to be force-fed, I use a "slurry" recipe for fish-eating birds which can be fed by spoon dribbles or medicine dropper (not too fast!) until the bird is strong enough to eat solids.

Slurry Diet for Weak Fish-eating Birds

3 or 4 small smelts (3 to 4 inches)
1 25-mg. vitamin B_1 tablet, crushed
3 drops Zymadrops liquid vitamins
2 oz. Gatorade

Put in blender and blend to a liquid consistency.

This diet might also be used for infant birds of the fish-eating species, though I have not tried it for this purpose.

Force-Feeding

Skimmers, we have found, must usually be force-fed at first, though I have been able to get skimmers to eat by dropping small whole fish into a wide dish or pan. Also, when dropped in a water bowl, a fish will spin and sink to the bottom, stim-ulating the bird's interest in picking it up and eating it.

The skimmer, in spite of its unequal bill construction, soon learns to eat from a dish, simply by cocking its head sideways and scooping up the fish at an angle.

If the bird must be force-fed, whether it is a tern or a skimmer, the technique is to open the bill by holding the bill base between thumb and forefinger and pressing, or by prying the bird's beak open with a thumb and forefinger. The fish or fish bits are poked as far down the throat as possible, and the throat is stroked gently a few times to help it go down.

These birds need plenty of fresh water to drink and, if they are not injured seriously, a large pan of water in which to bathe. They do not need salt water. I put Gatorade in their drinking bowl if they are thin and dehydrated.

Injuries, Capture, and Housing

Injured terns and skimmers are not going to be caught as long as they can fly. If they are badly hurt, capture is simply a matter of picking them up or tossing a towel over them.

Most of our tern and skimmer patients have suffered from concussion or broken wings. Concussion symptoms are usually evident; the bird is weak and unsteady on its feet, or it is unconscious. Broken bones are usually equally obvious; the bird cannot fly, flips around in an effort to do so, or drags or droops one wing.

Concussion patients need quiet, and we keep them indoors, in cardboard boxes lined with newspapers until they recover, seeing that they have clean boxes, fresh water, and fish. Broken wings (if not broken in the joint) are set by the vet, and these recuperating birds are housed in the same type of hospital box.

A very battered royal tern, swept in by a storm. We get many sea and shore birds after a hurricane.

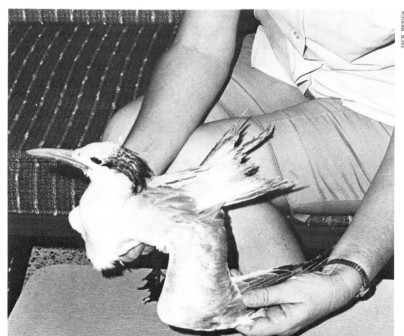
JACK BRIGGS

We have had terns and skimmers which we suspect had insecticide poisoning. They are thin and weak, and their droppings are greenish. Often the birds have convulsions, with the head arching backward and seizures of tremor. We know of no treatment for them, but we put sulfamethazine in their drinking water and try to keep them warm and quiet. Recovery rate for these birds is not good. Botulism symptoms are similar, and treatment is the same.

Terns and skimmers with smashed wings or joint breaks should be put out of their suffering. Their life is flight, and it is not humane to amputate or to heal them with a stiff or crippled wing. They do not do well when permanently landbound and are never happy in captivity.

When recuperating birds are stronger, they are moved to an outdoor wire pen which has a builder's sand floor and some shade. We provided some of our recovering tern patients with an aluminum doghouse, which they seemed to like because it afforded privacy and shelter from the weather.

We use big round plastic dishpans for their water in the outdoor pens. They can drink from them or bathe in them. Skimmers also like to take their fish from the water. The terns take theirs from a small dish.

Release

When these birds are well and strong, they should be released in the area from which they came. Ours, as do many of our birds, fly off over the back fence to the Gulf only three blocks away.

Terns and skimmers make a good recovery for release if they have only suffered mild concussion, or if their wing bones were not broken in the joint. We have successfully treated many birds for these injuries and find that if they get the proper treatment, and a little exercise in the outdoors before release, they can make a good recovery. The outdoors, of course, needs to be safe from any marauding wild animals or cats in the neighborhood. Even with our fenced backyard and the complete privacy of shrubbery and trees screening our "ambulatory area," we have to be on guard constantly against such dangers.

16

A LIFETIME ON THE WATER
Loons, Gannets, and Boobies

We have cared for over two dozen common loons in the past two years and have found they are very difficult to keep in captivity. We have never raised infant loons, gannets, or boobies, so we do not feel we can give any advice on that subject. I have deliberately grouped these species together in this chapter because they are seabirds, diving birds, with similar eating and living habits, and yet they differ from other shore and water birds.

COMMON LOON

The common loon is here in our area in the winter months, and at this time it is dark above and whitish below. The eye is a reddish brown and the bill is long, sharp, and powerful. The loon is 24 inches long, with a 58-inch wingspan. It is found throughout much of the United States and Canada at various times of the year, but its breeding range is in the far north.

Loons are diving water birds and spend all their life on the water. Their legs and feet are set far back under their bodies and they cannot walk or stand well on land, though they are marvels of grace and skill in the water. The buoyancy of water seems to be necessary to their health and well-being, and we have lost many of our loon patients in spite of all our therapy and care. If there were a way they could be kept in a convalescent water environment, we think they would do much better while being treated and cared for.

We have had many loons injured by motorboats, either struck deliberately by boaters running through a flock of loons resting on the water or injured by propellers when they were rising from an underwater dive. We have also worked with

A loon with the thin-weak disease.

JACK BRIGGS

loons afflicted by mysterious maladies which have struck loons here, both on the east and west coasts, and we have cooperated with the Florida Game and Fish Commission and the University of Florida in trying to determine the outbreaks and cause of the loon die-off. The illnesses seem to differ between the two coasts.

The university has determined that many loon deaths on the east coast were caused by a form of botulism, from eating contaminated food. The west coast die-off cause has not yet been determined. It is a possibility that pollution might be a factor. If so, it might also be a problem that could affect man.

Since loons seldom go ashore except to nest, and seldom approach beach and pier fishermen, we have had no hook and fishing line injuries in loons. Loons are shy, but we have found them seemingly intelligent, and certainly not the "crazy as a loon" types so celebrated in legend. (Actually, it is probably the eerie effect of the loon's lonely wild cry that gave rise to its reputation of "craziness.") They are fresh-water birds in spring and summer, frequenting lakes and streams in the northern climates. In winter many come to the Gulf of Mexico.

We have also treated oil-covered loons, receiving several during the Tampa Bay oil spill in 1970 which killed and crippled so many water birds. (See chapter 24.)

The loon has a long, powerful, and sharp bill. One must be careful when capturing loon patients, and use plastic garden gloves even when force-feeding, because the edges of their bills are very sharp.

Diet and Care

We have read that loons must always be force-fed and can never learn to eat from a dish or the hand. This has not been our experience. Some of our loons had to be force-fed the first twenty-four hours; then they quickly adapted to taking fish from a dish or my hand, or they simply picked up fish dropped in their pen.

Our loons each eat about 2 pounds of fish a day and do well on thawed frozen smelts or sardines. We always put a 50-mg. tablet of vitamin B_1 in a fish daily, either by slipping it in the fish's gill or mouth or by cutting a slot in the fish and putting the tablet inside. The same rule applies for gannets, boobies, and all other water birds, since B_1 is a very necessary addition to their fish diet.

If our loons have an unknown illness or are healing from wounds, we keep them indoors in a large cardboard box lined with newspapers. They get sulfamethazine in their drinking water for the first five days, and Furacin is applied to wounds as a first-aid measure. Keeping them quiet, clean, and dry is the best treatment until they are stronger; then they are moved to wire outdoor pens which can be moved regularly to clean grassy areas.

A very important rule for all seabirds is to keep their feet from drying and cracking. Web-footed seabirds living on dry land must have their feet oiled daily with baby oil or mineral oil. If cracks develop in dried-out feet, infection usually sets in rapidly.

Once a day, as soon as they are strong enough, we put our loons in the wading pool (or sometimes the bathtub) for swimming exercise. This is also good for their feathers, for after swimming they will preen, working the natural oils through their feathers. We usually "swim" them in the morning, so they will spend the afternoon preening. We oil their feet after their swim.

This recuperating loon enjoys a swim in the bathtub.

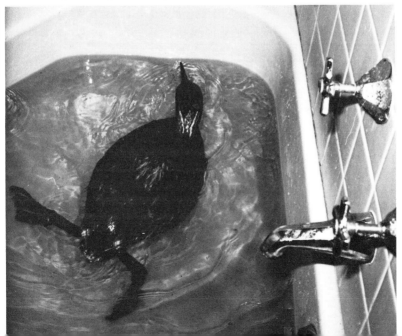

ROSEMARY K. COLLETT

Sometimes our loons will "dive" in our shallow wading pool for fish treats. This is fun for the loons, but it also tends to poke holes in the plastic pool.

The same will happen to a plastic pail if fish is dropped in the water to feed a water or wading bird. There will soon be a hole in the bucket. We use galvanized buckets for this purpose, and we buy a lot of plastic wading pools.

Occasionally we see loons that have a deteriorated flight feather condition, in which the feathers seem to have been stripped. Vets say mites are not the problem. The primary flight feathers on these birds have been literally destroyed, and they cannot fly north for the spring migration. If they can be kept alive until they go through a complete molt, it could be a solution. We have not yet found the cause of this condition.

We have enjoyed our loons and have had a little fun at their expense by giving them "loony" names. We recall with pleasure Claire de Loon, Panta Loon, and the Loon Ranger, three of our best-remembered loon patients.

Claire de Loon, recovering in an outdoor pen before her release.

ROSEMARY K. COLLETT

Claire was like the Cat Who Came Back, of legend and song, we had a very hard time getting her to stay released. Three times we released her, the first time taking her to the Gulf, where I waded out beyond a roaring surf and deposited her gently on the water. She immediately dived, surfaced, dived and came up with a fish, and took off into the west, swimming strongly, while we watched her proudly out of sight with field glasses. She was back in Venice in twenty-four hours, sitting forlornly on the beach, less than a block from where she had originally been found, and we were called to "come get a sick loon." This happened three times before Claire finally left us.

BOOBIES AND GANNETS

Our experience with both boobies and gannets has been limited because they are not usually found here. We have had one gannet, a diving bird generally found far out in the Gulf in the winter, farther south of our area. This was an immature bird which washed ashore at the Venice jetties one year, thin and weak. We were called to come for it, and we brought it home and did our best, but it was too weak even to keep food down and died overnight. As we often do in cases of this type, we froze its body and donated it to the University of Florida for study and analysis.

We have treated and released one immature brown booby, also an unusual bird in these parts. (This was the first recorded sighting of this species in Sarasota County; boobies normally live in the tropical Caribbean and the South Pacific.) It appeared at the Venice jetties, a popular fishing spot, and hung around for four days, becoming quite a pet with the local fishermen. Then, unfortunately, a fisherman accidentally hooked the bird, and we were called to come and help. The fishhook injury was minor, and the booby recovered rapidly, though it was rather thin and needed a lot of square meals before being strong enough to release.

Boobies are supposedly friendly birds by nature, but this one bit me hard enough to raise a bruise when I netted it. They have long sharp-pointed bills which are very powerful, and, like the loons and gannets, care should be exercised when handling them.

This booby soon learned to take fish from my hand or catch it on the toss, and it got the same B_1 supplement with its fish as our other fish-eaters. The wound was treated with Furacin, and the bird graduated from an indoor box to an outdoor pen within a few days. I banded it with an official band from the State of Florida and, by the time it was eating 2 to 3 pounds of smelt a day, decided it was ready to release. We wanted to do this as close as possible to its native environment, so I made arrangements with friends to drive to the Florida Keys, where it was released as far south as we could send it.

Release

Since these birds are all water birds, when they have recovered we take them back to where they were found for release. Loons cannot take off from the ground; they must be placed in the water. Boobies and gannets should also be placed on the water for release.

We wade out beyond the surf to set them down. This puts them back in their natural element with their natural diet at hand, since they all dive for fish. When released, they will usually dive immediately and then swim away.

17
WATCH THAT BILL!
Cormorants and Anhingas

Cormorants and anhingas hunt for fish by diving underwater. They are grouped together in this chapter because of similarities in their diet, care, and handling. The anhinga is generally found in fresh water, whereas in our area the cormorant is found most often in salt water.

DOUBLE-CRESTED CORMORANT

This is the most common species of cormorant, and the only one we have cared for. It is found on the east coast from the Gulf of St. Lawrence, south around the peninsula of Florida, along the Gulf coast, and on the Pacific coast from Mexico to the Aleutians. These birds most often frequent coastal waters but are also found in inland rivers and lakes.

The average adult is 27 inches long and has a 50-inch wingspan. Though it appears to be a solid black bird, if you look closely at the wings you will see that there is an effect of black scallops against dark brown. It has a bright yellow-orange pouch with a bill the same color. The bill is long, with a hook at the tip, and the eyes are a magnificent emerald green. In spite of the name, its crests are seldom apparent.

Nesting is from May to July, often on rocky islands. In Florida, the nests can be found on mangrove islands along with the pelicans, egrets, and herons. The bluish eggs number three or four, and the new-hatched young are blackish, naked, and blind—*very* homely. In about ten days, the babies begin to grow downy fuzz, and they are feathered fully by about six weeks. They are fed semidigested food from the parents' bills. The eager babies soon learn to plunge their heads into the parental pouch and grab for themselves.

The little cormorants stay in the nest until they are almost full-grown, but they take to the water and swim well once they are fully feathered. They can usually swim before they can fly. They take to the air at about eight weeks of age.

Fish is the natural food of the cormorant. These birds either dive from the surface of the water or swim underwater, hunting for fish.

Cormorants are easily tamed and have been used in the Orient for centuries as trained fish hunters for men. They are taken out in boats and are equipped with a ring around the neck attached to a long leash or cord, which is held by the handler. The ring allows only very small fish to be swallowed by the cormorant. Larger fish cannot slide down the neck past the ring and are held in the cormorant's gullet. The bird dives beneath the water, and when it surfaces with a good catch the handler pulls it back to the boat, removes the fish, and gives the cormorant a small tidbit to encourage it to continue fishing.

Since the cormorant spends a good deal of time underwater, it also spends a good deal of time on shore drying his wings. Cormorants are a familiar sight in Florida, characteristically perching on dock pilings with their wings spread to dry in the sun.

ANHINGA

The anhinga is commonly called a water turkey or snake bird. It does have a turkeylike appearance when perching motionless in the tree by a lake or stream, and, when swimming, often the only part that shows is a long snakelike head and neck gliding through the water.

The average adult is 28 inches long and has a 47-inch wingspan. The male is dark with silvery feathers on the wings. The long sharp-pointed bill is yellowish. The female is distinguished by a buffy breast and neck. The anhinga is found in freshwater swamps, ponds, and lakes of the southeastern United States and in the tropical Americas. It is often seen on tree branches with its wings spread, drying out, which it must do periodically because its plumage, resembling hair, soaks up water rapidly.

Willow clumps are a favorite nesting place, where three to five bluish eggs are usually laid. The young are fed regurgitated food and usually leave the nest only when fully grown and able to fly.

The anhinga's natural food is mainly fish, but it also eats aquatic insects, shrimp, tadpoles, water snakes, and other such delicacies. The anhinga spears fish with its sharp bill underwater, then rises to the surface, tosses the fish into the air, and, with the expertise of a pizza baker, catches its prize —and swallows it whole.

Capture and Transport

An early warning about capturing and transporting these birds: *Be careful!* Their bills are very sharp, and they use them as weapons when they are angry or frightened. You can lose an eye or need quite a few stitches if you ever relax your vigilance while working with anhingas or cormorants. Anhingas, particularly, are most intractable in captivity and must be handled with extreme caution.

The cormorant's bill, in addition to being very sharp, is equipped with a hook on the end of it. It can slash out and tear very quickly. I was once very careless in handling a cormorant patient with a broken wing. While holding it in my lap for the drive home (no box handy), I held onto its bill. The bird seemed to be uncomfortable, and in changing its position on my lap, I let go of the bill. The cormorant had seemed so calm and quiescent. It was not. In a flash, it whipped its long neck around and slashed me right across the mouth. My upper and lower lips were deeply gashed, and I bled profusely. It was two weeks before the swelling went down and I ceased looking like a Ubangi maiden. I have never again let go of a cormorant's bill while I was handling it, no matter how uncomfortable the bird looked.

The best rule, of course, if you are ever capturing one of these birds, is to use a long-handled net, get a firm hold of the bill, and wear garden gloves while doing it. Hang onto the bill, pop the bird into a cardboard box, and you will be wiser than I was.

Adult Diet for Cormorants and Anhingas

We have raised neither of these species from infancy, so I cannot advise on hand-raising them.

All our adult patients, both cormorants and anhingas, eat a straight fish diet. They can handle anything from small minnows to smelts, sardines, and pinfish. Our permanent cormorant resident, Stubby, loves small mullet, which are plentiful here.

Stubby is so fond of mullet that he grabbed a large 12-inch one from the pelicans one day, and before I could stop him he was in the process of swallowing it. I say "in the process" because the swallowing took some time. With a massive effort, he got the mullet partly down his throat. It was too large to go all the way, so he just stood around for quite a while with a bulging neck and the tail of the fish sticking out of his mouth. During the day, as the lower portion of the fish began to digest, we could see the balance slowly descend. It was several hours before Stubby's appearance (and our nerves) returned to normal. He didn't care for any more fish that day, but he was as hungry as ever the next morning.

These birds will take up to 2 pounds of fish a day each. One of their fish is dosed with a 25-mg. vitamin B_1 tablet inserted in the gill. Our birds have done best if their feeding time is split, so that they get half their fish ration in the morning and half in the afternoon.

Stubby, though much smaller than the pelicans, rules the

Stubby the cormorant, standing on my feet and demanding his fish. The pelicans keep a respectful distance until Stubby is served.

roost in our backyard. At feeding time, he is the first one at the back door, squalling at the resident pelicans to stay back, threatening them with his long neck and sharp bill. They stay back, too, until Stubby has had his fill. As I move around the yard, feeding other fish-eating birds in pens, Stubby supervises, following me like a puppy. If he is still hungry, he stands on my feet, and I am immobilized until Stubby gets another fish.

Housing

Our cormorants and anhingas live in wire pens in the backyard after recovering from wounds or injuries. (Stubby is an exception. He cannot ever fly again because of a crippled wing, so he has the run of the yard.) We keep clean builder's sand on the floor of the pens, which are partially roofed. An aluminum doghouse is provided in the pen for better shelter in inclement weather. We keep the birds' water in large plastic dishpans and change it often, for they like to use it for bathing as well as drinking.

Injuries and Care

Our cormorant and anhinga patients have suffered from a variety of injuries: broken wings, broken legs, propeller wounds inflicted by fun-loving boaters, and the mysterious thin-weak malady we find in so many shore and water birds.

Broken wings, if they are not joint breaks, can be set so they will heal properly. Joint breaks in these birds usually call for anesthetic termination of life, for rarely will the bird ever fly again, even if healed. Legs, if not broken in a joint, can be set and will heal. Leg injuries which cannot be restored to full use of the leg are hopeless cases. These birds must swim in order to hunt.

We treat wounds with our familiar standby, Furacin. If the birds are thin and weak, we house them indoors in cardboard boxes until they are better, force-feeding them if necessary.

Patients recovering from wounds or surgery also stay indoors, in cardboard boxes, on our porch. Newspaper linings in the boxes are changed daily. These patients get a large untippable bowl of drinking water treated with sulfamethazine

A cormorant with a broken leg, brought in from one of the Gulf beaches. It is wearing a Thomas splint.

for the first five days. If they are thin or dehydrated, we use Gatorade treated with sulfamethazine for the first three days. After a five-day period, they get plain unmedicated drinking water.

Force-Feeding

If force-feeding is necessary, I use extreme caution. With a lightweight glove on one hand—the hand holding the bill—I open the bill, slide a fish as far down the throat as possible, close the bill, and stroke the throat for a moment. Then I leave immediately. If the bird is left in quiet, it may finish swallowing the fish. If disturbed in any way, it will regurgitate it. If the first fish is swallowed, I give another in the same way and then leave the bird alone for twenty-four hours.

An Unusual Case

Sometimes we get sick birds that are hard to diagnose. Corey I, our first cormorant patient, was found just walking around disconsolately on the beach—he wouldn't fly away. He was a puzzlement, for he had no visible injuries and no broken bones. He was not emaciated, nor was he ill.

His appetite seemed a little off, for though he took fish directly from my hand in the most gentle way right from the beginning, he didn't seem terribly hungry.

We housed him in the bathroom, for it was a cold January for Florida. He enjoyed an occasional swim in the tub, and with a sigh I gave up my bathroom for a while and lined the floor with newspapers. Then I awaited developments.

He spent a week in the bathroom, and he and I designed a game I called "Wiggle-Waggle." This consisted of me getting on my hands and knees on the floor, while he perched on the edge of the tub. After a little preliminary eyeballing, I would shake my head back and forth, saying, "Wiggle-Waggle!" (No, I'm not crazy all the time, just when I'm being a cormorant.)

Corey, his green eyes glowing with joy, would wiggle-waggle right back at me, making soft *gronking* noises. He really enjoyed this game, which sometimes went on for fifteen minutes, and it seemed to be good for his morale.

One morning, I entered the bathroom to clean house and found a length of monofilament fishing line, attached to a metal leader line with a lead sinker, connected to a rusty fishhook. It had been expelled during the night by my puzzling patient, Corey. I wondered if perhaps he had suffered more

Corey the cormorant relaxes in the bathroom hospital ward.

than somewhat in that feat and watched him carefully for signs of dreadful internal injuries.

Corey's innards were tougher than one might think. From that day on, his appetite improved by leaps and bounds. He consumed huge quantities of fish for a week and, when he was taken to the backyard, immediately took off and flew strongly toward the Gulf. That was the last I saw of him, but I remember him fondly for his wiggle-waggle and his amazing insides.

Release

By now it has become obvious that releasing these birds when they are fully recovered is a simple matter for us here —we just let them out of their outdoor cages into the fenced backyard, and when they feel they are ready they take off.

If you are not near their natural habitat, take them to a good release site, open their box, and stand back. Most of them will hop out of the box and fly away. Anhingas are not always so cooperative, however.

McNarf I, our first patient, surprised me, when I opened his box in the backyard, by turning and attacking me. I scrambled backwards, caught off balance by expecting, if not thanks, at least trust and tolerance. Victorious McNarf then clambered up the drooping branches of a tree, working his way toward the top. When he reached the top, much to my relief, he took off.

While I was still having malignant thoughts about McNarf's ingratitude, the phone rang. A lady was calling from three blocks away, saying, "A strange-looking black bird is sitting in my driveway." I had a sinking feeling which was indeed warranted. When I arrived, there sat McNarf, looking belligerent. Evidently he had been strong enough to fly only a short distance and needed a little more time and fish to regain his full strength. We recaptured him, brought him home, and prolonged his convalescence. After two more weeks he was strong enough to be safely released.

18
THEY LOVE THE WATER
Ducks

In our work with wild ducks, we have cared for and released the lesser scaup, mallard, Muscovy, and red-breasted merganser. Mallards have been domesticated in many areas and may be found on ponds and in barnyards. The Muscovy, not even a native, has also been domesticated and is frequently seen not only on farms but also on lakes in cities and residential neighborhoods.

LESSER SCAUP

The lesser scaup is widely distributed in North America—including the United States, Canada, and Mexico. This wild duck breeds in the prairie regions of central Canada and the northern states of the United States. Essentially an inland species, it likes lakes, ponds, marshes, and streams. The adult is an average of 12 inches long and has a 29-inch wingspan. Nesting is from May to July, with six to ten pale gray or greenish gray eggs. The female broods the eggs for three to four weeks, and when the baby ducks hatch, she leads them to water and teaches them to swim and catch insect food.

Lesser scaups have an erratic flight and are a target of hunters. Their winter range includes southern North and Central America and the Caribbean islands.

Their natural food is small fish, tadpoles, mollusks, worms, water insects, and seeds. They feed mostly by diving for prey from the surface of the water.

MALLARD

Mallards are essentially freshwater ducks, found in North America. They breed in the northern portion of the Northern Hemisphere, mainly west of Hudson Bay and the Great Lakes but also in New York, New Jersey, and Virginia, as well as portions of the Pacific Northwest.

The mallard male is a handsome duck—he has a metallic green head, a white neck band, and a rusty breast. The female must be content with a dowdy costume of mottled brown. The average adult is 16 inches long and has a 36-inch wingspan. Nesting is from April to July, and generally the hatch is six to ten buffy or olive green eggs. Mama begins sitting on the eggs only after the full clutch is laid, so they all hatch at about the same time. She teaches the babies to feed and swim as soon as they are hatched; Papa doesn't help at all.

A surface-feeding duck, the mallard takes its food either from the surface of the water or from just beneath it. Mallards like duckweed, pondweeds, and things of that sort, and they also eat grain, such as wheat, barley, and corn. Sometimes they eat insects and fish, and also beechnuts and acorns.

MUSCOVY

The Muscovy is not a native duck. It was introduced into this country and is actually a native of tropical America. It is a large wattled duck which perches, something not every duck can do. Its bright-red wattled head is mounted on a body 28 to 30 inches long, and its coloration varies from almost entirely black, to a metallic green sheen, to mixtures of black and white.

This duck is very aggressive and often will chase native ducks away from their own feeding grounds and nesting sites. It is not entirely unsociable, however, as it interbreeds with other ducks, such as the mallard.

The female incubates the white eggs, a clutch of eight to sixteen, for about twenty-eight to thirty-two days.

The habits of the Muscovy seem to be similar to that of native ducks.

RED-BREASTED MERGANSER

A fish-eating, diving duck, the red-breasted merganser, like other mergansers, has a long thin bill with a sharp saw-toothed edge but may be distinguished from them by the reddish patch on the chest of the male and the longer crests on the heads of both sexes. It is found throughout North America, in both fresh and salt water. The average adult is 16 inches long and has a 33-inch wingspan. Mergansers nest on the borders of ponds, lakes, rivers, and sometimes near the seacoast. The female incubates the six-to-ten-egg clutch of creamy buff eggs, usually for twenty-six to twenty-eight days. Nesting goes on from May to July, and the young ducklings are active as soon as they are hatched and dry. The red-breasted merganser is chiefly a fish-eater but also likes mollusks, crustaceans, and crawfish. It winters mainly on the coasts of the United States —from Maine to Florida, on our own Gulf coast, and from British Columbia to Baja California.

Infant Care

We have hatched Muscovies from the egg (see chapter 11 for incubation instructions) and have hand-raised infant Muscovy and mallard ducks.

Scaups and mergansers do not breed in Florida, so we have had no experience with infants of these species.

Of course, everybody knows baby ducks are absolutely adorable. With their light golden fuzz, stubby wings, and indistinct dark markings, they are truly lovable. Those little flat webbed feet complete their charm. A baby duck can certainly never be mistaken for anything else, so you won't have any trouble identifying it.

We start our baby ducks in a large cardboard box with a 25-watt bulb clipped over one corner. Ducks are very messy and smelly, so their newspaper floors must be changed at least once a day. Muscovies, by the way, are higher on the messy-smelly scale than any other duck of our experience.

Baby Duck Diet

Like infant game birds, baby ducks must be taught to eat. We start ours on sloppy food—medicated turkey starter or game bird starter, mixed with lukewarm water to a sloppy consistency. We make about a cup of mixture at a time, with six drops of Zymadrops added. This will feed two or three ducklings. We don't mix more than they can eat, as it sours quickly.

One group of baby mallards that we recently raised preferred Gaines Meal dog food, soaked in lukewarm water for ten minutes and then drained. We sprinkled Vionate vitamins on it, and the babies thrived. The Gaines could certainly be used until turkey or game bird starter was available.

We change the food and water every four hours and keep fresh food and water in their box at all times. They get their water in a very small amount in a flat dish, so they can't get too wet if they decide to get in and tramp around. They must not get chilled, so we make sure they are not in a draft.

Teaching them to eat is easy. We dip their bills into the gruel until they begin to "daddle" around in the food on their own. "Daddling" is the natural duck process of stirring their bills and nibbling. They do this in their food, in their water, and to lawns and flowers when they grow up.

They also like bits of lettuce (washed clean), even when they are very young.

Penning and Growth

As they grow larger and more active, we move baby ducks to indoor portable pens with newspaper floors. They stay on their gruel diet until they grow a little more. At about six weeks, when they are reasonably well feathered, we move their pen outdoors, throw open the windows, and heave a sigh of relief. Duck odors are very strong.

Raising only one duck alone can be a problem—ducks tame easily, are great people-lovers, and can become spoiled rotten. Be prepared, if you raise an "only" duck, to have one that

These baby Muscovy ducks have just moved to a portable pen outdoors, since the weather is nice.

follows at your heels, always wants to be cuddled and to sleep in your lap, and is in constant danger of being stepped on, decapitated by slamming doors, and being shut up in cabinets. Also, the first time an only duck sees another duck, its first reaction is clearly "What's *that?*" followed by complete panic.

We hand-raised a baby Muscovy, named Dicky, who had somehow become separated from his mother. Dicky became a pet and was allowed the freedom of the house. He followed us everywhere. When Dicky was grown, we took him to the lakeside home of one of our friends, where many ducks were already in residence. We released Dicky in their yard, but when he saw the other ducks he went into absolute orbit and fled to the shelter of the front porch. He would only come out when the people appeared and the ducks left. After several weeks under the front porch, he finally joined the duck gang by degrees, but the front porch was still his refuge in bad moments.

Adult Care and Diet: Muscovy, Mallard, and Scaup

After our ducks are well feathered and have been moved

to an outdoor pen, we put them on dry crumbles as for adult turkeys or game birds, although some of our adult ducks have continued to prefer the "sloppy mess" mixture of warm water and turkey starter.

We also give adult ducks cracked corn, washed lettuce leaves, and bread. A number of our ducks love Gaines Meal dog kibbles, soaked and drained. One pair of our mallards is particularly fond of Puss 'n Boots canned cat tuna. They will fight with the backyard gulls for it, so when I feed it, I usually put out two dishes, one for the gulls and one for the ducks.

We have used the outdoor wire pens and the diet described here for mallards, Muscovies, and the lesser scaup.

In the outdoor pens, we use large plastic dishpans filled with fresh water for both swimming and drinking. After our ducks are acclimated to the backyard gang, we usually let them out into the yard, where they can use the wading pools along with the pelicans, gulls, and cormorants.

Anyone about to keep a duck should be forewarned that they can wreck a yard in short order. They dig holes all over our yard, searching for grubs and insect delicacies. They daddle in the pelican pool overflow, consuming every blade of grass and the root thereof, until there is a sea of mud around the pool. They are also fond of flowers, especially petunias and shrubs, and any growing thing that can be dug, nibbled, or tasted.

Merganser Diet

The merganser is a little different. Being strictly a fish-eater, he gets small fish, such as minnows or smelts, with a 25-mg. tablet of vitamin B_1 daily.

In force-feeding a merganser, as we sometimes do at first, we are careful of the serrated bill and wear light gardening gloves. The fish is put as far back as possible in the throat, and we follow the procedure of closing the bill and stroking the throat. (Detailed force-feeding instructions are included in chapter 23, First Aid for Birds.)

Most of our mergansers have learned quickly to eat from a dish. Sometimes they like to have their fish placed in their water bowl, so they can pick them out of the water. They do not need salt water but are perfectly content with fresh water for bathing.

Our mergansers are acclimated to the yard by a period spent outdoors in the portable wire pens. They have a plastic dishpan to swim in until we release them to the yard, where they use the wading pools.

Injuries and Care

We have had many ducks with broken legs, broken wings, concussion, and wounds from boat propellers. We have also had oil-spill victims and mergansers suffering from the thin-weak malady.

Wings and legs not shattered or broken in the joint can be set by the veterinarian and usually heal well. Concussion patients respond to quiet and isolation. Open-wound patients have their wounds stitched by the vet if necessary, and the wound is treated with Furacin. For the thin-weak malady, we give the only treatment we know: rest and quiet, force-feeding, Gatorade, and the sulfamethazine solution.

Ducks need their wings and legs in full operation to function. They cannot function in the wild without flying, and if a leg or foot is amputated they can only swim in circles.

Duck patients with concussion usually will have some of the following symptoms: holding the head or tail to one side, general dopey attitude, and inability to stand or walk properly. These birds should also be examined for head wounds or other injuries, usually indicated by broken or missing feathers.

Sometimes, when we have mergansers with the thin-weak malady, we give them a pat of butter or margarine to help cleanse the digestive system.

All our patients recovering from broken bones, wounds, concussion, illness, or surgery are kept indoors in cardboard boxes until they are strong enough to move to outdoor pens.

All our injured birds get sulfamethazine in their drinking water for five days to guard against infection. The thin-weak patients get Gatorade to drink, treated with sulfamethazine —1 tsp. sulfamethazine to 2 cups Gatorade.

Force-feeding is sometimes necessary. The only hazardous duck bill belongs to the merganser. The other duck species cannot do much personal damage with their bills, except maybe to pinch smartly.

We have had a good rate of recovery with our ducks, but some of them don't make it. We have had little success at treating ducks with the thin-weak disease, and some of our ducks who were oil-spill victims did not survive either, in spite of our best efforts (see chapter 24).

Speedy and Charlie, our mallard pair, came to us separately. Somebody left Charlie on our doorstep. He had a limp, and the vet discovered a slight fracture of the right leg but not enough to require setting. Charlie was confined to a cardboard box to recover. Then two kids brought Speedy. She was the same age, with the same injury. She had been caught by a dog.

After three weeks we introduced them, and they hit it off. When they had spent a week together in an outdoor pen, we released them to the backyard. Speedy is at this writing nesting on seventeen eggs under the boughs of our acacia tree, which droops to the ground, making a fine duck nest screen. Unfortunately, these are the very same boughs favored by the pelicans for playing "Mangrove," and they scramble up and down them all day, firing at will at poor steadfast Speedy sitting on her eggs below. I will say this for Speedy, she never flinches.

Speedy and Charlie are still with us simply because they have not chosen to leave. Many of our wild ducks just fly away when they are ready, but it looks as if our mallard pair has settled in for good.

We also have in permanent residence Daffy, a lesser scaup. His wing is amputated at the body, but we have kept him for the children to see. Though he spends his life on the ground and in the wading pool, he seems to be happy with the backyard gang. Because he has only one wing, Daffy couldn't make the climb over the edge of the wading pool, so we built him a cleated ramp. He can walk up it in grand style and fall into the pool. However, he can't figure out how to get out of the pool on the ramp. He just climbs to one corner of the pool, hurls himself over the side, and falls to the grass, where he sits preening himself, apparently completely satisfied.

ROSEMARY K. COLLETT

Daffy Duck, a lesser scaup, survived his wing amputation and learned to climb the cleated ramp into the pool for his daily bath.

Capture and Transport

It is almost impossible to catch a wild duck on the water, no matter how hurt it is. If it can fly, it is also very difficult to catch it on land. The stealthy technique sometimes works if the duck is badly disabled on land. We get between the injured duck and the water, pretend to be doing something else, then pounce on it with the long-handled net. Sometimes we toss a towel over a disabled duck, quieting it until we can get our hands on it. We carry our duck patients in cardboard boxes when we have them, and we usually keep a spare box in the car for just such purposes. If we happen to be caught without a box and have to carry one in the lap, we wrap it in a towel or sweater to keep it quiet and hold its bill so it can't peck. Ducks cannot do serious damage with their bills, but it is a good idea to use light gloves when holding a merganser's bill.

Release

We have no problem releasing our duck patients. They will fly from the backyard when they are strong enough, and we let them into the fenced backyard from their pens when we think they are ready to get the exercise they need before flight. Even scaups are released from our backyard. We usually take the mergansers back to the beach. Since they are diving birds, we like to release them at the waterside.

We do not release domesticated mallards and Muscovies in the wild. The mallard is often so tame, it is akin to murder. And the Muscovy, of course, is not properly a native species. Both these species would be better off on a civilized lake or pond somewhere. We find that farmers are usually glad to take them in once they are mature. These ducks have a tendency to settle in, once established, and won't leave otherwise.

Birds which have recovered from oil-spill damage should not be released until they are surely waterproof (See chapter 24). "Swimming" an oil-spill patient until preening restores feather oils is the only way to be certain that such victims are ready to return to nature.

OTHER DUCKS

The ducks discussed in this chapter have been our patients, but it is likely that other species can be handled and fed in a similar manner.

We have had as boarders two white Pekin ducks, pets of the writer John D. MacDonald. His ducks, Trampas and Duck-Duck, stay in our backyard when John is out of town, living with the backyard gang. They are always welcome, especially as John sends along with them a 200-pound bag of cracked corn.

The white Pekin duck has become very popular in this country, but is an introduced species, once a native of China. These ducks have been domesticated so long, they have only rudimentary wings and can no longer fly. They can live only a domestic life and should never be released into the wilderness.

19
ROYALTY OF THE MARSHES
Herons, Egrets, and Bitterns

Aside from a green heron and a little blue heron, we have not raised any marsh birds from infancy—they nest on isolated islands, and their young are seldom seen by man. Most of them are shy, elusive creatures. However, we have cared for snowy and cattle egrets, the American and least bittern, and an immature sandhill crane.

We have also worked with the adult little blue heron, the Louisiana heron, the night heron, and the common egret. Methods of capture and transport, housing, and diet are similar to those described for the other herons and egrets in this chapter.

GREEN HERON

This handsome little bird stands about 14 inches tall, and has a wingspan of 2 feet. Its back is a dark, metallic blue-green, and its legs are yellowish or orange. The crest is not always visible, and its bill is yellowish.

The green heron is found in fresh- and salt-water areas of the United States and southern Canada east of the Rocky Mountains, and in Central America.

Its natural diet is quite varied: minnows, tadpoles and frogs, water insects, and crayfish. It also eats crickets, grasshoppers, snakes, and even small mammals.

We raised one green heron from infancy. One night during a storm, with a wind from the west, we received a call from a Sarasotan who had found a heron's nest washed ashore with one baby green heron in it. We took in the fuzzy little mite and dried it off. Its nursery was a laundry basket lined with soft towels and a heating pad underneath.

The diet we used might also work for infant young of the other species in this chapter (but see also infant diet given for the little blue heron, below) with one exception, the Florida sandhill crane (or any sandhill crane), which needs grain added to its diet.

We fed the baby heron tuna cat food sprinkled with Vionate vitamins. This was supplemented with freshwater minnows. We had local children catching the minnows for us with a seine, but they are probably available at any live bait store.

The method of feeding this little fellow was to push small bits of tuna far back in its throat with the fingers. The minnows (dead ones, but fresh) were fed the same way. These birds, we found, become excitable quickly and then lose their interest in food, so when our baby seemed to reach this state, we stopped feeding it for a while. However, in its fuzzy infant stage, we fed it all it would take once every hour all day, alternating the tuna cat food with the minnows. It thrived and grew on this diet, and when it began to grab at the minnows, I put them in a dish but continued hand-feeding as well until I could see that the youngster was completely self-feeding.

Our heron soon became quite active, trying to pop out of its laundry basket, so we moved it to a very large cardboard carton (such as television sets come in) and lined it with newspapers. We put a bowl of water inside and a screen across the top.

As soon as the heron became too active for the box and was well feathered, we moved it to a large outdoor pen and taught it to fish for itself by putting live minnows in the water pan. Occasionally, for boot training, we put the heron in the bathtub, partially filled with water, and created a nice swamp atmosphere with rocks and branches. The kids would bring in live minnows, rushed from the waterside, and dump them in the tub. The little heron had a grand time catching them. It was a little puzzled at first, because they were alive instead of dead, but it soon caught on.

When the heron became proficient at catching fish in the tub and water bowl, we opened the pen door. It was two days before it ventured out. After it had entered the social world of our backyard, explored it, and met all the gulls and pelicans, it flew around the yard occasionally. We kept food out for it.

After four weeks, the heron flew away. In a week it was back. It stayed two weeks, this time, and then left again. It returned once more but only stayed a few days on this visit before it flew away forever. Since there are mangrove islands and watery environments near us, I didn't worry about the heron's finding its home climate.

This method of release would probably work well for other birds of this type, as they need the security of familiar surroundings and regular food supplies while they are readapting to the wild. If you should happen to have such a bird away from its natural environment, you would, of course, need to take it back where it belongs before releasing it.

LITTLE BLUE HERON

This shy little heron stands 22 inches tall and has a wingspan of 41 inches. Its body and wings are a dark blue-gray, and its head and neck are brown. Its long legs are bluish green, and its bill is bluish gray with a black tip.

This bird prefers freshwater ponds and marshes but is also found in coastal areas of the southern Atlantic states, ranging from New Jersey southward, throughout Florida, on the entire perimeter of the Gulf Coast, and into Mexico. It often nests in willow thickets on islands.

Its natural diet consists of frogs, lizards, minnows, crabs, shrimp, grasshoppers, locusts, and other insects. Our adult patients have done well on minnows and shrimp, with the addition of any insects or frogs we could catch for them.

We have cared for a number of adult little blue herons for various lengths of time. One of the most beautiful was with us for less than a day. It was a magnificent specimen in full breeding plumage. We picked it up at the edge of a small lake that had been sprayed to control mosquitoes and insects. The bird died within twenty-four hours with symptoms indicating possible pesticide poisoning.

At this writing we are successfully raising an infant little blue heron. Tiny and featherless, it was brought to us when its nest, dislodged from a mangrove island, had floated ashore. Its eyes were barely open and it called pitifully with a great gaping mouth. I decided to experiment with a new diet:

      6 to 8 medium smelts
         ¼ cup water
         1 100-mg. tablet vitamin B_1, crushed
         1 teaspoon Vionate

Chop smelts in thirds and place in blender with other in-

This baby little blue heron is all legs and bill.
ROSEMARY K. COLLETT

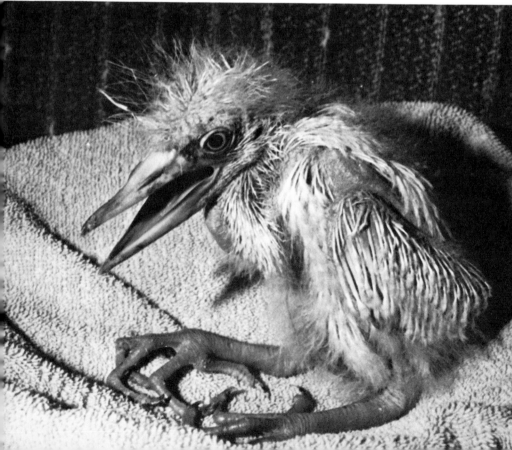

The baby blue heron is getting its feathers, but its legs are still pretty wobbly.

gredients. Blend on low speed to a mushy consistency. Keep refrigerated and use as needed.

I fed small amounts on the end of my finger. At first it would not willingly open its mouth, so I gently pried its bill open and poked in some of the slurry mixture. As soon as the baby found out it was food, it opened its mouth greedily and often. I fed as much as it would take every hour all day long.

Now it is half grown, feathered and healthy and able to take small whole fish.

GREAT BLUE HERON

We have had several adult great blue herons as patients. Some recovered and were released; some simply were thin and weak or injured so badly they did not make it. We now have one, Ben, in permanent residence with a crippled bill.

The great blue herons range across the continent and into Canada. They are a very large and striking bird, standing over 3 feet in height, with a 70-inch wingspan. They are stately and dignified, and are unmistakable. They fish in both fresh

Ben, the great blue heron, being placed in his original cage after treatment and before the injury to his bill. I am wearing light plastic gloves to protect my hands.

JACK BRIGGS

and salt water and generally nest in colonies or groups, preferably in the trees. Like other marsh waders, they are very excitable and do not generally do well in captivity. Their natural diet consists mostly of fish, but they also eat frogs, tadpoles, eels, and sometimes mice, young rats, and small birds.

Ben, our permanent boarder, came to us after he was found wandering in a vacant lot. He could not fly, but he could run, and George and I collected quite an audience trying to run him down. When we finally caught him, we found he had a broken cotton rope around his neck. Evidently someone had captured him and tied him to something, with no food or water, but he had broken away. Though by no means a baby, he was a young bird. He had no injuries but he was thin and weak. He injured himself in his cage after we had him a short while. Something, we don't know what, upset him, and he caught his long bill in the wire and broke off the upper beak about half way. He bled profusely, and I held him and applied gauze with pressure for about an hour before the bleeding was stanched.

We learned a lesson from that terrible experience: Never put these birds in cages so constructed that they can injure themselves. Ben now has solid walls on his cage, with large wire openings on the front, but his bill is so damaged we can never release him to fish in the wild again.

Ben had to be force-fed the first three days we had him. Then he learned to take fish from a dish, and now he takes them from my hand. His favorite is pinfish. Like all fish-eating birds he gets vitamin B_1 with his daily diet, a 25-mg. tablet either in the fish's mouth or gill or inserted in a slit.

Ben likes both fresh- and salt-water fish. We give him a variety of small ones. He will not eat Spanish sardines, which is his own peculiarity; our other great blue herons liked them. This is a good example why it is never possible to give a hard and fast diet for any one species—they are all individuals and all have individual tastes.

Our stories about great blue heron are often sad ones. Blue Boy was brought to us totally blind. Our local ophthalmologist, Dr. Douglas Williamson, was kind enough to come and examine Blue Boy. After examining a healthy heron's eyes, he

ROSEMARY K. COLLETT

Ben is now a permanent resident.

determined that Blue Boy had incurable retinitis and would never recover his sight.

We force-fed Blue Boy for a week. Then he learned that when I tapped the edge of his bill with a fish and said, "Fish, fish!" it was dinnertime. He would open his mouth and I could slip in the fish. Finally he learned to open up just at the command, "Fish, fish!"

We tried hard with Blue Boy, but he was terribly nervous and upset because he could not see. I hoped that I could calm him down enough to use in my educational work, but it was no use. After two months, during which he became increasingly nervous and frantic, we turned him over to the vet for an end to his misery. He was not able to ever enjoy life, and it did not seem fair to keep him alive when nature would not have done so.

SNOWY EGRET

The snowy egret is found throughout much of the United States and even as far north as southern Canada. It stands about 20 inches tall in the adult size and has a wingspan of 3 feet or more.

Snowy egrets, as do many other egrets and herons, nest in colonies on islands, which protects them from man and raiding animals.

Their food in the wild includes shrimp, small fish, frogs, aquatic insects, and snails. Any of these, if available, can be added to their diet, for the more natural food they get the better off they will be.

The snowy egret was almost wiped out in the early 1900s because of fashion's demand for their feathers. Thousands of adult birds were slaughtered for their plumes, and the young were left to die in the nest. The federal government finally banned the killing of egrets, and they have made a remarkable comeback. The Audubon Society also played an important part in preservation of this lovely species.

We cared for a young adult we called Snowy. He was brought to us with a broken wing, and the veterinarian set it, using a lightweight aluminum splint, padded on one side with

A snowy egret, recuperating in the fenced backyard.

foam rubber. He bent the splint to fit the shape of the wing and taped it on. Snowy's wing healed within three weeks.

During his convalescence, he lived in one of our wire pens in the backyard. He had a water bowl large enough for drinking, but not for bathing, because the vet did not want him in water until the splint was removed.

We force-fed chopped smelts, sprinkled with Vionate and a 25-mg. tablet of crushed vitamin B_1 for the first forty-eight hours. From then on, he ate from a dish by himself. We also gave him minnows and frogs whenever we could get them.

After his splint was removed, we kept him in his pen for two weeks, but his wing seemed to be fine and did not look damaged or crooked, so one day we left his door open. He came out and bathed in one of our plastic wading pools, chased the gulls in the yard, and returned to his pen at dinnertime. He stayed in his pen all night. For two months he continued this routine, sometimes even flying around the yard.

With the coming of spring, Snowy flew away, and he never returned. We like to think he is not far away, at our Red Lake rookery—a mangrove island where many of these birds nest—busily raising families of little Snowies.

We have cared for many other snowy egrets, some with broken wings, some with the mysterious thin-weak malady. Some made it, some did not.

For all our wading birds that were healing from wounds or illness, or with the thin-weak symptom, we kept sulfamethazine in their drinking water the first five days as per the instructions in chapter 23. All did well on small fish, minnows or chopped smelts, with an occasional frog.

CATTLE EGRET

Every motorist who has visited Florida has seen cattle egrets following the cows in the vast pasturelands of our state. These birds came here, no one knows just how, from Africa in the 1940s, where they follow the rhino and other animals across the veld in the same way. They do this because the animals, while walking and feeding, stir up insects in the grass and provide an easy meal for the egret. These birds are now found in many parts of the southeastern United States. They have adapted so well to our mechanized society that they have learned to follow bulldozers, mowing machines, and golf carts just as they once followed the rhino. We have dozens of them standing about the tees on our golf course here, waiting for the action.

When grown, they stand about 18 inches tall, and are white birds except in breeding season, when they have beautiful buffy-orange plumes on their heads, breasts, and backs.

We have had many cattle egrets as patients. They have a lot of severe injuries, such as being stepped on by cattle and horses, being shot, or flying into power lines. We have saved some of them; some we could not. We think many of them have suffered from pesticide poisoning, but we cannot prove it.

They do well on chopped fish or small minnows, lean ground beef (chuck or round), and horsemeat, which can be bought canned or frozen in pet food departments at markets. Of course, they are fond of insects from the fields and pastures, but it is impossible to catch enough to give them the protein diet they need.

AMERICAN BITTERN

The American bittern is found throughout most of the United States and into Canada. The bittern is a shy, secretive bird and lives a solitary life in bogs and swamps. It has a habit of hiding among reeds or tall grasses, holding its neck straight up with the beak pointed heavenward, and "freezing." This camouflages it so that it looks like just another reed or cattail. It often nests in cattail marshes. Its food is frogs, small fish, lizards, snails, small mice, grasshoppers, and insects.

LEAST BITTERN

The least bittern lives in much of the eastern United States and parts of the Pacific coast. It stands less than a foot tall with a 1½-foot wingspan. It is rarely seen, for it stays hidden in reedy marshes. Its natural food is flies, caterpillars, insects, small fish, frogs and tadpoles, lizards, snails, and beetles.

Our bitterns have liked small whole fish such as minnows or small smelts. When feeding small fish we put a 25-mg. tablet of B_1 in the mouth of the fish; when force-feeding chopped fish, we sprinkle a crushed B_1 tablet on the food.

Basically the same care, caging, feeding methods, and diets apply to the bitterns as to the herons and egrets.

SANDHILL CRANE

The sandhill crane ranges through the western United States (west of the Mississippi River) and up into Canada and Alaska.

The adult stands about 3 feet tall, has a near 80-inch wingspan, and builds its nests of reeds and grasses in the water. It is a handsome buffy to grayish bird with a bright red cap. In nature it eats grain, along with rats, mice, frogs, lizards, worms, grasshoppers, beetles, and other insects.

We have worked only with the immature Florida sandhill crane, which is a subspecies and a smaller bird.

We have fed our immature cranes the turkey starter and meat formula, as for insectivorous birds (see chapter 9), because it meets their need for high protein and provides the grain which is a natural part of their diet.

> ½ cup medicated turkey starter
> 1 drop Zymadrops vitamin supplement
> 1 25-mg. tablet vitamin B_1, crushed
>
> Mix with warm water.
> Add ¼ pound lean ground beef (chuck or round)

Adult sandhill cranes, as well as the other adult birds described in this book, should have fresh food kept in front of them at all times, because birds eat periodically and not on any regular schedule. If the food gets stale or sour before it is eaten we throw it out and replace it with fresh food. We always keep their water bowls or buckets filled with fresh water.

These birds do well in our wire pens in the backyard while recuperating. The only special point I might mention on injuries is that, like other wading birds, the sandhill crane does not recover well from broken leg injuries. All the waders, having long thin legs, can be splinted if the break is not in the joint or is not severe, but these birds must wade and stalk in order to hunt, and joint injuries and compound fractures do not heal evenly. It is better to have a wading bird put to sleep if it has a severely damaged leg.

Diet

These birds are all fish-eaters, with the exception of the sandhill crane, and we feed them small fish such as minnows, smelts, and pinfish, all of which we buy frozen in bulk. The fish are thawed before feeding, of course, and a 25 mg. tablet of Vitamin B_1 is slipped into one fish daily.

We often need to feed chopped fish at first, especially in force-feeding, but it is always better to feed whole fish (or in many cases even frogs, if they are available), because they look like what they are to the bird—food it can recognize. Birds will become self-feeding sooner if they can see food they know.

We have found a simple method of encouraging some of these adult birds to accept dead fish. We drop the fish in their water container. It swirls around for a few moments, perhaps appearing alive to the bird, which grabs it. One of the biggest stumbling blocks in working with these nervous birds is getting them to eat.

Since all these birds have long sharp bills, we have found a metal bucket or washtub to be the best water container. We discovered this after our great blue heron went through three plastic buckets in one week. Each sprung a leak within a day or two. We finally noticed tiny holes in the bottom of the buckets, caused by the rapierlike tip of the pointed bill. Ben now has a large metal bucket. It is scrubbed out and refilled with fresh water each day.

Some of the smaller birds such as the green heron don't seem quite as destructive and have large plastic dishpans of water.

Capture and Transport

The birds described in this chapter all have long, sharply pointed bills. Remember this if you ever capture an injured bird in this group: They have long muscular necks, and when cornered they will strike out, aiming for the eyes.

If you do not have a long-handled dip net, you can use a large towel, bedspread, or sheet to toss over the bird, provided you can get close enough. Then you can move in and get a firm grasp on the bill. Always grab the bill first, and wear plastic gardening gloves to protect your hands.

It is best to use two people, one to make the "netting," and one to move in and immobilize the bird. The bird will flap around a lot unless it is very weak or sick, but don't mind that; just hang onto the bill, then get the body firmly tucked under your arm.

Our old standby, the cardboard box, is what we normally use for bird transportation, either to the vet or home for care and treatment. Even a 3-foot-tall heron can be put in an average-size box—it will squat down very nicely. Use a lid with air holes. The dark and quiet of boxes has a calming effect on these birds, although they are always very nervous, no matter what.

We have found all birds in this group difficult to keep and raise in captivity, but it can be done if you are willing to exercise a great deal of calm patience and loving care in dealing with them.

Release

If you live near the natural habitat of these creatures, as we do, you can release them in your own yard, as we released our green heron and snowy egret.

However, if their natural habitat is some distance away, it would be best to transport them there in the usual cardboard carton and release them in a suitable spot. The bird always has a better chance for survival after all your hard work in curing it if it is in the proper surroundings near its natural food supply and others of its own species.

20
MORE MARSH BIRDS
Rails, Coots, and Gallinules

We have worked with a small number of birds in this group: the sora rail, king rail, coot, Florida gallinule, and purple gallinule.

Their diet and care are similar. All are found generally in freshwater marshes. They are long-legged birds, with the exception of the coot, and many are somewhat chickenlike in appearance and manner.

The coot swims and dives better than any other bird of this group. These birds eat mostly vegetation, and all are considered game birds, especially the rail, which is a favorite of hunters.

SORA RAIL

This is a small bird, the most common of the rails. It stands about 6¾ inches long and has a 12½-inch wingspan. It is light gray below, with brownish upper parts, and has a black facial mask from the base of the bill to the eye and down the throat. Its reddish eyes and yellow bill and legs are the only bright colors.

The sora rail nests in Canada and the northern part of the United States, usually in dense thickets of cattails. From six to sixteen eggs are laid, buffy gray with reddish brown spots, and they are incubated by both parents for about two weeks. The babies are covered with thick black down, and their chins have a silvery tuft of curly hairs. They leave the nest soon after hatching and are taught by the parents to hunt for seeds and insects.

The natural food of the adult is mollusks, some insects, vegetable matter (such as weed seeds), and wild rice.

The sora rail has always been a popular game bird. With its fairly slow and steady flight, it is easy to shoot.

KING RAIL

The king is a larger rail, 14 inches long, with a 24-inch wingspread, rust-colored, with barred markings. The bill and legs are long. This species is generally found in freshwater marshes in the eastern half of the United States, Mexico, and southeastern Canada. Usually nesting in May and June, the king rail hatches five to seven eggs, cream colored with brown speckles. The young, like those of the sora, are covered with thick black down, but they have pale white bills. They leave the nest immediately after hatching and are taught to feed on tadpoles, seeds, and insects. The natural food of the adult is small fish and mollusks, insects, tadpoles, and seeds.

The king rail is also a popular game bird.

AMERICAN COOT

The American coot is often called a "mud hen." It is a dark gray bird with black head and neck, reddish eyes, chicken-like white bill, and a white facial disk on the forehead above the base of the bill. The coot has lobes along the sides of its toes, handy for paddling or walking on marshy bogs and lily pads. It is an excellent swimmer and diver and feeds on the shore, on the surface of the water, and under the water.

The coot nests from April to August, depending on the area, and usually lays from six to sixteen grayish eggs, finely speckled with black. The young leave the nest immediately and can swim and dive right away. "Crazy as a coot" might have originated from these odd-looking babies—they are balls of black down, with bright red head and shoulders, and almost bald. A scarlet bill completes the funny getup.

The natural food of coots is aquatic vegetation, meadow grasses, sprouting grain, seeds, small fish, tadpoles, worms, and snails.

COMMON GALLINULE

This bird in Florida is called the Florida gallinule. It averages 10½ inches in length and has a 21-inch wingspan. The common gallinule is dark gray underneath, with a brownish back and a bright red bill and forehead. The tip of its bill is yellow, and its legs are greenish-yellow.

Found throughout the eastern United States and also on the lower Pacific coast, the common gallinule nests from May to July and has an average hatch of twelve eggs. The parents incubate the spotted buff-colored eggs in about twenty-one days. The babies look like long-legged black bumblebees, except they have the funny bald red head of the coot baby, with a few black hairlike "feathers" sprouting from the dome. The babies leave the nest right away and are taught by the parents to look for food.

These birds have very long toes and can walk right across a lily pad mat on the water, searching for food. Their natural food is seeds, the roots of water plants, mollusks, grasshoppers, and other insects and worms. Much of their diet is vegetable.

PURPLE GALLINULE

The purple gallinule is gloriously costumed in shades of deep blue and purple, with a greenish back. Its bright red bill has a yellow tip, and there is a silvery patch on its forehead. The legs are yellowish-green. It is about the same size as the common gallinule but starts nesting a little earlier, from April to July. The eggs are fewer, six to ten in a clutch. The little black bumblebee babies have the almost-bald head, sprinkled with black down, but are distinguished by silvery white hairs on the crown, cheeks, and throat. They leave the nest quickly, too, and learn to hunt for the natural food of their species: wild grain and seeds and also cultivated grain and rice. They also eat some insects.

Infant Diet and Care

Among these species, the only infant bird we have raised is the common gallinule. However, the diet we used might do well for all the species discussed here, as they lead similar lives.

With 1 cup medicated turkey starter, we mix enough water to make a sloppy mush. This food is placed in a flat dish, and the baby is taught to eat by dipping its bill in it or by tapping the dish till the baby gets curious and pecks for itself. Replace the food every three hours—it sours easily. It is best to put down only what the baby will eat and keep the rest refrigerated. Sometimes I put a couple of live mealworms on top of the food to encourage interest in pecking.

Our first baby gallinule was found by friends in a ditch during a rainstorm, with no signs of parents anywhere. We named him Baby George, after my husband, because of his bald head. (Of course *my* George's head isn't bright red, thank goodness, unless he stays out in the sun too long.) Baby George, with his inky-black bumblety body, long legs, and red bald head, was a very funny sight. Also, he had such tiny stubs of wings that it wasn't hard to look at him and say, "It'll *never* fly!"

We kept our baby gallinule in a cardboard box nursery with a heating pad on low heat under one end. We put a screen over the top, as these babies can hop very high even when small.

Baby George liked tiny bits of smelt and smidgens of cat tuna. After force-feeding at first (gently prying open the bill and putting a tiny bit of tuna or smelt far back in the throat), we fed him by putting the bits on the end of a long wooden applicator stick and waggling it in front of him, tapping his bill lightly. He was smart and caught on quickly to grabbing bits of food off the swab stick and pecking his food from the dish. I fed him off and on all day long, whenever I was passing by, until he learned to eat from his dish well. His cafeteria-style dinners of starter mix and tuna and smelt bits were sometimes augmented by bits of lean ground beef, a special treat. We taught him to drink by dipping his bill into a flat jar lid of water.

When he was larger and well feathered, we moved him into a portable indoor pen lined with newspapers. Baby George was with us at the same time as Dicky, a baby Muscovy duck, and they stayed in the same indoor pen. They got along famously. Baby George even liked to share Dicky's lettuce bits.

When he was two months old we released him at a friend's lake home, where other gallinules dwelled. He took off so fast our photos of his release were a blur. He flew out and looked over the lake, explored the reeds along the shore, and settled in immediately. He still lives there, has a mate now, and seems to pay no attention to people any more.

Adult Diet and Housing

Our adult gallinules, rails, and coots are housed in pens in the yard until they are acclimated, and then usually we release them to the freedom of our fenced backyard for a while to get their strength back.

All the adult species will eat the same medicated turkey starter diet as the babies, augmented by bits of lean ground beef and horsemeat. They also like fresh minnows, live ones when we have them. They enjoy aquatic weeds from nearby streams. And they will eat any insects they can get.

Injuries and Illness

Most of our patients in this group have broken wings and legs, and some suffer from the thin-weak ailment, the mysterious disease possibly caused by pesticide poisoning or botulism from contaminated food.

For all these patients, we provide a cardboard box lined with newspapers during recovery. Broken bones not broken in the joint or shattered are set by the vet. They then get the five-day treatment of sulfamethazine solution in their water bowls. For thin, dehydrated birds, we use Gatorade with the sulfamethazine.

If force-feeding is necessary, we feed bits of fish, cat-food tuna, or ground beef. Fresh moist turkey starter mixed with water is kept in their food dishes. Placing mealworms or live food on the turkey starter encourages eating.

Rest and quiet is provided for injured and ill birds as well as for concussion patients.

Birds are usually put to sleep if they are badly mangled or maimed, or if they have wings or legs broken in the joint. We did have one coot, named Cootsie, who had a bad wing break in the joint right next to the body. We tried to save her wing, but it did not heal properly and she could not fly. We released her in the backyard with the other birds, and she seemed to enjoy life. She was shy, though, and always scurried under a bush when she heard strange voices. She shared the gulls' and ducks' food and spent a lot of time swimming and diving in the pelican pool—but she always waited until the pelicans

ROSEMARY K. COLLETT

Cootsie had the free run of the fenced yard.

were finished because they were so raucous and boisterous. If the pelicans came in while she was having her private swim, she tumbled over the edge of the pool in a hurry and stayed out until they left. Cootsie lived in the backyard for a number of years and eventually died, apparently of old age.

We treated one sora rail which we assumed was suffering only from exhaustion (we think from migration). A friend found it lying beside the road and brought it in. It had no visible injuries but was thin and weak. We kept the bird and fed it for a few days, until it seemed to be rested. It was then released in the yard and took off strongly right away.

Our little sora rail soon left us. It was apparently suffering from exhaustion after its long migration.

ROSEMARY K. COLLETT

Release

As we often do with other species, we release these birds in our backyard when they are well, and they usually fly away of their own accord, as their habitat is not far away.

Sometimes we take them to a nearby pond or marsh, if we know the area from which they came or know a place where birds of their species congregate.

These birds are usually very eager for release. They fly up immediately and head in their own private direction, or sometimes, if released near a pond or marsh, simply dash off into the reeds and undergrowth.

They seem completely confident of where they are going, and we never worry about them.

21
RULERS OF THE HEAVENS
Falcons, Eagles, and Ospreys

The American and Arctic peregrine falcon and the Southern bald eagle are now on the endangered species list. Ospreys also seem to be on the decline in recent years. These are birds of prey, and they live on other living creatures. Some species have been known to eat carrion. They do not eat seeds, grain, or fruit.

We have never had any of these birds from infancy and for this reason cannot give advice on raising them. It is possible that infant falcons could be raised in a manner similar to infant hawks and owls—that is, on an all-meat diet.

We have worked with immature and adult birds of all these species, including the sparrow hawk, which is the smallest falcon in North America.

SPARROW HAWKS

Sparrow hawks are, in the adult stage, about 8½ inches long and have a wingspan of about 21 inches. They are the most commonly seen falcon, both in the open country and in civilized areas, where they perch on power lines, watching the roadsides for insects stirred up by the traffic.

Sparrow hawks eat insects mostly, though they do occasionally prey on very small birds, mice, and frogs. They are found throughout the United States, Mexico, and Canada.

We have had a number of sparrow hawks hurt by flying into power lines, or with broken-wing injuries of various types. They are rarely damaged by cats. We have had some success in setting wings not broken in the joint. The veterinarian has used paper tape, and the bone usually healed in two weeks. (See Veterinary Reference for further information on tape and tape removal.)

When these birds are recovered, we put them in a large outdoor flight cage to exercise, and also to see if they are fully able to fly before releasing them.

We feed our sparrow hawks 2 to 3 ounces of raw beef heart daily, sprinkled with vitamins, bone meal, and calcium gluconate. Calcium gluconate is a calcium supplement, obtainable at the drugstore. The bone meal we feed is *not* the kind sold at the garden shop for fertilizer. It is bone meal for animal consumption, obtainable at most pet shops.

For ease in administering the powdered supplements, I use a large salt shaker, combining the following amounts:

> ¼ cup Vionate vitamins
> 3 tbs. bone meal
> 2 tbs. calcium gluconate

This is then sprinkled liberally on each serving of beef heart.

The beef-heart diet is varied by adding grasshoppers, crickets, moths, dragonflies, tiny mice, and little green frogs. These birds need natural foods in their diet to stay really healthy. Feeding live mice and frogs is a little unpleasant, but birds of prey are just that, and they are not concerned with the niceties.

We raise laboratory mice specifically to feed our birds of prey. It may seem a little incongruous to be rearing wild field mice on the one hand and feeding laboratory mice to falcons on the other, but nature is unchangeable in her diet laws, and live mice and frogs are part of a sparrow hawk's natural diet.

We have found the most painless way (for us and the mice)

is to take the mouse by the base of the tail and rap its head sharply on a table top or any hard surface, stunning it. The sparrow hawk does the rest. Small green frogs can be dispatched in a similar manner, holding them by the legs.

Live frogs and mice can simply be put in the cage, letting nature take its course. The bird doesn't care, just so it gets the necessary fresh-killed natural food.

This is Diana, the sparrow hawk. She is the only falcon which became tame enough to ride about the house on my shoulder.

JACK BRIGGS

We always keep a large dish of water in the sparrow-hawk cages, because they love to bathe. They are very fastidious birds.

Diana, one of our sparrow-hawk patients, lived in an indoor cage in our home. She was comfortable in a cage 3 feet long, 2 feet high, and 1½ feet wide, with tree branches for perching and a small stump, on which she loved to preen after her bath. We allowed her to exercise in our house daily, since she did not live in a flight which permitted flying room. We had no insect problem while Diana was patrolling in our house. And in Florida that's a novelty.

Diana became a very tame bird and would often ride about the house on our shoulders. This is a habit I would not advise with larger birds of prey, because of their painfully sharp talons and large powerful feet.

PEREGRINE FALCON

The peregrine falcon is found worldwide, though the plumage varies in different areas and locations. However, the species is losing ground, and they no longer breed on the Eastern seaboard of the United States. I believe there are some breeding peregrines in the western states.

The peregrine is from 13 to 19 inches long and has a wingspan of nearly 40 inches. This bird is truly the ruler of the heavens. It preys almost exclusively on smaller birds, which it kills in flight. It can stoop (dive) at a speed of close to 200 miles per hour. It is the most favored of the species which is trained for hunting, and the use of the peregrine in falconry was originally reserved exclusively for royalty. The average adult weighs 1½ to 2 pounds. As with most birds of prey, the female is larger than the male and darker in color. In the terminology of the falconer, the female is properly called the falcon, and the male is called a tercel.

We have a peregrine falcon named Juno, after the mythical queen of the heavens. Juno came to us because of a reported broken wing. She was found down on a beach ten miles south of our area. She had no broken wing, we found, but could not fly properly. When we approached her, she flew up into a tree and then fell.

I used heavy leather gloves to pick her up, and we took her to a veterinarian for examination. He found no injuries or broken bones, but her entire left side was weak. She was not paralyzed, but her muscles on that side did not function properly.

We have had Juno three years, and the condition has never cleared up. She is not releasable. We don't know where she came from, or her exact age, but her plumage showed she was on her first migration. Cornell ornithologists have shown an interest in her; they think she is from an arctic hatch.

Juno lives in an extremely large flight outdoors (we are planning bigger quarters for her eventually). It has a 15-inch-wide shelf of ¾-inch exterior plywood mounted at the rear of her cage, covered with Astroturf (an outdoor carpeting). The cage is protected by the roof and the back wall. In the wild, peregrines like to perch on ledges, and the shelf serves this purpose. The Astroturf serves as a more natural surface and helps guard against the foot problems to which falcons are prone. Juno also has a large perching rock, to simulate the same in nature. Her favorite preening perch is our own creation, a birdbath pedestal with an inverted clay flowerpot mounted on the post. This regal perch seems exactly to suit Juno's needs after her bath, which she takes early in the morning, in a very large bath bowl. The floor of her cage is covered with clean builder's sand, which is cleaned and raked regularly and completely renewed every six months.

Her basic food is 5 to 6 ounces of raw beef heart daily, liberally sprinkled with a Vionate, bone meal, and calcium gluconate mixture. Some authorities say that any amount of meat over 2 to 3 ounces daily is overfeeding a falcon of this size, but Juno seems to thrive on her ration. She gets it once a day, late in the afternoon between four and six.

Since her natural food is mainly birds and her health depends on eating whole birds (that includes intestines, feathers, and all), I try to see she gets them when available. Whenever, we have an instant fatality, such as an injured dove or similar bird brought in which soon expires, the carcass goes immediately into Juno's cage. She also gets live mice and day-old chicks when available. We never, of course, feed her any bird that has been diseased or mysteriously ill. But sometimes we feed her fresh road-killed birds which are in good condition.

Since Juno is a permanent resident, we have tamed and "manned" her. "Manned" is the term used by falconers for the practice of attaching short leather jesses (thongs) to the bird's legs and training it to sit on its handler's fist.

ROSEMARY K. COLLETT

Jan works with Juno, the regal peregrine falcon. Member of an endangered species, Juno is a permanent resident because of her injuries. She is manned and sits on the gloved fist.

In handling Juno, we use heavy leather gloves with a long gauntlet. When she is perched on the glove, the jesses can be wrapped around the thumb, and the bird cannot fly off.

We are training Juno in this practice, which is only a very elementary step in falconry technique, so that we can handle her well enough to take her to the schools and use her in our wildlife programs for the children. Peregrine falcons are rarely seen by the average person, and we hope to give Juno as much exposure as possible to promote the cause of preserving her beautiful species.

BALD EAGLE

The bald eagle, our national bird, is found throughout the United States and parts of Canada. Its best-known breeding colonies are now in Florida and Alaska. Bald eagles return to the same nest yearly if they are left alone, enlarging it until it is 15 to 20 feet across.

While at present only the Southern bald eagle is an endangered species, all bald eagles seem to be somewhat on the decline. Some suspected and known causes of this are shooting (strictly illegal), destruction of their habitat by man, and DDT poisoning through their natural food. There are fines and jail terms for harming them or disturbing their nests, but crimes against bald eagles continue to reduce their numbers.

The full-grown bald eagle is about 32 inches long with a wingspan of around 50 inches. It is easily identified by its size, its dark body and wings, and its white head and tail feathers. The bald eagle is not bald, of course, but in flight the white feathered head may look that way. The young bald eagle is dark brown all over and does not grow white head and tail feathers until the age of about four years.

These birds' favorite food appears to be fish, and they usually nest near some body of water. They also eat small animals, such as rabbits, rats, and chipmunks. They have been known to eat carrion in the absence of live game.

Bald eagles in captivity will eat the same diet of raw beef heart and vitamin supplements as the peregrine, with the addition of whole fish (raw, of course, and not gutted or beheaded). They may also be housed in the same manner.

Our only bald-eagle patient was a young male. He had been hanging around the pier, mooching fish, at the nearby community of Englewood, and federal authorities asked us to come and get him. For some reason, he didn't know how to hunt or feed himself and was in danger of being fouled in a fishing line or hook.

The required special federal endangered species permit

A very angry bald eagle is untangled from the net lines after being captured by Bill Wimbish.

was issued to us, and we captured him with the help of a local high school biology teacher, Bill Wimbish. Bill is handy at casting a mullet net. He made a spectacular throw and dropped the net right over the young eagle, while George and I moved in, wearing heavy jackets and gloves. We took the eagle home, put him in a large wire pen in the backyard, and fed him half a beef heart and several mullet daily. He seemed to thrive, and after three and a half weeks the federal authorities moved him to a permanent home at the Boyd Hill Nature Center in St. Petersburg.

We had found our eagle to have a huge appetite, but five days after he was moved to the Nature Center the director called us and said the bird had not yet eaten. This was strange, for he was not bashful about eating at our house and had begged fish from the pier fishermen at Englewood for several days before we picked him up.

We drove up to St. Petersburg (sixty miles away), taking along the eagle's feeding block, his perching stump, and a supply of beef heart and mullet, and found our friend sitting disconsolately in a barren wire cage. The only perch was a smooth metal pipe, on which his talons could get no purchase. The cage was exposed on three sides. On the left was a cage of screaming monkeys and on the right a pen of gabbling turkeys. People passed by the front constantly, stopping to exclaim, "Look at the eagle!" No wonder he was a nervous wreck and couldn't eat!

I had the keeper put the stump, a wooden perch, and some shrubbery screening in the cage to give the bird a little natural privacy, and then I went inside. The eagle just sat there, his back to me, hunched up. I walked over, talking to him just as I always did, and he suddenly turned and began squawking and flapping in recognition. However, he refused my offers of beef heart and mullet. I spent five hours in that cage trying to get the bird to eat, but he wouldn't. He was just too upset.

At one point he had come quite close to me and was reaching to take a bite of food. Just at that moment an excited youngster banged on the cage front, yelling, "Hey, Mom! Look at the lady with the eagle!" The bird backed off and I could not re-tempt him.

I asked the keeper to cover the cage with canvas for a while and keep the eagle quiet. I intended to come back and force-feed him if necessary. However, two days later the keeper called me and said the bird had started eating. Evidently he finally made the adjustment to his new surroundings.

I doubt that he will ever be released, because he seemed incapable of caring for himself. We visit him occasionally, and he often bows his head and calls in recognition.

AMERICAN OSPREY

There are five subspecies of ospreys found throughout the world, except in the polar regions. They live near fresh or salt water, as they are fish-eaters.

The American osprey breeds in North America but then wanders to Central America and on to South America. It is believed these birds mate for life. Their plumage is dark above and light below, and their 54-inch wingspan supports a body about 22 inches long. They have two toes pointing forward and two toes pointing backward.

Like the bald eagle, they return to the same nest each year and enlarge it annually with new material. Their nests are enormous, but three creamy brown-splotched eggs is the usual clutch, and they hatch in about twenty-eight days. The female rarely leaves them, while the male dives for fish and brings them to her. The young leave the nest after about eight weeks.

Ospreys are seen here in Florida in watery areas, diving from a height of 30 to 100 feet for fish on the surface or just under the water. They strike with their talons, and their dive sometimes carries them completely under the water. Their plumage is extremely waterproof. Ospreys have been known to tackle a fish too big for their size and, rather than release it, be dragged under the water and drowned.

After an osprey makes a successful dive and catch, it may be seen carrying the fish dangling head down, as the hit is most often made from behind. Often the hard-won catch is stolen by the bald eagle, which is the osprey's prime enemy.

This species is struggling to survive. Many scientists blame the ospreys' dwindling numbers on destruction of their habitat and possibly DDT in their food. DDT in the diet can cause thin-shelled eggs which will break before they hatch.

We have had two osprey patients. They came from adjacent Florida counties, and both of them had been shot.

The first one, shot in the wing, was also blind in one eye from unknown causes. A veterinarian treated and bound the wing, and we fed the bird small fish. It had to be force-fed, but it retained the fish. It died three days later, however, and an autopsy showed that the fish had not been digested properly; many were still in the crop.

The second osprey patient had been hit with buckshot in the body and wings. It, too, ate small fish for several days but did not survive.

Both birds were too badly injured to survive, and we did not have an opportunity to work with them toward rehabilitation and release. Severely wounded birds in this category are very difficult to save, but it is always worth trying.

General Housing

We have found the best housing for our short-term osprey patients is the large traveling dog kennel, the type used and sold by airlines. The seclusion offered by these crates is most desirable for sick and sensitive birds. They need privacy, while recovering, and do not like to be disturbed or watched. These boxes are solid wood on all sides, giving protection as well as privacy. A barred door covers the front opening. We line these with newspapers, put a heavy log inside for perching, and keep fresh water (treated with sulfamethazine) available.

The smaller sparrow hawk may be kept during recuperation from injuries or illness in a cage about 3 feet long, 2 feet wide, and 2 feet high. A larger cage will be needed later for recovery and exercise.

Larger birds, such as the osprey, may be kept in the large enclosed dog traveling crates for short periods.

For recovering birds which need more exercise room, we use a large outdoor pen, at least 8 feet long, 4 to 6 feet wide, and 6 feet or more high. This pen has a walk-in safety door (see Cages and Housing). The bird's activity here usually shows us whether or not it is ready to be released.

Water bowls, of course, must be large. We use the largest, deepest birdbaths we can find for the outdoor pens. Sulfamethazine should be added to the smaller indoor water bowl if the bird is still sickly or healing.

Since these birds eat by holding down their food and tearing off bits with their beaks, we provide them with a feeding block—a heavy patio stone, a rock, or a large tree stump—on which they can seize their food and hold it down securely without messing it up with dirt or sand while they are eating (at least in the beginning; the food often ends up off the block and in the dirt before they have finished it).

Force-Feeding

We use extreme caution when force-feeding any of the

eagles, ospreys, and peregrine falcons. They are very powerful birds, well equipped with talons, beak, and a fierce nature, and can seriously injure any human who is careless.

It is easier if there are two people to do the force-feeding. The person holding the bird wears heavy leather gloves with gauntlets, such as welder's gloves, grasping the bird and firmly holding the wings and feet. The person doing the feeding can use lightweight plastic garden gloves if he wants (they just get in my way and I rarely use them).

I press gently on each side of the base of the bird's bill until the mouth is forced open, then place small chunks of beef heart (½ to 1 inch square) or fish (for an osprey) as far back in the throat as possible. If the bird will allow it, I stroke the throat for a moment to encourage swallowing.

If the bird will accept *live* food from the beginning, this may eliminate the need for force-feeding. Often after several meals of live food—frogs, mice, small birds, baby chicks (or fish, if you are feeding an osprey)—the bird will then eat beef heart without prompting.

When feeding live food or beef heart to see if the bird will eat for the first time, we put the food as near the bird's feet and talons as possible. We have found that if you toss the food onto a bird's feet, it will often automatically grasp it, which is the prelude to eating it. In other words, the eating reflex seems to be triggered by its talons, not by pushing food at its beak.

When force-feeding ospreys or prompting them to eat, we never forget to include the vitamin B_1 tablet, inserted in the fish's mouth or gill or in a slit. And at all times we keep uppermost in mind that the talons are the prime object to avoid. While the bill can do damage also, the powerful talons are the bird of prey's most formidable weapon.

Release

Since some of these birds mate for life, we try to release the bird at the place where it was captured. The mate may still be in the vicinity, if not too long a time has elapsed.

These birds can be carried to the release site in a stout cardboard box or in wooden traveling crates.

When we arrive at the release site, we just open the box or

crate and stand back, letting the bird come out on its own. Birds of this type usually take off immediately.

We always bring along our heavy leather gloves and our long-handled net, however, because it is possible to misjudge the bird's strength, and it may have to be captured again. These birds should never be released until they are ready, because they must fly well to be able to survive in their natural environment, and they must be strong and alert and in good physical condition to hunt for their natural food.

22
THE WISE ONES AND THEIR COMPATRIOTS
Owls, Hawks, and Vultures

We have cared for young and adult common screech owls, barn owls, barred owls, and great horned owls. Owls are extremely sensitive birds and must be handled with great care and gentleness. They die easily of shock and heart failure and do not like to be handled any more than necessary.

There are many species of owls found throughout the world. The ones discussed here, along with some background information on their particular species, were all cared for in our home, and some are permanent residents.

We have also cared for a red-shouldered hawk, a red-tailed hawk, and a black vulture. I have included hawks and vultures in this chapter because much of their feeding, care, and housing is similar to the owls. Although hawks and owls are birds of prey, the vulture is not. It eats meat but does not kill its own, feeding on dead animals killed by other means.

COMMON SCREECH OWL

The common screech owl is found throughout the United States and in parts of Canada and Mexico. These are small owls, ranging in size from 7 to 9 inches. In the United States they have two color phases: some are grayish, and some are reddish. Both colorations have "ear" tufts and large golden eyes.

They like to build their nests in tree hollows at least 5 feet from the ground and sometimes as high as 40 feet, depending on which tree they choose. They generally lay five to eight white eggs. The incubation period is about twenty-six days. The male brings food to the female while she is on the nest and helps feed the babies when they hatch. The young owls leave the nest at about four weeks, but the parents often feed them for several more weeks.

We had a pair of screech owls nesting in an old dead royal palm tree in our front yard, so we had a chance to observe them closely. The male often perched on our porch light, looking very ornamental indeed, and we learned to use the back door so we wouldn't disturb him. When the young were hatched and out of the nest (there were two), they stayed around the yard while the parents fed them. We contributed lean beef cubes occasionally, which the father would take to his family. One baby was stupid and would not follow the others, even when Papa flogged him with his wings. But they grew up, and the whole family stayed about two months before flying away. It was a beautiful way to observe and enjoy an owl family, and we appreciated the opportunity to be admitted to their private lives.

The natural food for these birds is mice and small mammals, birds, insects, lizards, and frogs.

BARN OWL

The barn owl is found throughout the United States, Mexico, Central America, and parts of South America. Variations of this species are found in many parts of the world.

This is an intermediate-sized owl, 15 to 17 inches long. Their color has light and dark variants, and there is a white-breasted phase and an orange-breasted phase. They are easily identified, however, by the heart-shaped face disc and dark eyes.

The barn owl likes to nest in old barns, naturally, but will also haunt old steeples and other old buildings if they suit its owlish tastes. These owls also nest in hollow trees, caves, and other shelters provided in nature. The barn owl generally has a clutch of four to seven white eggs and sometimes will raise two broods in one year. The incubation period is about thirty-two days, and the female stays on the nest while the male brings her food. The young are usually flying at less than three months of age.

Their natural food is mice, rats, and woodland rodents. It is a lucky farmer who has a barn owl in residence.

BARRED OWL

The barred owl varies in size from 16 to 18 inches. It is barred in varying shades of buffy brown and cream and has black eyes. This owl is found in many parts of the United States, the Midwest through the East, and also in parts of Mexico and Canada.

This species hatches two to four white eggs, using nests in hollow trees or even secondhand hawks' nests which have been abandoned. The incubation period is about twenty-eight days, and the male feeds both the mother and the young. The babies leave the nest at about six weeks but often stay with their parents throughout the summer.

These owls are nocturnal hunters, feeding mostly on mice and small mammals. However, they will also eat insects, crayfish, and small amphibians such as frogs.

GREAT HORNED OWL

This large owl is found throughout the United States, Mexico, Central and South America, and in parts of Canada and Alaska. The adult is 19 inches in length and comes in a white-breasted and an orange-breasted phase. It has "ear" tufts and big golden eyes. This species is a fierce predator, hunting both by day and by night. The two to four white eggs are laid in secondhand nests abandoned by hawks and eagles, and sometimes in hollow trees. The incubation period is around thirty-four days. The male feeds both mother and young during the nesting period. The babies often leave the nest at about five weeks. They can hop around among the tree branches, but they don't really fly until they are nearly ten weeks old.

Their natural foods are rodents, small mammals, birds, snakes, frogs, and fish.

RED-SHOULDERED HAWK

The red-shouldered hawk is found in the eastern United States and into Canada and may also be found occasionally along the Pacific coast. It is 18 to 20 inches in length, a broad-winged bird, with yellow feet and legs and brown eyes. This species usually nests in tall trees. The female lays three or four white brown-spotted eggs, which hatch in twenty-seven days.

The natural food of the red-shouldered hawk is mice and squirrels, and it also will eat toads and minnows.

We have a red-shouldered hawk, Reddy, as a permanent resident. He has a healed broken wing, which, though properly set by the vet, has never functioned. We tried releasing him, and he flew like a lead balloon. We are now working at fitting him with leather jesses and teaching him to perch on a falconer's glove, so that he can be taken to schools for our wildlife programs. Many children have never seen this species of hawk.

RED-TAILED HAWK

The red-tailed hawk is found throughout the United States, including Alaska, as far north as Canada and as far south as Mexico. This broad-winged hawk has a blue-black beak, brown eyes, and yellow legs and feet. It comes in several color phases in North America and usually nests in tall trees. The adult's tail is reddish above and pink beneath. Eggs—white spotted with brown—number two to four, and both the male and female share the chore of sitting on the eggs during the thirty-four-day incubation stage. The young leave the nest at about six weeks. The natural food of this bird is rodents (including large ones as big as hares), insects, reptiles, amphibians, and birds.

We have never raised infant hawks or buzzards, though we

Wiley, the red-tailed hawk baby, had huge feet.

did attempt to rear a young red-tailed hawk which had fallen from its nest in a tall pine and suffered a broken wing. Though the vet put a pin in the wing and we nursed the hawk carefully in a laundry basket on our dining room table, constant care did not save the bird. Baby Wiley, as we called him, died of complications after a month.

BLACK VULTURE

The black vulture, often commonly called "buzzard," is found in the southern United States, Mexico, Central America, and into much of South America. This big black bird ranges to 24 inches in length. Its head and neck are naked. It has dark eyes. The wing feather primaries have light patches.

This bird nests in tall trees, in hollow stumps, or even on the ground. The hatch is two bluish white eggs, spotted with brown, and the parents share the duties of keeping the eggs warm for the incubation period, which is from thirty-nine to forty-one days.

The young and the adults will regurgitate their food from the nest if disturbed, not to be vengeful of trespassers, but because they are nervous birds.

Our one and only vulture patient was Buz, who was a young bird with a downy head but fully feathered. He was found, unmoving, in a backyard in the community of Englewood, south of here. He was unhurt, though thin and weak. He was friendly at first, and liked to have his head and neck scratched, but as he grew older he became downright mean. Then he escaped from his pen in the backyard and was found a block away by a priest, who helped me to recapture him. I leave it to your imagination to visualize the priest and me chasing a huge hopping black vulture across many front lawns. We collected quite a crowd. We also collected Buz, as he could not fly, but only took great leaping bounds like an earthbound pterodactyl.

Buz never did become "flyable," but he became very large, and I finally placed him at the Crandon Park Zoo in Miami, since we really did not have the proper facilities for a full-grown vulture.

Infant Diet and Care

My first experience with infants in this category was with Baby Wiley, the red-tailed hawk youngster.

Baby Wiley's laundry basket nursery was lined with towels, which we changed several times daily, though after a week or two he would try to raise his little fanny and shoot out over the basket edge in the manner of hawks. They do this, as do vultures and some other birds, to keep their nests clean. We were finally forced to cover the table and surrounding area with newspapers to handle this new development.

We fed Baby Wiley small bits of beef heart, liberally sprinkled with the mixture of Vionate vitamins, bone meal, and calcium gluconate we use with eagles and falcons.

Because (again as with eagles and falcons) these birds must have roughage in their diet, we also fed him small baby mice. All birds of prey need to regurgitate pellets of undigested material such as fur, feathers, and bone periodically. Scientists say this keeps their crop cleaned of mucus and keeps them healthy. Thus they need whole animals to eat, such as rodents and small birds.

If no small whole animals are available to feed, you can chop up bird feathers and tuck them into the bird's meat. However, this is only a substitute. The real thing is better.

We fed Baby Wiley as much as he would eat, every two hours, throughout the daylight hours. He eventually died of his injuries, and we have had no further experience in rearing young hawks. However, I feel this diet would work well with many infant bird of prey species.

Diet and Care for Baby Owls

We had never raised any baby owls, but while this book was in progress we acquired an infant great horned owl which we named Oliver.

Oliver was creating a neighborhood crisis because he had fallen from his nest in a tall pine, and although his mother frantically defended him for two days on the ground, neighbors finally asked us to take him before their nerves gave out. He was unhurt, but he wouldn't have lasted long in an area teeming with cats, dogs, and nighttime predators.

Oliver turned out to be about four weeks old, and a more darling specimen of owlhood I have never seen. He was a very large baby, of course, with wings much too big and heavy for his body, the beginnings of horn tufts on his head, and Clementine-sized feet. He was covered all over with a wild array of fuzz. With his large, golden, expressive eyes, he looked somewhat like a frazzled Phyllis Diller. We put him in a towel-lined box, with a heating pad on low under one end, and clamped an infrared light on a stand about four feet above his box, to give additional warmth without glare.

At this writing, he is 8 or 9 inches tall and likes to stand with his back against the rear of the box, peering out owlishly at all the activity from his nursery on the dining room table. I keep him there so he can watch me in the kitchen (where I usually am), for he seems to get lonely without company and activity.

Oliver, age five weeks, sits on my shoulder as I read about birds of prey.

He is so young, he can't really stand alone, and his wings are terribly heavy and droopy, so he often leans on them rather like a person leaning on his elbows. Sometimes he goes to sleep that way, with his head bending lower and lower until his very large beak is also resting on the floor of his box. Occasionally, though, he sleeps on his side, with one wing and one leg stretched out. When awakened or startled, he clacks his bill, just like a grown-up owl.

I hand-feed him, wrapping him in a towel to hold him on my lap. I know I said owls don't like to be handled, but Oliver does; he even likes to be cuddled. Maybe it's because he's a baby.

While working with Oliver, I discovered a food prepared especially for birds of prey. It is Carnivorous Bird Food, made by Hill's, the people who make dog food. It was originally developed for zoos, however, and comes only in large quantities—5-pound rolls, made up like sausage, and available only in 40-pound cases. It must be kept frozen until ready to use. We find the rolls are easier to handle if they are presliced by a butcher, so we can put out slices to thaw before we need them.

This is a great diet for carnivorous birds, because it has everything they need. Thawed, it looks and smells somewhat like predigested food and includes bone, blood, liver, various meats, and moisture, plus all the important vitamins and minerals these birds must have to be healthy.

This is hand-fed in small bites to Oliver, who seems to like

At six weeks Oliver begins to explore. Rhani, the Afghan hound, isn't sure she likes this togetherness.

ROSEMARY K. COLLETT

it very much and is thriving on it. It even contains the roughage he needs to cast up pellets to remain healthy. It probably could be fed right on through adulthood, but I plan to include chicken necks, beef heart, and live food in Oliver's diet as he progresses, so he will learn what real meat and live animals are like. Otherwise he might not survive when we release him.

I would think this prepared food could be used with any infant or adult bird of prey. However, since I release all my patients, I would recommend that releasable birds get other meat and animal kills as a supplement to prepare them for life in the wild.

Since Oliver is a new resident, I will learn from my work with him as he progresses, but he seems to be doing well in the few weeks I have had him.

Adult Diet

The basic diet for adult owls, vultures, and hawks is beef heart, with the fat trimmed from it. Sprinkle the raw beef heart with the mixture of ¼ cup Vionate vitamins, 3 tablespoons bone meal, and 2 tablespoons of calcium gluconate used for other birds of prey. (I mix these dry ingredients in a large salt shaker, so I can apply them easily when I feed the meat.) Raw chicken necks with the fatty skin stripped off can also be fed, either as an alternate or in place of the beef heart, if none is available. Lean stew beef can also be fed. Make sure it is *lean.*

We feed our adult barred owls 4 to 5 ounces of beef heart, once a day, usually late in the afternoon. This is the nearest to their natural feeding time for our convenience, as they like to hunt at dusk.

Adult great horned owls get 5 to 7 ounces of beef heart once a day, late in the day. If we are able to give our owl a fresh whole rabbit, we eliminate the beef heart feeding, for it will feed on the rabbit that evening and eat more the next day. After twenty-four hours, we remove any of the carcass that remains.

The adult red-shouldered and red-tailed hawks get 4 to 5 ounces of beef heart, usually in the morning, as hawks are daytime hunters.

Buz, our young vulture, would eat 5 to 7 ounces of beef heart or five or six chicken necks daily, usually in the morning. Buz also occasionally ate stew beef. He was especially fond of chicken necks, ripping the meat off them with great gusto.

These birds usually get plenty of fluids in eating whole game. However, though they do not need much water in the wild, we keep fresh drinking water in their cages for them while they are in captivity, because they are forced to eat a lean-meat diet.

It is always best to feed their natural food—whole small animals—whenever possible. We pick up fresh road kills, such as rabbits or doves, for our birds, after making sure they were healthy, not diseased or sickly in appearance. We also feed mice, rats, and day-old chicks. The owls like theirs live or stunned. The vultures like theirs dead. These birds *must* have whole animals, at least occasionally, to maintain their health.

Injuries

Almost all our injury cases among these birds have consisted of either broken bones or concussion, from flying into

George seems to have misplaced Diogenes, the screech owl.
The owl, however, is quite alert.

ROSEMARY K. COLLETT

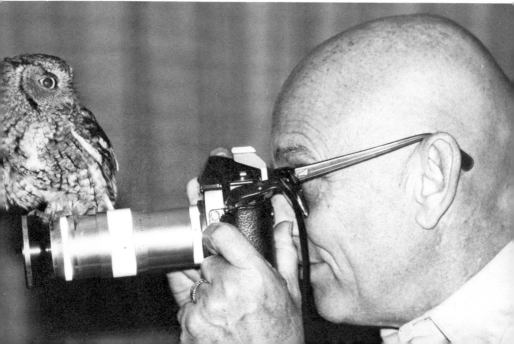

cars or some other object while pursuing their prey. Some have had gunshot wounds. (Buz, our vulture patient, was an exception—we never did know why he couldn't fly.)

Our very first screech-owl patient, Diogenes, had an injured wing. He lived on our screened porch in a cage while he was healing, and his great golden eyes, fixed in an unwinking stare, made some of our visitors uncomfortable.

We keep most of our owls indoors while healing, especially if their injuries are broken bones. Concussion patients, though they need quiet and solitude at first, usually recover fairly quickly and can be moved to outdoor cages, unless they have trouble with their balance. Otus, a screech-owl concussion patient presently in residence, lives in an outdoor cage, which has a hollow tree trunk for protection from the weather.

Owls are extremely sensitive and can die of shock even while having a broken bone set. It is very hard to treat them and to keep them in captivity. I always try to release our owls just as soon as possible after recovery.

The general rule in treating these birds, again, is:

Wing smashed in the joint—have it put to sleep.

Wing with a clean bone break—have the vet set it and keep the patient quiet while healing, preferably undisturbed except for feeding time.

Concussion—if the weather is cold, a warm bed in a box and a heating pad under the hospital carton; quiet and rest until the patient comes around.

Remember that these birds depend on flight to live and hunt; flight is their very existence. It is never merciful to save a cripple for no reason except to keep him alive. It is true that there are handicapped birds now in residence at our home representing injuries that did not heal properly, but they do serve a purpose in helping us to teach children what can happen if someone senselessly hurts these magnificent hunters and coursers of nature.

Capture and Transport

If you ever are about to capture and handle birds of prey, be very careful. They are large strong birds, have vicious beaks and talons, and are equipped with a fierce nature. The vulture is more bad-tempered than fierce but is also a strong and difficult bird to handle.

Wear heavy leather gloves with long gauntlets, such as welder's gloves. Use a net with a long handle—at least 6 to 10 feet—and a big diameter; if none is available, use a blanket or sheet, which can be tossed over the injured bird. A blanket not only immobilizes the bird but quiets it somewhat.

If the bird is unable to fly and is on the ground, the capture is relatively easy. After plopping the net or blanket over it, you can move in and extricate it firmly with your gloved hands. Pick it up by the feet.

If the bird is badly crippled, you can sometimes just move in and, as it takes the defensive position—on its back with its talons in the air—grasp the feet with gloved hands. The talons will automatically lock around your hand, and you can pick up the bird easily. Tuck it carefully under one arm, keeping a firm hold on the feet and keeping your face away from the beak. The bird can also be wrapped in a towel or sheet, thus further immobilizing it until you can get it to a box or crate.

Large birds of prey, such as the great horned owl, have talons that can pierce even heavy leather gloves, but they cannot penetrate deeply enough to cause serious injury—at least, I have never been seriously hurt in this way.

These birds can be transported to the vet or to your home in a large cardboard box or a wooden dog-kennel crate. They tend to travel quietly once they are enclosed in darkness.

While examining these birds for injuries or treating them, we cover their heads with a towel (leaving breathing room). We find this tends to quiet them while we are working with them.

Housing

If the birds are ill, or healing from broken bones or surgery, we keep them on our screened porch in large cardboard cartons, or dog travel crates, lined with newspapers. We keep the crate or box clean by changing the papers daily. In a cold climate, sick and injured birds must be kept indoors until they are recovered enough to move to outdoor pens.

We always furnish the hospital carton or crate with a log for perching and a large dish of water. Sulfamethazine is always added to the drinking water for the first five days during convalescence to guard against infection.

When our patients are well enough to live outdoors, we put them in large flights or pens. They like seclusion, so we pick an area screened by shrubbery, and we furnish the cage with a large nest box or hollow log. They can always retire to these sanctuaries when they don't really want to be bothered, and these furnishings also provide shelter from the weather.

These birds are very sensitive and do not like to be stared at, poked or prodded, or handled any more than necessary for their care and feeding.

Our large flights are made of wire and are 8 to 10 feet wide, 6 feet high, and equipped with a safety walk-in door. (See Cages and Housing section for details on construction.) In these flight cages, we provide stumps and large rocks for sitting purposes, and also a perch made of a large tree limb with rough bark. The water supply is a big birdbath; many of these species like to bathe regularly. In fact, I have even seen our vulture take a morning bath. The floor is covered with clean builder's sand and is raked and changed as needed.

In the case of a hawk too crippled ever to release, it is possible to man it with leather jesses and keep it on a screen perch. This is simply a frame, somewhat like a hitching post frame, with screening nailed on it. If the bird tries to fly and falls, it can catch itself on the screen panel and climb back to the perch, rather than be left dangling. Hawks seem to like such a perch arrangement better than an enclosed cage or flight.

None of these birds is easily tamed. Though you can work with members of the hawk species to some degree, adult owls are almost impossible to tame. They do not like to be handled. Barry, the barred owl that works in our school programs, is one of the few exceptions I have seen.

Release

When these birds make a full recovery, they should be released if possible in the same area in which they were found. A mate may be waiting nearby.

Preparing to release a red-shouldered hawk. The heavy gloves and jacket are a must when dealing with these birds.

If the bird cannot be returned to its original habitat, it should be released as far away from civilization as possible. It is taken to the release site in the box or carrying case. The door is opened, we stand back, and let it go. It will fly away immediately if it is fully recovered. However, if it is unable to fly well or flutters to the ground after a short try, we recapture it. These birds *must* fly well to hunt and live in the wild.

23
FIRST AID FOR BIRDS

We are not veterinarians and we have never tried to substitute for one, but we do administer simple first aid to ill or injured wildlife. If our patients need a vet's attention, we take them to him and then carry out his instructions, including postsurgical care, if it is needed, or care following the setting of bones.

When you find an injured bird, or one that appears ill, determine if you can what kind of a bird it is and examine it for the cause. Does it have a broken leg or wing? Is it thin and emaciated? Is it unconscious? Are its droppings abnormal?

If a bird is thin or emaciated, you can feel the breastbone sharply—a bird's breast should be smooth and plump if it is healthy. If its droppings are very green, it may indicate intestinal problems. Very dark droppings, we have found, sometimes indicate a bird is near starvation; black droppings might mean internal bleeding. Broken bones may be indicated by a leg or foot twisted out of proper position, a drooping wing, or a wing held at an odd angle. Compound fractures are easy to spot. Never try to set or manipulate a bone yourself, for you may do more harm than good. And never attempt an amputation; this is also a vet's job, and only he can do it properly with a minimum of injury, infection risk, and bleeding.

Occasionally a bird will have a dislocated wing. In some instances we simply keep the patient quiet in a box with food and water for a week or two. In other cases, the veterinarian tapes the wing with paper tape (see Veterinary Reference), keeping it in its proper position for a couple of weeks. If the bird can be kept quiet, the wing often will return to normal and the bird can be released.

When a bird seems to be ill, isolate it from all other creatures until you have some idea of the nature of the illness. Contagion is possible in many diseases through air-borne virus, so isolation is always a good idea when dealing with an unknown malady.

If you or your veterinarian need further information which may be helpful in treating wild birds, check the Veterinary Reference section at the back of the book.

Birds can suffer from shock. This may occur from being mauled by a cat or dog, being handled by humans, or just being transported by car or examined by a vet. The treatment for shock is quiet, isolation, and warmth.

Heart attacks can also occur in birds. Hawks and owls are especially prone to these attacks, as they are extremely sensitive birds. We have seen this happen when the vet must set a broken bone, for instance. In fact, our vet has made "house calls" to treat an injured owl, because owls are so prone to heart attacks when frightened.

It is seldom that a wing joint break will heal well enough to permit a bird to fly again. Breaks in the joint, we have found, tend to stiffen when they heal, making correct manipulation of the wing no longer possible, at least for flying purposes.

Broken or amputated legs are another matter. Many birds can get along very well on one leg and are releasable in this condition. However, birds such as ducks and other water birds, which depend on swimming for feeding purposes, can then only swim in a circle, so amputation is not practical here. Birds of prey also need their legs because they depend on their talons to seize prey, and waders, such as herons and cranes, need their long legs to maneuver in the streams and to balance their long bodies. For these, too, amputation is impractical.

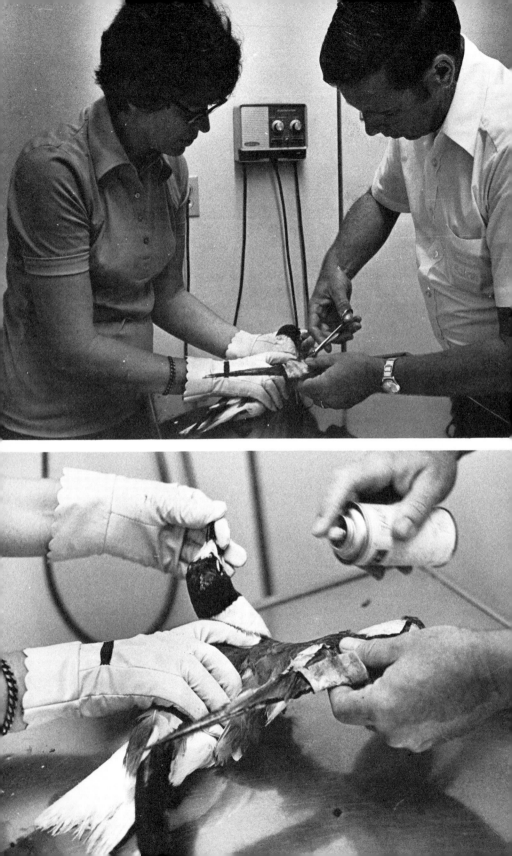

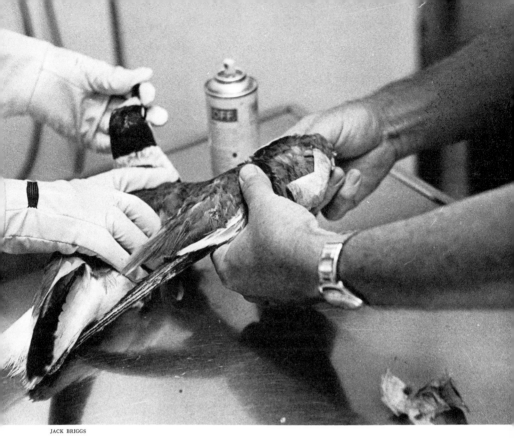

*Dr. Suddaby prepares to take the tape from a sea gull's
healed wing while I assist. Spraying with solvent as the
tape is removed from the wing takes some of the "ouch" from
pulling. (Note the plastic garden gloves; the gull pinches
smartly.) When the tape is almost off, the wing is found to
be well healed but a little stiff. This gull will fly again.*

Sea gulls do all right with one leg, and most song and
garden birds can manage very well. There are several one-
legged birds about town in this category which have often been
reported to us, but they do not need any special care (so long
as they can fly) and have learned to hop around and feed with
no difficulty.

Some birds that come to us have lost a toenail or talon. It
is possible for a bird to die from loss of blood from something
which appears as minor as a broken toenail. In cases where
bleeding is quite profuse, we apply Monsel's salts (available
at a veterinarian's). This generally stops the bleeding. We
always keep a bottle of Monsel's on hand. When bleeding is

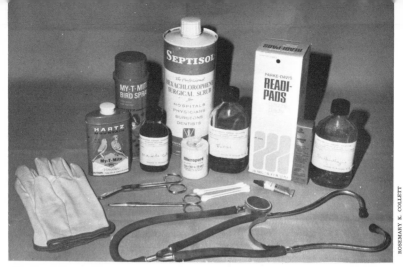

First-aid supplies: lightweight plastic gloves, Hartz Mountain mite powder, Hartz Mountain mite spray, Monsel's salts to stop bleeding of cut toenail, Septisol for cleansing hands after handling patients, Micropore paper tape for birds, Furacin medication for wounds, gauze pads, Panalog ointment, sulfamethazine, bandage scissors, toenail scissors, cotton swabs for applying medications, Mycitracin ointment, and stethoscope.

less, we place a gauze pad over the wound and apply pressure for one to ten minutes. Bleeding from a large vein or artery is another matter. Get the bird to a veterinarian as soon as possible, applying pressure to the wound in the meantime to stanch the flow.

When a bird is sick or hurt, warmth and isolation are what it needs first. Birds have a high rate of metabolism, and their normal temperature runs about 102 to 103 degrees. When they are sick, their temperature drops.

A good hospital cage for bird patients is one protected from drafts with three solid sides and a wire front. Under one end of the cage, place a heating pad on low setting. Or you can clamp a 25-watt bulb directly over one end of the cage. This allows the bird to seek warmth when needed and move away when overheated.

The cage need not be too large. It depends on the size of the bird. An ill or injured bird should not move about too much. Do not use perches, for the bird might injure itself further.

If it is a small bird, put in a jar lid of water and sulfamethazine. This is a good all-round medication and is available from your vet. It comes in liquid form, and you mix it with water at the rate of one tablespoon per gallon. (See preceding chapters for diet instructions for individual species.)

Leave the bird alone for thirty minutes to three hours to get used to its surroundings, if it is not seriously injured. It is not necessary to feed a bird the moment you get it unless it is obviously dehydrated or starving.

Gatorade (available in the fruit juice department of most supermarkets) is excellent for birds suffering from dehydration. It can be substituted for water and sulfamethazine or can have sulfamethazine added to it for patients with obvious infections.

When examining a bird, handle it carefully but don't be afraid—it's a lot sturdier than you think. Don't ever squeeze any bird. Most birds do not like to be held and are very nervous about it. Always move slowly and speak softly to reassure it. Use gloves when handling owls, hawks, egrets, herons, or any bird with a long sharp bill or talons.

If you are injured by the bill or talons of any of these large birds, see your doctor about a tetanus shot. Such wounds might possibly be dangerous.

We always wash our hands, or any scrapes or nips, thoroughly with an antiseptic solution such as Septisol after handling patients. This is simply a precautionary measure to help avoid any possible infection.

Many birds knock themselves unconscious flying into picture windows or sliding glass doors and suffer from what resembles a concussion. They need to be placed in the hospital cage and left in quiet with a little food and water. A number of my "concussion" patients came around in from two to forty-eight hours and were then released.

If a bird is badly injured and beyond help, or if an amputation is necessary for some birds who depend on flight for life, have the vet put the bird to sleep. It is the only merciful way. It is not a charitable deed in our opinion to amputate the wing of a bird such as a nighthawk or chimney swift, and most owls and hawks. Nighthawks, for instance, are not built for life on the ground. They have tiny weak feet. They rarely learn to pick up food from a dish and must forever be hand-fed if they are kept in captivity. However, we have pelicans who have had wing amputations and they can live happy lives even though earth-bound. They cannot be released, of course, but anyone seeing our pelicans romping around our backyard can testify that they are happy and well-adjusted birds with big appetites.

Poisons

We have cared for many birds which seemed to have symptoms indicative of poisoning. These symptoms can include: no visible injuries; partially paralyzed legs; thin, emaciated condition; tremors or convulsions; and, occasionally, greenish droppings.

Sometimes these birds recover and sometimes they do not. The cause may be pesticides, botulism, or, in fish-eaters, contaminated fish. We know of no cure. Our treatment is to keep the victim warm and quiet and give him the sulfamethazine solution to drink. Refer to the specific bird chapters for further information if force-feeding is necessary.

We had one royal tern which did survive such an illness after six weeks with us. It was released in good health.

Diseases

Some common diseases we have seen in our bird patients are a good reason to follow the isolation procedures recommended earlier in this chapter.

Fowl pox is one of these and can develop in nestlings as well as adults. Lesions appear around the bill and mouth. As in poisoning cases, some survive and some do not. We use Panalog ointment (see Veterinary Reference) in treating the lesions, applying it twice daily.

Doves and pigeons are prone to canker. This is an ailment which develops in the mouth and throat, with nodules and swelling. It can be treated by a veterinarian in the early stages, but if it is well developed it is best to put the bird to sleep. It is highly contagious and can spread through the bird's drinking water or bath.

Pelicans often suffer from roundworms. These can be diagnosed by examining fish portions regurgitated by the pelican.

If he has roundworms they will be evident. The treatment for roundworms, Piperazine, is discussed in the Veterinary Reference section.

Fishhooks and Fishing Line Injuries

A whole chapter could be written on the removal of monofilament fishing line and fishhooks from pelicans and other shore and water birds, we have treated so many.

The general procedure is this: Have two people in on the job when dealing with a pelican with a fishhook embedded in its pouch or body. One holds the pelican, grasping the long bill with one hand and tucking the bird securely under the other arm. (That, in itself, is a job! I usually wind up holding the bird.) Watch out for the pelican's beak. The bird can use it, and it has a sharp hook that can inflict a nasty injury.

The barbed tip of the fishhook must be pushed through the skin and the barb cut off. Use wire cutters to clip the barb, then slide the hook shaft back out.

If stitches are needed in a pelican's pouch, the veterinarian might like to know that a pelican's pouch should be stitched on the inside as well as the outside if the tear is fairly long. Otherwise it may break open again. It was discovered that there is both an inner and outer lining involved in the pelican's pouch. Stitching both sides adds strength.

Monofilament fishing line is often embedded in flesh and feathers on a bird, and you must get it all when you take it off, either cutting or untangling as the case demands. Examine the legs carefully for embedded line, and try not to cut any flight feathers if you cut the line from the wings. Embedded areas may be swollen or infected and should be treated with Furacin (see Veterinary Reference). We keep our pelicans in an outdoor pen until the swelling goes down and the infection heals, or until they stop limping. Sulfamethazine is given orally during the convalescence.

We treat many pelicans, gulls, and terns with this problem, as we live on the Gulf of Mexico, where sea and shore birds sometimes compete with the fishermen to see who gets the fish. Many birds die of hook and line injuries, as the skeletons in our local rookeries will testify.

Capture and Transport

A long-handled net and gloves are essential in capturing hurt birds of prey, large water and shore birds, or any other bird which may inflict injury if you don't take proper precautions.

Smaller birds can be captured with a fine-meshed net (often available at pet shops). The handle should be 3 to 4 feet long. If the bird cannot fly but can hop about, slip up on it and pop the net over it. In removing the bird from the net, handle it gently. It can pinch and peck but can't seriously hurt you. Small birds can be transported in a shoebox or small cardboard container—just be sure to punch pencil-sized holes to allow plenty of ventilation.

Large birds such as pelicans, eagles, ospreys, hawks, and owls, as well as smaller ones such as gulls, terns, and loons, require a fish landing net with a handle at least 6 to 10 feet long and the largest diameter net you can get.

When capturing birds on the beach or shore, always approach from the water side, else the bird may escape into the water, where it is very hard to catch. Many birds can swim when they cannot walk or fly. Read Chapter 13 for details on how to slip up on wounded pelicans, loons, cormorants, and the like before they reach the water.

Always wear heavy clothing and gauntlets when handling large birds of prey. I use welder's gloves for this purpose. Lightweight plastic garden gloves are handy for many birds, such as gulls, loons, egrets, and even pelicans. The edges of these birds' bills are often razor sharp. Long-billed birds like herons and egrets will go for the eyes, and they have amazing accuracy, so watch it. Generally, once the bill is firmly in hand, the rest of the bird can kick and flap but cannot seriously injure you.

Birds of prey are often most easily captured by approaching them slowly until they take the defensive position, which is on their back with their feet and talons in the air. When you grab their feet, the talons instinctively lock on your gloved hand, and the bird can be lifted and placed in a box or cage.

If the bird of prey cannot fly but can move about, and does not assume the defensive position, you may want to pop the long-handled net or towel over it. Use caution when removing the bird from the net. If you use a towel, simply pick up towel, bird, and all to place in the traveling box.

For large birds, you can use a heavy cardboard box with air holes and a lid. Birds of prey like darkness; it is quieting. When handling or treating them, drape a towel over their heads (leaving breathing room) to keep them from becoming excited. This is why falconers keep their birds hooded when they are not hunting or exercising them. When examining a bird of prey, poke a thick folded towel at its feet. It will often lock onto the towel, keeping those talons occupied during the examination.

Dog or cat carriers—the kind that are enclosed on three sides with a door on one end—are also useful in transporting large birds.

When capturing an injured bird, two people are best. One can maneuver the net, while the other handles the bird when captured.

Remember always to grasp the bill of a large or long-necked bird when handling it to keep your own injuries to a minimum.

If, even after your best efforts, your patient dies, don't be too quick to blame yourself. We have lost patients, too, in spite of all we tried, and we have had patients which we found later would have died anyway, because they had a chronic or fatal illness.

It seems that sometimes wildlife abandon their young for just this reason—whether they know instinctively that their young are doomed, we do not know. But we have had both birds and mammals which died, and they seemed to fit this category. Many of our abandoned baby birds have died of unknown causes.

The real tragedy is when a wildlife patient dies because of ignorance or neglect. If you are caring for sick or injured wildlife, make sure you are well informed—and then take good care of your patient.

24
GLUNK!
Oil Spills

Oil spills have been much in the news, and the toll of wild birds and animals has been tragic. It was estimated that the Santa Barbara oil spill in January of 1969 destroyed 50 percent of the normal bird population—about 3,000 birds were lost. The San Francisco oil spill in January of 1971 cost more than 2,000 birds their lives. Oil spills came to our area in February 1970 when the tanker *Delian Apollon* ran aground in Tampa Bay and spilled more than 10,000 gallons of bunker-C fuel oil over a 100-square-mile area. The Florida Audubon Society estimated a loss of 1,000 birds along just one ten-mile stretch of shoreline. The dead included pelicans, grebes, loons, ducks, gulls, and mergansers.

As people have been doing everywhere, concerned citizens rushed in to try and save as many birds as they could. Many of them did more harm than good. Knowing what you are doing is the first step in helping anything, including oil-damaged birds.

In addition to being coated with heavy oil so they cannot fly, the birds swallow more oil in trying to clean themselves. In the struggle to reach the shore, many die of heart failure and exhaustion. Chilling and infection of the respiratory tract also cause death. Even the stress of being handled can kill an oil-sickened bird.

Cleaning

The first three rules for oil-damaged birds are:

1. Do not clean immediately. Wrap the bird in flannel securely, so it cannot preen its feathers and swallow more oil. Keep it quiet and warm in a cardboard box with a heating pad under it—75 to 80 degrees Farenheit is about right.
2. Force-feed one to two tablespoons of soft butter. This helps clean the oil out of the bird's digestive system.
3. Do not try to clean the oil from the bird's feathers for at least twelve hours. It needs a chance to rest and recuperate from shock before being handled.

It takes two people to clean one bird. One person must hold the head and bill (to avoid injury to humans), while the other handles the cleaning process. You must *avoid stress* to the bird as much as possible. Stress can cause death. Handle it roughly, and you may have a clean but dead bird. In cold climates, clean the bird indoors, away from drafts.

The two handiest household items for cleaning oil-soaked birds are cornmeal and salad oil. *Do not use* kerosene, turpentine, or gasoline. You will kill the bird. *Do not use* detergents. You will destroy natural feather oils.

It takes three to five hours to clean one bird properly using the cornmeal-and-salad-oil method, so be prepared for a long ordeal. Have plenty of rags and old towels on hand. Be very careful not to damage, break, or rub the feathers the wrong way. If the feathers are damaged, the bird will no longer be waterproof.

First, work salad oil gently into the bird's feathers. Use rags to wipe the oil off, squeezing carefully to remove the excess oil from the feathers.

Second, dust the bird with fine cornmeal. Wipe the cornmeal off the bird in the same manner. It takes up the oil residue.

Repeat the salad oil treatment, then the cornmeal, and so on, until the bird is as clean of oil as you can get it. You can occasionally rinse the bird with clear, warm water to help

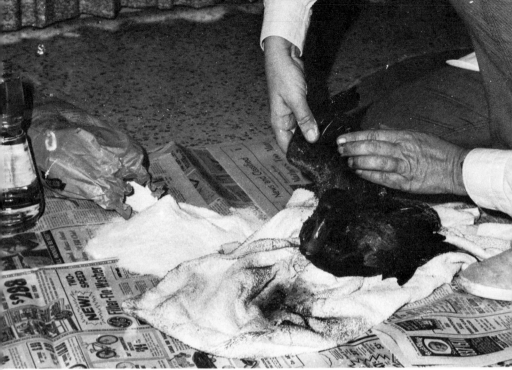

Cleaning a victim of the 1970 Tampa Bay oil spill, using cornmeal and salad oil. This scaup had to be cleaned many times before it was free of oil.

along the cleansing process. Finally, blot with a towel or use a nozzle-type hair dryer blower on a warm setting.

Aftercare

When the bird is clean, place it in a warm box, wrapped in clean flannel or a towel, and place a 75-watt bulb overhead for warmth. Put a heavy nontippable dish of water in the box. Oil-spill victims must be encouraged to drink water to avoid dehydration, but they must not get into their water dish. To encourage drinking, dip the bird's bill into the water a number of times until you can see it is drinking on its own. Oil-spill birds may, at first, show a fear of the water, but they must be encouraged to drink.

Badly damaged birds must be kept warm and dry for several weeks after the salad oil-cornmeal cleaning method. We house these birds, often singly, in indoor cartons or boxes. Loons do not seem to be particularly social and may jab at each other. Cormorants are the same. Scaups and some other ducks may be kept two or three to one large box.

We line the boxes with newspapers (preferably shredded) and change the papers twice a day. Sanitation is most important.

While the bird is recuperating, the feet should be kept oiled with a baby oil or mineral oil to prevent cracking. If the birds feet are allowed to dry out and crack, infection may set in.

Diet

For fish-eaters such as loons, gannets, and cormorants, we feed whole frozen smelts (thawed), usually available at the grocery store. Vitamin B_1 is extremely important when treating oil-damaged birds; the bird should have 100 milligrams daily. We administer it by making a slit in the fish we feed and inserting a 100-mg. tablet.

Our patients often needed force-feeding for the first few days. To force-feed, open the bill. Slide the fish as far back in the throat as possible, holding the bird's bill and neck up. Close the bill and gently stroke the throat. All my loons, gannets, and cormorants learned to take fish from my hand or from a dish (or simply dropped in front of them) within a few days. Remember again, when force-feeding pelicans, to put the fish down the *bird's right side* of the throat.

Terns and gulls may be fed very small fish, such as minnows, or chopped smelts. Often a bird will not take a piece of chopped fish, because it doesn't look like a fish, so force-feeding as just described may be needed for a while.

Gulls will often also eat soaked and drained dog kibbles.

We fed our ducks turkey or chick mash, mixed with water to a sloppy consistency. To start a duck eating, stick its bill in the mixture a few times. It will get a taste and soon begin eating on its own.

Release

If the feathers have not been damaged, and *if* the bird is completely free of oil and is waterproof, you can consider releasing it. The earlier the release, the better the chance of survival.

*Panta Loon, a victim of the Tampa Bay oil spill, is
exercised in a pool to check her waterproofing.*

Before releasing, you must be *sure* the bird is waterproof.
Check by placing the bird in a tub or a wading pool. Do this
for brief periods for several consecutive days, even up to a
week or more. At first it may seem to get waterlogged and
sink low in the water, but after a swim it will usually preen.
This will help restore waterproofing, provided the feathers are
not damaged and the oil gland is still functioning. Application
of baby oil, olive oil, or mineral oil to the feathers will *not* en-
sure waterproofing. It is only wasted effort.

When the bird finally swims well and stays afloat at the
proper level, you may consider releasing it. Try to release it
in the area from which it came, if there is no longer any
contamination. If that area is still unthinkable, find another
place with similar surroundings.

If a bird has suffered severe feather damage, or has completely lost its waterproofing because of lack of natural oils,
it may have to be cared for over a period of several months
to a year. After a complete molt, the bird should then be

ready for release. A premature release can result in the bird sinking and drowning.

Care of Nonreleasable Birds

Birds that cannot be released fairly soon after cleaning are kept indoors up to one month after initial cleaning, particularly in cold weather.

They can be placed in outdoor pens when the weather warms and there is no chance of pneumonia or chilling. We use wire enclosures, with clean builder's sand on the floors, or pens on the grass, which can be moved to clean the areas daily. We sometimes allow birds such as loons, which cannot take off from land, the freedom of the yard.

Remember to keep the feet of seabirds oiled to prevent cracking and infection.

New Methods

The cleaning methods discussed here have the advantage of utilizing ingredients available in any household and are certainly worth trying with a few isolated cases. But they often involve keeping the birds for a rather long period of time. It is difficult to keep most of them alive while recuperating, and many die in the process.

New methods have recently been developed, and they are especially applicable to use in a large, well-organized undertaking, such as a collective effort at a university after a major oil spill. The most comprehensive and successful have been worked out by Dr. James L. Naviaux, D.V.M., Director of the National Wildlife Health Foundation, 450 Boyd Road, Pleasant Hill, California 94523. Utilizing Dr. Naviaux's methods, birds may be released in just a few days.

Dr. Naviaux and his foundation have published an excellent booklet, "Aftercare of Oil-Covered Birds." It is a wealth of knowledge and information, based on the most thorough studies I know of, and it contains the latest and best methods of cleansing and treatment.

By all means, if you need help, contact Dr. Naviaux for further information. We have joined his foundation membership and support him in his work with oil-damaged birds.

25
WILDLIFE SPEAKS FOR ITSELF

As a part of our work, we give slide programs about wildlife and our environment at schools, libraries, hospitals, and nursing homes in our area. We travel up and down the west coast of Florida in our red van, the Ark, carrying our projection and sound equipment, along with some of our wildlife patients. Our aim is to show how important these creatures are to the balance of nature.

In the schools, we have found that direct contact with the living bird or mammal is important in helping children relate to the world of nature. After the slide program, the youngsters have a chance to ask questions and are allowed to pet the animals. We take along only well animals, some of whom have become permanent residents and are accustomed to being petted.

Brownie the rabbit was always a favorite, as well as Lovey the skunk, and both were veteran performers in our cast of characters. The children loved the contrast between stroking Brownie's soft fur and Lovey's coarse hair. The petting is important. A child who is able to touch a live, real, warm, living creature learns that it is something quite different from a target for rock throwing or BB practice.

Some of our animals cannot be petted. Snowflake the crow

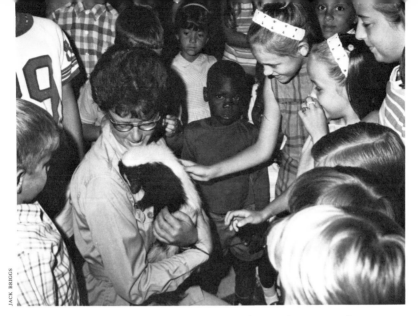

Lovey being petted by a group of children after one of our summer programs at the Venice Area Public Library.

only perches on my hand. He sometimes heckles the audience with his jabber, which delights everyone. It was in a classroom that he made his first flight from babyhood, and the kids enjoyed the unrehearsed part of the program—me climbing a chair to the top of a bookcase to get him down from what was suddenly to him a fearful height.

Snowflake the crow greets the children from my hand at an elementary school program.

Neither can Barry, the barred owl, be petted, but he impresses the children with his dignified manner, his round-eyed stare, and his powerful talons clutching my glove. When I tell them his wing was shattered by gunshot and he can never fly again, there is a moan of sympathy from the audience.

The children love especially the baby birds and animals, and we take infants along when we have them. They like to watch me feed a baby bird, poking food into its gaping little mouth while I make mama-bird noises.

Willy, a baby gopher turtle, presents a contrast for them when shown with his adult cousin, Tommy, who measures about 1 foot across the back and weighs close to 15 pounds. I let Tommy crawl around after the show, and the children stroke his broad back while I explain the difference in coloration and size between him and little Willy.

Baby raccoons are especially popular, but I only take them to programs when they are quite young. They are hard to handle and unpredictable as they grow older. Baby opossums, bunnies, and squirrels are always a big hit because they are so cute, tiny, and cuddly.

One of our new stars is Christopher, a gentle ferret that I recently liberated from a pet shop. Christopher is a girl ferret, but I named her after St. Christopher, the patron saint of travelers, because the day I acquired her our van had a series of breakdowns and only just made it home. Christopher likes to yawn and grin at the kids, showing her set of sharp little teeth.

After we have visited a school, the children sometimes write us letters and send us drawings of our performers. Many a rescued animal or bird has been brought to our door by children who have seen our program. Children's groups often tour our home to see the animals and birds, and the Scouts are regular visitors.

We will always remember with special affection a program we gave at an elementary school one winter day. We could not accept an invitation before Christmas, because of our crowded schedule, but managed to get there on January 6. We noticed while we were setting up our equipment in the classroom that there was an unusual stir of excitement among the children. After the program of slides and talk, but before the animal

Lovey and I doing a program for the children of Venice Elementary School.

petting session, there was again much whispering and bustling about. We soon found out why. The children produced from the closet several mysterious boxes decorated with Christmas tree ornaments and ribbons and marked "Christmas in January." As each child passed by to pet the animals, a gift was presented and placed in the boxes: a carrot with a Christmas bow on it, an orange wrapped in shiny foil, a bag of birdseed decorated with a bright red ribbon, a box of raisins wrapped in Christmas paper, a can of dog food wrapped in gay tissue. It was a lovely time. I like to think the children enjoyed that Christmas in January as much as we did.

Older children have also been responsive to our work with wildlife. The Ecology Club at the Venice Junior High School has taken an active interest, and several of its members have helped by coming on weekends to build large flights for our birds. We have furnished material and tools, and they have supplied the labor and a generous amount of their free time. At this writing, they have made seven flights and are still building. It is a joy to see our birds flitting around in their new roomy quarters in the backyard sunshine. Such a grand gift makes us realize that there are plenty of other people in this world who care as much as we do and know how to show it in a very practical way.

One day we were asked to do a program for the mental health unit at a nearby hospital. When the invitation was made, I was a little apprehensive. I was afraid that I might say something wrong, or that the pictures of some of our hurt birds and animals might upset the patients. But the nurse who invited us thought the program would be good therapy; she said the patients were almost well enough to leave the hospital and would benefit from such an opportunity to relate to the outside world again before going back to it. We accepted.

We loaded up the Ark with our projection equipment and took along our prize actors: Lovey, Tommy Turtle, Brownie Rabbit, and, for a special treat, Thunder, a crane hawk.

We carried our equipment into the hospital dining room, where a bulletin board was posted with news clippings about our work. I set up the sound system while George readied the projector and slides and brought in the animal cages. We were going to do one of our most popular and basic wildlife programs, beginning with "Nature's Creatures," a general show on wildlife, and followed by "Wall to Wall Wildlife," a look at us caring for our wildlife patients in our home.

The hospital patients filed in, not looking at us or at one another. Some of them just sat down in their chairs and stared at the floor. Usually when I give a program, I chat with people as they arrive, if it's no more than "Good morning," or "Nice day," but my overtures got no reaction from this audience. There were no answers, no smiles, just total withdrawal. Some reacted only by hanging their heads to my "Hello." The patients ranged in ages from sixteen to seventy, but there was no variation in their total lack of response to us and what we were doing. It gave me an uneasy feeling to smile and speak to someone and get no answer. So I hurried to get the show under way as soon as everyone was seated.

I made up my mind to go ahead and do the show just as I always did, with cheerfulness and enthusiasm and energy. I hoped it might get through to somebody.

I started with my usual brief introduction. No reaction. I signaled for lights out and began the slide show. During the first half of the program they were still quiet. When we reached the second half, and a slide flashed on showing our baby raccoons, there were a few chuckles from the darkness. The pelican in the bathtub brought a few more, and the atmosphere had lightened considerably by the time the show ended.

Then we brought out the animals. Tommy the turtle was greeted with a noticeable lack of enthusiasm, Thunder the crane hawk caused a stir of interest, and Brownie Rabbit rated a few smiles and nods.

With Lovey, I gave the invitation to come forward and pet him. No one did.

I sat down next to a little old man in the front row and said, "Wouldn't you like to pet Lovey?"

He didn't flinch away from Lovey but only said shyly, "I'll just look at him if you don't mind."

But then someone near him reached over and tentatively stroked Lovey, and the ice was broken. Others began to come forward, and soon I was surrounded by reaching hands, stroking shy quiet Lovey and timid gentle Brownie. They asked questions. Where did they get their names? What did we feed them? Where did we get them?

The show broke up in a cheerful relaxed atmosphere. And no one was more thrilled than we were to see the change in those people. The nurse was so pleased with the results of the program, she asked us to come back again. We were glad to accept. After seeing the miracle wrought by our wildlife actors, we never worried again about doing a show there.

Nursing homes enjoy our animals, too. At one program, I noticed an elderly lady in a wheelchair in the front row, dozing and snoring lightly throughout the slide presentation. Hardly the best audience, I had ever had, I thought—but then her eyes snapped open as the animals were brought in. Lovey the skunk was there, and she wanted to pet him. Altogether, Lovey and I made four trips to that old lady's wheelchair. She kept wanting to pet Lovey "just one more time."

We cannot go everywhere we are asked. We charge nothing for programs given to schools, libraries, and hospitals, and the east coast of Florida is too far away and too expensive for us. But we try to cover cities and towns within an 80-mile radius of our home when our schedule permits.

Our Ark is old and journeys with difficulty now, and some of our beloved "actors" in our cast of characters have lived out their life spans. But we still wend our way to the classrooms and the hospital wards, bringing the world of nature to young and old whenever we can.

Our chief purpose is to make others aware of the importance of protecting animal life, but we also like to share some of the enrichment that these wild creatures bring to our own lives every day as we work with them. For as people help them, they help people, and it is rewarding to see how the animals and birds work their magic with different groups. The children seem to feel a particular bond with the living, warm, breathing creatures that are dependent on them in a trusting way yet completely independent in their natural element. The elderly get a special pleasure out of the attention an animal gives to them alone. The ill appear to be drawn out of themselves and their problems for a little while—long enough, perhaps, to get a better perspective of relationships again.

The benefits conferred are impossible for me to measure. But I am convinced, from my own experience, that anyone who involves himself actively and intimately with the wild creatures around him will find unexpected personal rewards. Maybe they have to do with gaining a sense of the unity of all nature—a feeling that in preserving nature we are preserving a part of ourselves. I don't pretend to know what the rewards of such involvement will mean to others. I can only hope this book will encourage them to find out for themselves.

Many hands pet Snowball the rabbit after a schoolroom wildlife presentation. Petting the animals is the most popular part of our wildlife program.

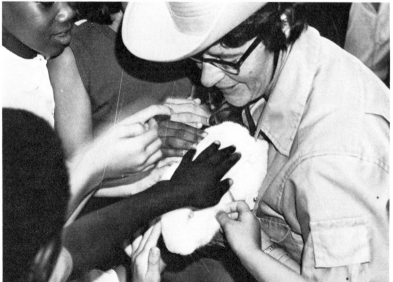

JANICE COLLETT

Appendix I
Cages and Housing

The basic construction for all cages is the same, utilizing the same type of wire mesh and tools. Variations occur in dimensions, type of door or entrance, and flooring. There are also differences in cage furniture, such as nest boxes, perches, and shelves.

Small cages can be constructed fairly easily by one person. However, it is helpful if two people work together on larger cages or flights. In one instance, when building a rather large cage, George and I found that we needed a third pair of hands while attaching the roof wire, because the wire, which comes in rolls, has a tendency to buckle. We enlisted the help of our daughter, Jan, who was then seven years old. We popped Jan into the nearly completed cage, and she held up the roof wire while we went around the sides, clipping it on. Since we never cut door openings until the cage is completed, the outcome in this case was a fully completed cage, with Jan inside but with no entrance or exit cut.

As we fastened the final roof portion and were about to cut a door opening so Jan could emerge, the doorbell rang. It was an acquaintance who had long wanted to visit and meet some of our unusual patients. Imagine her surprise, when entering the backyard, to find a cage with no door, housing our seven-year-old! Jan was always a quiet, patient child, and she had seated herself, cross-legged, on the cage floor, waiting till Mom and Dad had time to cut an opening. She was softly humming to herself.

Our visitor, inspecting a number of patients, kept glancing over her shoulder at Jan in the cage. She was finally driven to ask, "Does she spend much time in there?"

My reply was, "She outgrew her other cage."

The visitor left shortly thereafter, and we have never seen her again.

Materials

Most of the cages we build are freestanding affairs. Only the largest outdoor walk-in types need any sort of framing.

Materials and tools for basic cage construction are simple:

1. Galvanized welded wire, purchased in 100-foot rolls through hardware stores or feedstores.
2. Cage clip pliers, purchased at feedstores or from agricultural suppliers, and occasionally from hardware stores.
3. Cage clips (also called ferrules), ordered through feedstores and some hardware stores.
4. Metal tape measure.
5. Four-inch eye screws, found in hardware stores.
6. Heavy-duty wire cutters, obtained at hardware stores.

We always use galvanized welded wire rather than hardware cloth. The welded wire is sturdier and lasts longer. It must be galvanized to resist rusting.

Galvanized wire comes in rolls of assorted widths. These can vary from 18 inches to 6 feet. For small indoor cages we find the 2-foot width useful, while for large outdoor cages 4- and 6-foot widths are the best.

Planning

Appropriate types and sizes of cages have been discussed in each chapter. While the sizes given are approximate, for guidance only, generally speaking it is better to make the cage a little bigger than you might think necessary. So when in doubt, add a bit to the dimensions you are considering. Birds and mammals need room in which to move about to keep healthy and to avoid cage paralysis.

The tall, narrow, round birdcages so popular with some people may be decorative, but they are a disaster for birds. Birds need a cage that is *longer* than it is high or wide. This provides flying room, which is essential to maintain a healthy bird.

Exceptions to this are outdoor cages temporarily housing patients such as gulls or pelicans, prior to release. Also, birds such as our permanently disabled barred owl, Barry, do not need great height and length. Barry can no longer fly, so his cage is not very high, but it is long and wide enough to allow freedom of movement on the ground.

When planning your cage, you will find it will generally come under one of the following categories:

1. Smaller indoor cages to house birds or small mammals.
2. Medium-size outdoor cages to house songbirds and others prior to release, or very small mammals such as chipmunks. The wire floor on these cages is raised above the ground to permit droppings to fall through.
3. Large outdoor cages and flights for larger birds or mammals, prior to release, or for permanent residents. These cages have a flooring of clean builder's sand. Depending on size, they may need a framework to support them. They often have a safety door.
4. Portable pens for nonflying birds. These are a simple circle or oval of wire, with no roof or floor, and can be moved to fresh areas daily.

INDOOR CAGES

Cage Construction

STEP 1: Planning and Design

The first step in cage construction is to design the cage on paper and choose the proper width and mesh of wire.

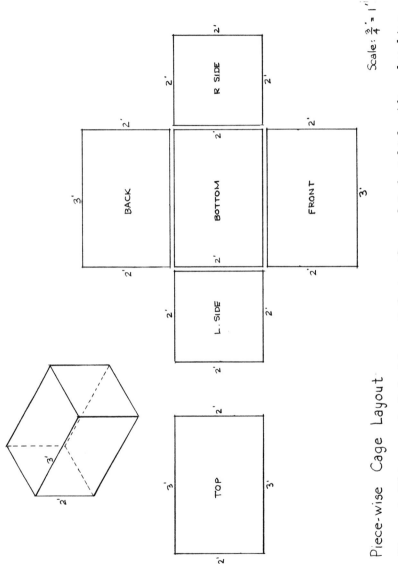

Piece-wise Cage Layout

Scale: $\frac{3}{4}'' = 1'$

Figure 1. This cage is 3 feet long, 2 feet wide, and 2 feet high. After sketching the six cage sides needed, labeling dimensions, you will cut four pieces of wire 3 feet long by 2 feet wide (for the top, bottom, front, and back) and two pieces of wire 2 feet long by 2 feet wide for each side (or end) piece.

Smaller cages are easy to build. We use ½-by-1-inch mesh wire for small birds and mammals. Larger cages can also be designed using the basic method below.

STEP 2: Cutting the Wire

After you have drawn the plan on paper and figured the number and sizes of various pieces needed (see figure 1), it's time to start cutting.

Handling a roll of springy wire can be dangerous and requires caution. The wire comes tightly rolled, and I have often envisioned myself caught, as the wire springs back when I unfasten it, and rolled up inside! Luckily, this has not yet happened, because in order to protect myself when cutting wire, I utilize eye screws inserted in the mesh before unfastening the roll to keep the wire from springing open or shut.

Stand the roll of wire on end. Insert a 4-inch eye screw into the mesh, twisting until the eye portion is almost even with the wire. (Same technique as inserting a screw into a piece of wood.) Be sure to keep the eye portion adjusted so it cannot slip through the mesh, releasing its hold. Use two or three eye screws. Place them vertically in the roll, one above the other, at 1- or 2-foot intervals, to prevent the wire from unwinding.

You generally cannot unroll the full amount you need at one time. You must unroll to the eye screws and then move them around the roll, one at a time, placing them as far back in the roll as possible, and gently unroll some more, repeating these steps until you have enough. The roll must be kept under control at all times.

Now measure length of wire needed, using tape measure, and cut with wire cutters. If the cutting line, measured precisely, will bisect the open spaces of the mesh, move the line over to include the next vertical strand of wire and crop closely to eliminate any horizontal wire spikes. We start at the top and work down carefully along the vertical strand. This leaves, of course, a row of wire ends bristling along the beginning edge of the next piece to be cut. They are cut off, and the next piece is measured from this vertical strand, and so on.

Plan the size of your wire pieces carefully to make the best use of your wire and to avoid wasting it. For instance: If you are using a 4-foot-wide roll of wire and you want two finished pieces 2 feet long and 2 feet wide, you must remember that you cannot simply cut the 4-foot-wide piece in half. You must take into consideration the size of the mesh. Even using ½-by-1-inch mesh, one of your pieces would be at least half an inch too short. Study a piece of wire closely. Measure it as if you are about to cut, and you will see what I mean. When cutting the wire, you always lose one width of mesh on the remaining piece.

If you have carefully laid out the plan on paper beforehand, you will avoid much wasted wire and time.

We try to have our front, back, and side panels finished with the larger dimension of the mesh running vertically. We find it more attractive in appearance and easier to install doors, perches, and water bottles.

Top and bottom panels can have the mesh running in either direction, just so the outer measurements of the finished piece are correct.

STEP 3: Wire Dance

Assuming you have cut the correct number of pieces in the correct sizes (see figure 1 for a basic example), without entangling yourself too seriously, the next step is the "wire dance."

Since the wire has been tightly rolled, the cut pieces have a tendency to curl. This makes them a bit hard to work with, so we invented the "wire dance." The steps are not intricate and are quite easy to learn. Here, again, it's handy having two people for the dance if the piece of wire is fairly large.

Find a nice flat firm surface. We use our concrete driveway. (I advise against performing this dance indoors, since the wire is really rough on hardwood and polished floors.) Lay the wire, concave side down, on the hard surface, hop on before it curls up, and begin to dance—flat-footed. If you're a lightweight like my Coonrad Hilton friend, Mary, you may be somewhat ineffective. It takes a good heavyweight to do the job properly. George and I have no trouble.

Start at one end of the wire and stomp about. Travel up and down the length, and back and forth across the width. Use any variation of steps you choose. It's your dance. Just keep it up for a while, and soon you will find that the wire has flattened out considerably and is much easier to handle.

Waltzes and tangos are not suggested. Flat-footed polkas or jitterbugging work better.

George and I frequently gather quite a crowd of spectators when performing the wire dance in the driveway.

STEP 4: Putting It All Together

As figure 1 shows, you now have six pieces of wire, cut to the correct dimensions and partially flattened by the wire dance. Now comes the chore of hooking them together. This is where you utilize the cage clip pliers and cage clips.

The pliers have specially curved jaws, into which the small cage clip fits. The jaws are placed around the two pieces of wire to be joined, with the partially curved clip encircling them. Squeezing the pliers locks the clip around the wires. Be sure both wires are caught within the clip.

We begin with the cage bottom and the front, lining up the edges and clipping them together. We place a clip every two or three spaces (meshes). Then we clip the back piece and the two side pieces to the cage bottom.

Then, with the cage bottom still flat, we raise the front section and one side section, so that they meet at right angles, and clip their edges together, starting at the bottom and working all the way to the top. We do the same with the back piece and the other side piece, joining all edges carefully.

Remember: Be sure to match the mesh as closely as possible when clipping all edges together. Otherwise you may end up with one piece sticking out an inch too far in one direction or another.

Last to be done is the top. This occasionally initiates a struggle between cage builder and wire, but can be accomplished with a little effort and much patience. Lay the final piece on top of the whole shebang. Starting on one long edge, carefully clip the top to the upper edge of the cage, placing a clip every two or three spaces. Work your way around a side, along the other long edge, and across the final side.

Voilà! You have a cage! Well, almost.

STEP 5: Doors

You now have a square or rectangular cage—a little lopsided, maybe, on your first try, but you'll improve with practice. Next you need a door. How else will you place a crittur inside or put in food and water? We always cut door openings *after* the cage is completed, to avoid excess bowing or weakening of the wire during construction.

Making the door is a simple matter. Cut an opening as large as needed. Then cut a spare piece of wire larger than the door opening. In both cases cut flush along the parallel wire strands so there will be no bristling wires to hurt you or your animal. We overlap the door at least 2 inches all around on standard cages. Attach one door edge to the cage wire with several cage clips. They make an excellent hinge.

Small doors can be fastened shut with a spring-type clothespin, a spring hooked from door to cage wire, or a snap such as is used on dog leashes. Just be sure it will latch and hold securely.

On cages for birds, we find it best to place the door opening low on the cage. A bird's natural tendency is to fly *up* when startled. Since you will be using the door to place food and water in the cage daily, there is less chance of a bird's escape if the door is low. Do *not*, however, cut the opening at the very bottom of the cage. This weakens the entire structure and gives no room for overlapping the door at the bottom edge. Stay up a couple of inches.

(*Note:* Placing perches high in the cage will also lessen the possibility of escape.)

STEP 6: Cage Flooring

For small indoor cages, the bottom can be covered with newspapers which can be changed daily through the door opening.

We have had specially constructed trays made to fit some

of our indoor cages, but the procedure is a bit complicated, so I shall not detail it here.

It is helpful to place a piece of heavy-duty plastic under the entire cage to protect the surface upon which it rests.

For small indoor cages housing mammals such as chipmunks, we have our local welder build a pan of galvanized metal a couple of inches wider than the cage base. The pan has a lip about 2 inches tall on all four sides. The cage is set into the pan, and cedar chips are sprinkled on the wire floor. The chips are absorbent and have a nice odor, and the lip of the pan keeps them from scattering all over the living room rug.

OUTDOOR CAGES

As explained in previous chapters, we have many outdoor cages for recuperating patients. These cages, some as large as 6 feet long, 4 feet wide, and up to 6 feet high, can be built using the method described for indoor cages. If no larger than the above measurements, and built of heavy-gauge welded wire, these cages will be freestanding and need no framework.

The wire most frequently used for all our cages, indoors and out, has a ½-by-1-inch mesh. For larger creatures, such as owls, hawks, eagles, and raccoons, we use a 1-by-2-inch mesh.

Using the same method of design and construction discussed, build the outdoor cage you need. Set it on level ground. Put clean builder's sand on top of the wire floor. This can be removed and renewed as needed. The wire beneath the sand holds the shape of the cage and prevents entrance of any digging intruders such as rats, mice, or snakes.

If you are housing mammals such as raccoons, skunks, or opossums in an outdoor cage, it is best to raise the wire floor a couple of feet above the ground. This allows droppings to fall through and is more sanitary. You may build a wooden frame of 2-by-4 lumber and set the cage on this. Or you could support each corner with a stack of concrete blocks.

Be sure to provide a roof and back to give protection from hot sun, rain, and cold winds. These can be made of exterior or marine plywood, as shown in figure 2.

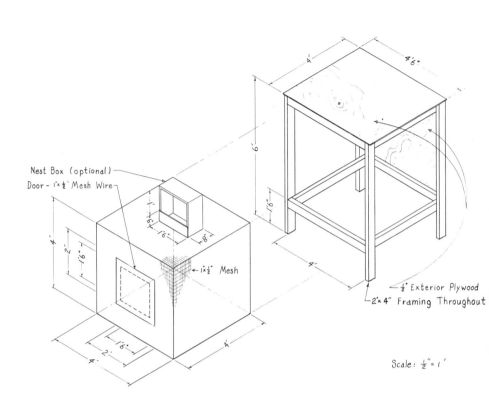

Figure 2. *This type of stand and cage can be used outdoors for small mammals or birds. The wooden frame of the stand can be made of 2-by-4s, with exterior or marine plywood roof and back. (Partial sides of plywood may be added if needed.) The freestanding cage made of welded wire slides into the stand, resting on the 2-by-4 framework at least 18 inches above the ground. (Wire here is ½-by-1-inch mesh but can be 1-by-2-inch mesh for mammals.) Nest box as shown in upper corner would be ideal for raccoons or squirrels. For opossums or skunks, place nest box at floor level.*

Doors of the larger outdoor cages need reinforcement. We build a frame of 1-by-2 lumber and attach the standard wire door to this with heavy staples, leaving at least a 2-inch margin of mesh on all sides. We then attach the door by clipping one mesh edge to the cage in the usual manner. (The wooden frame will be on the *outside* of the door to allow for easy closing.) The door on larger cages overlaps the opening by 4 to 6 inches. We use spring clips as door fastenings on these cages, rather than cage clips.

Door openings usually begin about 4 inches from the cage bottom on this type of cage and are fairly tall. The enclosed bird or mammal can then easily leave the cage at release time. We have kept recuperating pelicans, cormorants, gulls, herons, and others in such cages.

Flights

Larger cages, often called flights, can be 8 feet or more long, at least 6 feet tall, and 4 or more feet wide. Flights of this size will need a framing for support.

Our local welder has made frames by welding sections of pipe together in whatever size we need. We use pipe frames because they are more easily cleaned than wood and can be moved if necessary.

We clip the top and all four sides of the wire together, slip it over the pipe frame, and attach the bottom edge of the wire to the pipe frame with galvanized wire, wrapping it around the pipe and through the wire mesh.

These flights generally have no wire floor, as most of the birds kept in them cannot dig their way out. Should any other creature dig its way in, the cage occupant would enjoy an extra meal. We once found a very large, very dead rat carefully draped across the stump in our raven's cage. Edgar looked at us as though to say, "Aren't you proud of me?"

We place these flights on level ground with clean builder's sand on the bottom. We can rake it once or twice a week, removing accumulated droppings, and can dig out the old sand and put in fresh about every six months.

These flights usually have the standard plywood roof and back, as described earlier.

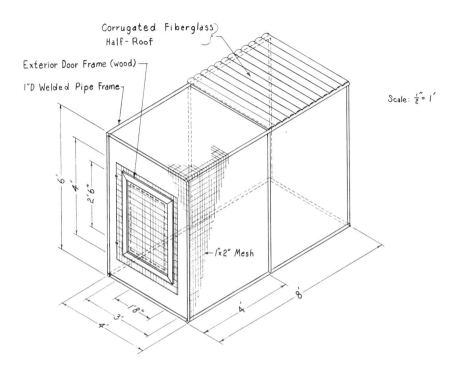

Corrugated Fiberglass
Half-Roof

Exterior Door Frame (wood)

1"D Welded Pipe Frame

Scale: $\frac{1}{2}$"= 1'

6'

4'

2'6"

1"x2" Mesh

1'8"

3'

4'

4'

8'

Figure 3. This type of flight, with its welded pipe frame and 1-by-2-inch-mesh galvanized welded wire, would be ideal for birds of prey and large birds such as ravens. We use corrugated fiberglass for the roof rather than plywood on many of these flights. The fiberglass is lightweight. Using a roll of fiberglass, you can simply extend the length down the back end of the flight or cage to provide more shelter at the back. Note the large wire door with its wooden frame for stiffening. The frame is made of schedule-40 ½-inch galvanized water pipe, welded. (The dimensions shown are just an example. Larger flights may be constructed in a similar manner.)

Safety Doors

Safety doors are a very important feature of large flights to prevent the escape of the occupant. They serve both permanent residents and those not quite well enough to be safely released.

The safety door is simply an extra "cage" placed in front of the flight's main entrance and attached to the flight at the top and side edges. It need only be large enough for you to enter, carrying food, water, or other essentials, and close the outer door before opening the inner door to the main flight.

Should a bird or animal dash past as you enter the main doorway, the safety door, or vestibule, keeps it from escaping. It is a simple matter to coax it back into its main flight.

Portable Pens

Portable pens for smaller flightless birds are easily made. Cut a piece of 18- to 24-inch-wide wire to whatever length you need. (Most of our cages of this type are anywhere from 12 to 30 feet in circumference.) Curve it into a circle or oval and clip the two ends together. Set it on grass, and you have temporary housing for loons, grebes, and other birds which cannot take off from land. The pen will need no top as long as you have no marauding cats or dogs in the neighborhood. Place it where a portion of the pen is shaded so the bird will not become overheated. In the event of a heavy rain, you can place a sheet of plywood across the top until the rain stops. Even in the wild, wild creatures usually seek protection from a downpour. Move the pen to a clean area daily.

Cage Furniture

Cage furniture—perches, shelves, nest boxes—are discussed in individual chapters.

When building shelves or nest boxes, use exterior or marine plywood. If you paint such items, use nonlead paint so the occupant cannot suffer lead poisoning.

Wooden barrels, minus the lid and mounted horizontally, often make good nest boxes. For climbing animals like raccoons and squirrels, mount the nest box in an upper cage corner. For nonclimbing animals like striped skunks, place the box on the cage floor.

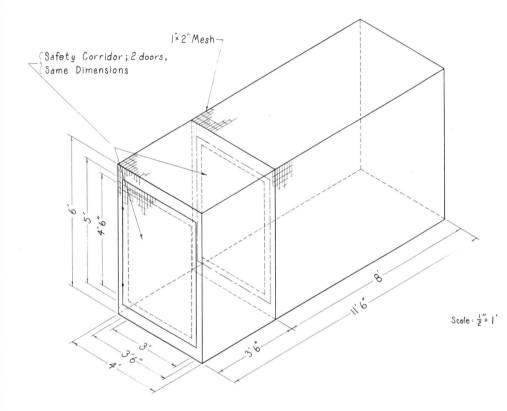

Figure 4. To construct a safety door, build a smaller, five-sided cage. Match the open side with the flight front and clip together with cage clips at side and top edges. Be sure the outer door swings out. If the flight is large enough, you may want the inner door to open into the flight. This leaves more room to maneuver in the vestibule.

The temperature rarely drops below freezing in our area, but we do provide old towels or burlap bags for animals to use as cover in cooler weather. I would advise against using metal nest boxes in extremely cold climates.

Natural tree limbs make the best perches for birds. They are better for a bird's feet than smooth wooden dowel rods. Be sure to use branches from nonpoisonous trees.

EMERGENCY MEASURES

Not everyone will want to buy a 100-foot roll of wire. We do, because our work is done on such a large scale. The average person may want to build only one or two cages. In this event, you may be able to purchase shorter lengths of welded wire or find leftover pieces near construction sites.

If no welded wire is available, heavy gauge hardware cloth may be used, though I do not advise it as it lacks the strength and durability of welded wire. A small cage may be constructed of hardware cloth, using the same method as for welded wire. This will generally not be suitable for larger cages, or for cages meant to house such creatures as raccoons or birds of prey.

Helpful for the person who has but one or two small songbirds to nurse back to health are the large flight cages made for finches and sold in pet stores. They have a removable tray for easy cleaning and will serve the purpose if the bird is fairly small. We use many large finch cages for our young songbirds until they are ready to graduate to an outdoor flight, and we always have at least a half dozen of the old faithful standbys—cardboard boxes—around for nonflying bird patients. Ours come from Television of Venice, our friendly TV dealer, who saves them for us.

And, of course, there's always the bathtub for sick shore and water birds. Just keep the cleanser and Lysol handy!

Appendix II
Natural Diet of Some Common Birds

Once you have established the identity of an infant bird, this chart may help you choose the correct baby bird formula. The foods checked indicate the diet of the bird in the wild.

If you find yourself with a nighthawk in hand, the chart shows you that this bird eats only insects. Therefore you will want to refer to the diet in chapter 9 on insectivorous birds.

If you have a cardinal, catbird, or mockingbird, which eat a variety of things, you will find their diet in the preceding chapter on song and garden birds.

Bird	Seed	Fruit	Insect	Insect Only
Bluebird		x	x	
Blue jay	x	x	x	
Bunting	x			
Cardinal	x		x	
Catbird	x	x	x	
Cedar waxwing		x	x	
Chickadee	x		x	
Chuck-will's-widow				x
Crow	x	x	x	
Cuckoo				x

Bird	Seed	Fruit	Insect	Insect Only
Dove	x	x	x	
Finch	x			
Flycatcher				x
Gnatcatcher				x
Grackle	x	x	x	
Grosbeak	x			
Junco				
Mockingbird		x	x	
Nighthawk				x
Nuthatch				x
Oriole		x	x	
Purple martin				x
Raven		x	x	
Red-winged blackbird	x		x	
Robin		x	x	
Scrub jay	x		x	
Sparrow	x			
Starling		x	x	
Swallow				x
Tanager		x	x	
Thrasher				x
Towhee	x		x	
Vireo				x
Warbler				x
Woodpecker	x	x	x	
Wren				x

Appendix III
Veterinary Reference

Many veterinarians are not familiar with treating some of the species of wildlife mentioned in these chapters. If your vet would like to see references on some of these species and their problems, refer him to the following guide. It lists medications and treatments we have used successfully with our patients.

Little is generally known about drug tolerance in certain wildlife species, and there are still many unanswered questions. Perhaps those answers will come in time.

MEDICINAL

Furacin ®: This comes in liquid or ointment form. We have successfully used the liquid form on birds for fresh lacerations. It stimulates healing. (Eaton Laboratories, Division of Norwich Pharmaceutical Company, Norwich, New York 13815.)

Kaomycin ®: We have used this preparation on infant raccoons with diarrhea at the rate of 5 to 6 drops, twice a day, administered orally with a medicine dropper, until the stool appeared firm. (The Upjohn Company, Kalamazoo, Michigan 49002.)

Monsel's salts: This liquid is used to stop bleeding of minor injuries such as a bird's broken toenail. I keep this on hand at all times and apply with a cotton swab. (Available from a veterinarian.)

Mycitracin ®: An ophthalmic ointment, containing three antibiotics, with petrolatum base, it is extremely useful in treating active eye infections in water birds. We have applied the ointment two or three times daily, when needed, to many birds, including pelicans, loons, herons, mergansers, ducks, and gulls. (The Upjohn Company, Kalamazoo, Michigan 49002.)

Panalog ®: This is an antibiotic ointment which we have used with excellent results on both birds and mammals for lacerations and chronic lesions. (E. R. Squibb, 909 Third Avenue, New York, N.Y. 10022.)

Piperazine: We have used this liquid for pelicans afflicted with roundworms. Dosage was ½ cc. per pound of body weight (approximately 2½ cc. for a 5-pound pelican). This can be repeated in ten days if necessary. The method of administering we used was by syringe, minus needle. The tip of the syringe is placed as far back in the pelican's throat as possible, on the *right* side. (That is, the *bird's* right side, which would be to your left when facing him. See chapter 13 for further information.) Squirt the liquid in the throat, and follow with a fish.

Prednisolone: On occasions when birds have been stressed and refusing to eat, prednisolone 5 to 10 mg. has been used to alleviate symptoms of stress and to stimulate appetite. We have always used antibiotics with this, and the injectable antibiotics we have used have been procaine and penicillin G and streptomycin, usually combined with benzathine penicillin G.

Procaine penicillin G in crystalline dihydrostreptomycin sulfate solution, 200,000 units penicillin, −.025 g. per cc. dihydrostreptomycin. In same syringe: benzathine penicillin G, each unit 150,000 units. Inject into pectoral muscle.

Sulfamethazine: See Sulmet.

Sulmet ®: This is a 12.5 percent sodium sulfamethazine drinking water solution. Mix 1 tablespoon Sulmet in 1 gallon water. This is half the recommended dosage for chickens, turkeys, and ducks. We have used this successfully with many birds, from tiny sparrows to blue jays, hawks, or pelicans. We frequently put new patients suffering from broken bones or any type of respiratory problem or wound on this immediately. We use this mixture instead of plain water, for a period of five days. The next four days we give plain water. Then we give Sulmet for three more days if needed.

I have also used undiluted Sulmet for pelicans suffering from various ailments, such as digestive tract infections. The dosage is usually 2 cc. daily, administered as with piperazine. (If the pelican will accept fish, the Sulmet can be injected in the fish fed to the bird.)

In cases of dehydration and weakness, especially in shore and water birds, and when infection is also suspected or apparent, I often add Sulmet to Gatorade. This can be done at the rate of 1 tablespoon Sulmet to 1 gallon Gatorade. However, for smaller amounts, I often add 1 teaspoon Sulmet to about 1 quart Gatorade. This solution is then given the bird in lieu of water for five days. (Agricultural Division, American Cyanamid Company, Princeton, New Jersey 08540.)

SURGICAL

Anesthetics: Local anesthetics such as procaine ½ to 1 cc. have worked well in pelicans for wing amputations. Fluothane administered by trachea tube has been very effective for more prolonged procedures.

Micropore surgical tape ®: We have found this paper tape far better for use on birds than regular adhesive. It does less damage to a bird's feathers and is lightweight. We use the 1-inch-wide tape most frequently. We have found it better, also, when taping a broken or injured wing, to tape only the one wing, leaving the good wing free. This helps the bird keep its balance. Also, tightly binding both wings may cause respiratory problems, by interfering with the normal abdominal movements. (Minnesota Mining and Manufacturing Company, Medical Products Division, St. Paul, Minnesota 55119.)

Sutures: Suturing the stumps of amputated wings with 3/0 chromic catgut has produced no problems and solves the need for removing sutures.

Tape-Off ®: This aerosol spray is very useful in removing paper or adhesive tape from birds. It leaves no oily residue on the feathers. (Coastal Medical Supply, Inc., Houston, Texas 77021.)

DIETARY

Bone meal: I use the steamed veterinarian type made for animal consumption. This is added to bird-of-prey diets as per instructions in those chapters. (Available through pet shops or veterinarians.)

Calcium gluconate: This is a powdered substance I also add to bird-of-prey diets. (Available at drugstores.)

Esbilac ®: This is a substitute bitch's milk made primarily for dogs and cats and available through your veterinarian or pet shop. We have found this the ideal formula for all small mammals and have used it successfully on infant raccoons, squirrels, rabbits, opossums, rats, mice, and armadillos. Many zoos use this product for babies ranging from chimps to tigers. (Smith-Douglass, Division of Borden Chemical, Borden, Inc., Norfolk, Virginia 23501.)

Gatorade ®: This imitation citrus drink, containing glucose, is used particularly on shore and water birds exhibiting symptoms of dehydration. We supply this liquid for the first three days in lieu of water. Sulmet is added, if infection is visible, at the rate of 1 teaspoon per 2 to 3 cups Gatorade. (Stokely-Van Camp, Inc., Indianapolis, Indiana 46206.)

Pet-Tabs ®: These are vitamin-mineral tablets. We give one of these chewable tablets daily to raccoons and skunks. (Ste-Med Pharmaceuticals, Division of the S. E. Massengill Company, Veterinary Department, Bristol, Tennessee 37620.)

Theralin ®: This is another vitamin-mineral powder supplement that we have used when Vionate was not available. (Lambert-Kay, Inc., Los Angeles, California 90018.)

Vionate ®: This is a vitamin-mineral powder supplement available at many pet stores. We give this to birds of prey, song and garden birds, and others. See individual chapters. (E. R. Squibb, 909 Third Avenue, New York, N.Y. 10022.)

Vitamin B_1 (thiamine hydrochloride): This vitamin is very important for all fish-eating species. It is given in quantities ranging from 25 to 100 mg. daily, depending on bird's size and requirements. See individual chapters for amount used. B_1 is also extremely important in the diet of baby mockingbirds and other infant song and garden birds. (See chapter 8.)

Vitamin B_{12} (cyanocobalamin 25 mcg.): One tablet per day has proved effective as an appetite stimulant for pelicans. Place the pill in a fish, either in the mouth or a gill opening, and feed.

Zymadrops ®: This is a liquid multiple-vitamin supplement often used for human babies and available in drugstores. We add Zymadrops to certain infant and adult mammal formulas, as well as to baby bird formulas. See individual chapters for details. (The Upjohn Company, Kalamazoo, Michigan 49002.)

Appendix IV
Permits and Conservation

If you plan to keep and care for wildlife in your home, most states require that you have a permit to do so. Almost all birds and mammals are now protected by state or federal laws, or both, and since laws vary in different states, you should check with your state wildlife agency or local state game warden.

This might be a good place to remind you to teach your children never to take a baby bird or animal from nest or den. It always has a better chance of survival with its mother. Handling and rearing young animals and birds, as you can see from earlier chapters, is very time-consuming and difficult. Also, it is not legal, a point which many people probably don't know.

If you find a hurt, ill, or orphaned creature and intend to care for it, probably the first thing you should do about the permit situation is to contact your game warden. He can help you identify the species and inform you about the permit required.

There are different types of permits, depending on the species involved and whether or not it is on the Endangered Species list. The taking and keeping of the bald eagle, for instance, is allowed only by a federal endangered species permit, usually obtained from the regional office of the Department of the Interior in your area. All federal permits are obtained through this department and are issued by the U.S. Fish and Wildlife Service. We have such a permit (ours was received through our regional office in Atlanta, Georgia) because we work with many brown pelicans and have also worked with bald eagles and peregrine falcons, all of which are on the Endangered Species list.

If you are working with birds, a federal Migratory Bird Permit is required. By the way, it is not legal to band birds without special permission. If you wish to band birds, you should check with your state wildlife agency for advice.

State permits for local wildlife may be obtained from your state agency, probably located at your state capitol. We get ours from the State of Florida Game and Fresh Water Fish Commission in Tallahassee.

If you are not in the business of selling animals, there is no charge for a permit. It is issued on the guarantee that your patient will be released when recovered or adult enough to care for itself.

Interested citizens can be of great help to many of the agencies concerned with wildlife conservation. We are now working with the Fish and Game Commission on several projects. One is a survey of brown pelicans, their nesting sites and movements. Our coast is one of the last strongholds of these birds. Though they are the state bird of Louisiana, they have disappeared from that state's coastline, and Louisiana has imported a number of brown pelicans from Florida, hoping to reestablish breeding colonies.

In this important survey, the pelicans are tagged by state officials with colored streamers and bands. We watch for these, report the birds sighted, the color of the streamer, and, when we can, the number on the band. This study is very useful in learning about the movements and life cycles of our endangered brown pelican.

When a bird dies, we also freeze it for study by the University of Florida, which is working with the Fish and Game Commission on unusual and unexplained deaths of pelicans and other shore and water birds. Disease and pollution in the wildlife community is becoming a major problem which requires much scientific study and effort to solve.

The health of our wildlife community is an indicator of the health of our planet and of the future health of man himself.

Suggested Reading

The books listed here will help you with identifications of species, natural diets, and habits and personalities. By means of drawings, descriptions, and maps you can discover what bird or mammal you have in hand and in what habitat it may be found. In ascertaining the natural diet of a creature, you can create a suitable diet for captivity. And researching the habits and personalities of a species will aid you in handling and understanding individual animals.

These books are only a few of the hundreds available for research, but they are the ones we use most often in our own work.

MAMMALS
Burt, William H., and Richard P. Grossenheider. *A Field Guide to the Mammals*. 2nd ed. Boston: Houghton Mifflin Co., 1964.
Cahalane, Victor H. *Mammals of North America*. New York: Macmillan Co., 1961.
Sanderson, Ivan T. *Living Mammals of the World*. Garden City, N.Y.: Doubleday & Co., 1961.

BIRDS

Bent, Arthur Cleveland. *Life Histories of North American Birds.* New York: Dover Publications, 1963. (This is a series of books, each covering a group of related species.)

Gilliard, E. Thomas. *Living Birds of the World.* Garden City, N.Y.: Doubleday & Co., 1958.

Grossman, Mary Louise, and John Hamlet. *Birds of Prey of the World.* New York: Clarkson N. Potter, 1964.

Laycock, George. *The Pelicans.* New York: Natural History Press, 1970.

Peterson, Roger Tory. *A Field Guide to the Birds.* Boston: Houghton Mifflin Co., 1962.

———. *How to Know the Birds.* New York: New American Library (Signet Books), 1949.

Reed, Chester A. *North American Birds Eggs.* Rev. ed. New York: Dover Publications, 1965.

Robbins, Chandler S., et al. *Birds of North America: A Guide to Field Identification.* New York: Golden Press, 1966.

Scott, Peter. *A Coloured Key to the Wildfowl of the World.* London: W. R. Royle & Son Ltd., 1965.

TECHNICAL MATERIAL

Allen, Glover Morrill. *Birds and Their Attributes.* New York: Dover Publications, 1965.

Armstrong, Edward A. *Bird Display and Behaviour.* Rev. ed. New York: Dover Publications, 1965.

Beebe, C. William. *The Bird: Its Form and Function.* New York: Dover Publications, 1965.

Headstrom, Richard. *A Complete Field Guide to Nests in the United States.* New York: Ives Washburn, 1970.

Lanyon, Wesley E. *Biology of Birds.* New York: Natural History Press, 1963.

Lorenz, Konrad Z. *King Solomon's Ring.* New York: Thomas Y. Crowell Company, 1952.

Petrak, Margaret L., V.M.D., et al. (eds.). *Diseases of Cage and Aviary Birds.* Philadelphia: Lea & Febiger, 1969.

Scott, John Paul. *Animal Behavior.* Garden City, N.Y.: Doubleday & Co. (Anchor Books), 1963.

Worden, A. N. *Functional Anatomy of Birds.* London: Dorset House, n.d.

Index

My Orphans of the Wild

Rosemary K. Collett with Charlie Briggs

A pelican in the bathtub . . .
A tiny raccoon asleep in a fish tank . . .
Baby birds nestled in kitchen mixing
    bowls . . .
A red-tailed hawk in the laundry basket . . .

What a household! For nearly a decade, Rosemary Collett and her husband and daughter have been caring for sick, injured, or orphaned wild creatures in their six-room Florida home on a one-acre lot. Today, at least a hundred birds and small mammals are in residence at all times, lovingly nursed by the Colletts until they are ready to go back to their natural environment.

In this book, Rosemary Collett writes of her experiences with her animal babies— the wild assortment of mischievous, playful, quarrelsome, ornery, lovable creatures under her patient and constant supervision. Her day's work may include burping a baby raccoon, teaching incubator birds to eat and drink, force-feeding a pelican. Her nights are often spent waking every two hours to bottle-feed baby opossums, squirrels, and raccoons. Rosemary has given mouth-to-mouth resuscitation to a drowning sea gull, and she was the first to breed the white-tailed antelope squirrel in captivity.